Treating Traumatized Children

New Insights and Creative Interventions

Beverly James
James Institute
Kona, Hawaii

THE FREE PRESS
New York London Toronto Sydney Tokyo Singapore

THE FREE PRESS
A Division of Simon & Schuster Inc.
1230 Avenue of the Americas
New York, NY 10020

First Free Press Edition 1996

THE FREE PRESS and colophon are trademarks
of Simon & Schuster Inc.

Manufactured in the United States of America

20 19 18 17 16 15 14 13 12 11 10

Library of Congress Cataloging-in-Publication Data

James, Beverly
      Treating traumatized children: new insights and
creative interventions /Beverly James.
        p.   cm.
    Bibliography: p.
    Includes index.
  ISBN 0-669-20994-5 (alk. paper)
    1.   Post-traumatic stress disorder in children—Treatment.
  2.   Child psychotherapy.   I.   Title
    [DNLM: 1. Physician-Patient Relations. 2. Psychotherapy—in
infancy & childhood. 3. Stress Disorders, Post-Traumatic—in
infancy & childhood. 4. Stress Disorders, Post-Traumatic—therapy.
WS 350.2 J268t]
  RJ506.P55J36   1989
  618.92'8914—dc 19
  DNLM/DLC
  for Library of Congress   89-2397

Contents

Illustrations and Table

Illustrations

Table

Preface

This book is directed to the experienced mental-health therapist who provides treatment for traumatized children. The theoretical bases and the clinical techniques set forth here are those I have adapted or developed over a period of twelve years working with—and for—children debilitated by psychological trauma.

Many clinicians are horrified to learn of the experiences of the youngsters with whom they are working. Listening to a child victim of war tell of her experiences or seeing the horribly disfiguring results of an accident or learning of an act of violence against a small child can tax the resources of almost any adult, including the professional therapist. The therapist's defenses are particularly challenged when the traumatizing event has been deliberate, such as occurs with sexual abuse or as an expression of war policy. This is not an arena in which to hone clinical skills; it calls for knowledgeable practice by a trained psychotherapist who will not give improper messages to the child or to the child's caregivers, by word or by deed.

Therapists generally choose their work with the expectation that they will help people alleviate their pain and feel better. But this is neither necessary nor desirable, at least not initially, when treating traumatized children. Instead, one needs to develop a relationship with the patient and then deliberately take her back through the painful experience. Our natural inclination is to shield a child who must undergo a painful medical procedure, or to give solace to a child who has seen a parent killed, whether by accident or by intent. We must act in an *unnatural* manner, to facilitate the child's experiencing reality.

A basic tenet presented in this book is that healing is not likely to occur until the child has worked through the trauma: repressing the experience simply puts it in abeyance, leaving it available to surface and cause problems later. The therapist must often reopen doors to terrible places in order to help the child work the trauma through, and in so doing, he exposes himself to the stories and descriptions of these events. And yet if he responds, overtly or subtly, with his own feelings of horror, the child and his caregivers are given the message that even inured professionals cannot face the enormity of the trauma the child has suffered. This is not consistent with the child's need for a safe, holding environment in which he can acknowledge the reality of his life, affirm that he has survived, and move on.

In order to be effective and to refrain from inflicting greater harm, the therapist must (1) have a clear theoretical foundation; (2) have a wide range of effective techniques at his disposal; (3) be aware of the commitment needed in time and energy; (4) be able to work sensitively and directly with the realities of children's traumatizing experiences, while protecting himself from being overwhelmed by those experiences; and (5) be willing to consult and to learn from trusted colleagues.

Dynamic case-examples, and descriptions of techniques and exercises that range from silly to intense, provide the reader with specifics for working with traumatized children. The techniques are presented in a clinical framework intended to help the clinician understand the treatment needs of these children.

This book is written with the expectation that readers will not simply adopt what has been put forth, but rather will carefully consider what others have learned, mix those ideas with their own theoretical foundations and experiences, adapt any usable result to their own styles, skillfully apply what has been chosen, monitor the outcome, and then decide whether or not to incorporate what they have learned into their basic armamentarium.

The children most likely to be helped by what the reader learns here are those who were relatively intact prior to the traumatic event. If the child is particularly fragile, if his early life included deprivation of human ties, or if some other deeply rooted emotional condition exists which is not directly related to the traumatic event, the approaches suggested here may not be useful and in some instances may even be contraindicated.

Some children are stronger than others and are better able to deal with life's hardships. Indeed, there are children who have benefited from the challenges they have faced; we must accept the premise that such apparently negative events can teach compassion to the survivor and in other ways strengthen the child. We must be prepared to respect, acknowledge, and utilize a terrible event for the purpose of healing.

These children need the genuine caring of committed professionals whose expertise will facilitate the children's progress back through their pain, so that they can acknowledge their losses and gains and get on with their lives.

Although this book focuses on treating the traumatized child, the methods and practices described are often translatable for use with adults who were traumatized during childhood. In treatment, these people may well reexperience their past as the helpless children they once were; their treatment needs are often responsive to the techniques presented here.

A word about gender. I have referred to both male and female children

and therapists interchangeably throughout the book to avoid gender stereo-
typing and the awkwardness of continual dual references. I cannot think of
a single traumatizing experience or method of treatment that is gender specific. The sex of the clinician can be significant in that there may be some
advantages or challenges in a treatment situation due to the clinician's gender,
but it is clinically inappropriate to state that certain issues require treatment
by a clinician of one sex or the other.

Acknowledgments

Numerous friends and colleagues have assisted in my clinical growth, which, in turn, enabled me to write this book. And there would have been no growth without the children, for they are the best teachers of all. The editorial skills of Stephen Gross made this book happen, and I am especially appreciative of his dedication to this work. William Knittle did the wonderful drawings in chapter 3.

1
What Is Trauma?

Trauma, to paraphrase *Webster's New Collegiate Dictionary,* is an emotional shock that creates substantial, lasting damage to an individual's psychological development. As used in this book, "trauma" also refers to overwhelming, uncontrollable experiences that psychologically impact victims by creating in them feelings of helplessness, vulnerability, loss of safety, and loss of control. Although other emotional reactions may be seen (or may exist and not be seen), these are the states most likely to be present and to be uncovered by a clinician. The child victim may exhibit severe psychiatric symptoms or may superficially appear symptom-free.

The impact of an event in a child's life cannot be assessed in isolation.

An event traumatic to one youngster may be just a bad experience to another, or it may be traumatizing at one stage in life and not traumatizing earlier or later. The experience may, in fact, be a challenge to some children, who are strengthened by having met the challenge and coped with their situations. The child's constitution, temperament, strengths, sensitivities, developmental phase, attachments, insight, abilities; the reactions of his loved ones; and the support and resources available to him, all contribute to how an event is experienced, what it means to the child, and whether or not it is traumatizing at that specific time in the child's life.

The traumatizing event may be a single occurrence such as witnessing violence or an injury to self, or a series of interactions which, in totality, is traumatic. Examples might include incest, a long exposure to deprivation, a prolonged custody battle, surviving an airplane crash, or seeing people killed during war. The trauma may be directly physical, such as involvement in an accident, or solely psychological, as may occur when a child witnesses a disaster in which people are killed or injured, or when a parent whispers erotic longings to him.

Children have always been traumatized. It is only recently, however, that researchers and clinicians have begun to pay special attention to the effects of trauma on children—attention that is probably an outgrowth of social, political, and technological changes. Reporting systems and communication improvements have brought about an awareness of the widespread sexual abuse of children. Post-traumatic stress disorder has been identified in Viet Nam war veterans. The women's movement has brought us to a greater awareness of the problems of rape and incest. Trauma is not new, but how we recognize and deal with it is new.

Research suggests that the impact of trauma on a child may have lifelong psychobiological consequences, depending on the developmental stage of the child at the time of trauma, his coping abilities, and the meaning of the event to the child. As research continues and theories are developed and refined, we should expect new implications for treatment that will assist the clinician in working with these children.

2
Critical Aspects of Treatment

The treatment of traumatized children incorporates the methods and techniques typically used when dealing with most injuries to the psyche, in the sense that what we have learned elsewhere applies, with some reservations, to these children. Although the treatment goals are not unlike those we would establish for treating traumatized adults, dealing with children who have suffered trauma does require some special applications.

A number of aspects critical to the treatment of traumatized children are presented here. These considerations are not new to psychotherapy in general, but they do not appear to have been routinely incorporated by practitioners into their treatment of traumatized children.

1. The child needs to acknowledge and explore his pain while in therapy, in order to integrate his experience.

2. A serialized course of treatment, rather than one uninterrupted period of therapy, is often indicated. The treatment is sequenced over time so that it is responsive to developmental vulnerabilities that arise from the trauma over time.

3. The needs of the child usually cannot be effectively met by a clinician working alone, without the support of others involved with the child. The caregivers must be considered part of the treatment team, and their active participation is needed.

4. A direct, active treatment approach is needed to elicit material from the child that is unlikely to emerge spontaneously, and to demonstrate that the issues need not be shameful and can be dealt with directly.

5. Positive clinical messages have to be intense to be heard and felt through the child's defenses. The genesis and passage of these messages must be fun for both the child and the treatment team, in order to balance the hard work being accomplished.

6. The clinical course must include attention to the physical, cognitive, emotional, and spiritual parts of the child since the damage usually affects all these areas.

7. Many of these children engage in behaviors that are secret and dysfunctional, and that continue long after the traumatic incident itself. Dissociation and deviant sexualized behaviors, which often develop after traumatizing events, are not likely to be uncovered unless a determined effort is made to discover them by a knowledgeable clinician.

8. Working with traumatized children means dealing with gross, sometimes horrible, situations which may have a strong personal impact on the therapist; this impact may interfere with treatment.

Returning to the Pain

Helping children acknowledge and accept the realities of painful events in their lives is an essential part of treatment. If reality is not accepted, children continue to put enormous amounts of energy into avoiding what they find overwhelming and frightening, often by invoking defense mechanisms such as splitting, dissociating, and suppressing, which can impede their development. Children avoid anything that reminds them of what they want to forget. Avoidance mechanisms include extreme withdrawal, constricted physical and emotional expression, dangerous risk-taking, and aggression.

Traumatized children who have not come to terms with what has happened to them may be afraid to play, fantasize, or dream, because unbidden memories or thoughts might emerge. There can be within them a driven hunger to achieve, because they feel worthless. Academic achievement, for instance, counteracts their profound sense of worthlessness, but their intense reactions to both internal and external stresses often lead to learning problems, which consequently confirm their perceived inadequacies.

This failure to address the realities and consequences of the event make it impossible to uncover and deal with any misperceptions that exist or are likely to develop, which can get buried along with the actual circumstances of the trauma. The buried erroneous information festers along with everything else that has been suppressed, and, like a geological hot spot, can erupt without warning, causing grievous and possibly permanent damage. The following examples of such misperceptions were uncovered only after walking the children back through their respective traumas; prior treatment had not disclosed the existence of the misperceptions, nor was there any reason to believe the children had these concerns:

- The child believed that a knife was left in his body after surgery.
- The child believed that his mother's body was still inside the crushed car six months after she was killed in an accident.
- The child believed that the devil lived in his stomach.
- The child believed that wearing her pink nightie caused her grandfather to sexually molest her.
- The child believed that he had AIDS.

Medical professionals are commonly called upon to perform painful procedures necessary for the physical well-being of their child patients. So, too, mental health practitioners must guide and assist the child through the painful process whereby the event is carefully unwrapped, gone over in slow motion to gain some developmentally appropriate understanding and acceptance of what happened, and then put away. And when all appears to be finished, we must make the child understand that further painful work may be needed when he has attained a more mature level of development. The entire process requires exquisite skill and sensitivity.

Most adults, therapists included, are naturally inclined to shield a child from pain rather than help him confront it. To be clinically successful in the unnatural process of having the child examine hurtful experiences, the practitioner must understand and accept that the process is necessary for integration and mastery. Something like this may well have been in Coleridge's mind when he had his Ancient Mariner say

> Since then at an uncertain hour,
> That agony returns:
> And 'til my ghastly tale is told,
> This heart within me burns.
> (Samuel T. Coleridge, *The Rime of the Ancient Mariner*)

A more detailed discussion of returning to the pain will be found in chapter 14.

Developmentally Sequenced Treatment

The impact of traumatizing events on children often includes the establishment of developmental injuries. Sequenced treatment is necessary because past traumatic events will have different or additional meaning to the child as he matures, which can impair the progress of development. What was once experienced as generally confusing or disagreeable may become shameful or may be experienced as exploitation at some later time. Examples include a car accident and sexual abuse.

With an accident, the child's immediate sensations may be fear related to the loss of parental contact during hospitalization, and helplessness in the face of painful medical procedures. Days or even years after the accident feelings of guilt may emerge related to a sibling's death in the accident, shame regarding any possible feelings of happiness given the family's loss, self-blame for causing the accident (If only I hadn't run back inside for my doll), inadequacy, a driving need to succeed to justify his own survival, a negative body image, or an obsession with any disfigurement.

With sexual abuse, the child may initially experience physical excitement and the satisfaction of a reward, or may experience heightened stature as a result of sharing a secret with an adult. At later developmental stages he may experience guilt feelings for having enjoyed, or at least not having resisted, the experience. He may feel shame, believing himself responsible for causing the removal of a parent from the home. He may later long for the abusive parent; have feelings of shame and stigmatization; believe he is gay, gross, perverted, or that his only value is as a sexual object; or he may fear that he will be found out, or that he will abuse others. A therapist treating only a victim's presenting symptoms is usually aware that there are other clinical issues to be addressed—but one cannot treat what has yet to emerge developmentally. Therefore the therapist should, during the initial treatment sequence, prepare a foundation for future treatment.

Developmentally sequenced treatment can be likened to the association which develops in the traditional family-physician model, wherein the physician maintains an ongoing relationship with the child and family, providing professional services as needed. The relationship may last for many years, perhaps for a lifetime. The work at any given point is primarily with the sick child, although others in the family may provide home care as part of the treatment.

A thorough assessment of both child and family is an essential first step in developing a treatment plan. No list can identify every element to be covered in an assessment, but the clinician must minimally become knowledgeable about

- the child's past and present functioning,
- the specific traumatic events leading to the conditions for which treatment is sought,
- the experience and meaning of the events to the child,
- the child's strengths and problem areas,
- resources available to the child.

Utilizing this and other information developed with input from the child and his family, a comprehensive treatment plan with specific objectives is developed. The plan and its objectives should be changed as needed.

After the initial course of treatment has been completed, the therapist is available for consultation; the involved parties should understand that new issues may emerge. Checkups can be scheduled by the clinician on a regular basis, such as every nine months, or the family or child can contact the therapist as needed.

Following is an example of a sequential-treatment regimen for a girl who, at age four, witnessed the murder of her mother.

Age	*Treatment*
4 years, 3 months	Ten-month initial therapy focusing on the traumatic event, loss of mother, transfer to new school.
6 years, 1 month	Checkup/followup. Three sessions directed toward the child's belief she had some responsibility for the event, and her profound sense of loss.
7 years, 3 months	Five months treating the emergence of issues related to loss of birth-mother and adjustment to father's upcoming marriage and new stepmother.
8 years, 2 months	One month supportive treatment for family and school issues.
9 years	One session with child, and one with child and family, for assessment.
10 years	Six weeks of therapy dealing with puberty and sexual overtones of mother's murder.
11 years, 2 months	No therapy for child. Three sessions with parents discussing issues related to child's adjustment to new sibling.
13 years, 4 months	Eight months of therapy dealing with sexual misconduct and underlying adolescent conflicts.
15 years	Three-session checkup.
17 years, 4 months	Sessions regarding high-school graduation and impending separation from family.

It is likely this young girl will need some supportive therapy during her adult years. We can predict that she will be particularly vulnerable to emotional disturbances when faced with making her own decisions about mothering.

At first glance it may appear the periods of time shown are insufficient for the work to be accomplished. This would be true for typical psychotherapeutic work in which there is a traditional termination at the end of treatment. But we need to remember that the strength of the ongoing clinical partnership with the child enables work to proceed rapidly. This approach also significantly reduces the time spent dealing with termination issues such as loss of the therapist's support, feeling rejected, or engaging in behaviors designed to keep the therapy from ending.

A common error in working with traumatized children is to keep them in treatment for two to three years, attempting unrealistically to repair what has not yet surfaced. With that history, both parents and child can be resistant to returning to treatment at a later time when new difficulties relating to the trauma arise, such as problems stimulated by puberty, or by a significant loss. The parents and child can feel exhausted by the previous long course of treatment, be unwilling to repeat the experience, and feel as if they have failed, and that past treatment has been unsuccessful.

Treatment guidelines are presented here using a developmentally sequenced model. These guidelines will not apply to each individual situation, and should be looked upon, as with most other guides in this book, as the foundation on which the individual therapist can build his own approach for each specific child.

1. Conduct a comprehensive evaluation of the child and family.

2. Make a careful differential diagnosis.

3. Develop a specific treatment plan with clearly stated objectives, including the possibility of additional treatment at a later time.

4. Treat the child and caregiver as respected partners in treatment who will actively assist in the planning and implementation of therapeutic work. The additional involvement of teachers, coaches, and extended family, among others, may be desirable.

5. Develop a strong relationship with the child.

6. Use a combination of directive and nondirective techniques to assist the child in reviewing traumatic events, working through conflicts and behaviors related to the events, and establishing a foundation for future clinical work, to·be invoked when new developmental issues emerge.

7. End initial treatment when objectives are met, not necessarily when all loose ends are tied up.

8. Make termination of a course of treatment "open door," that is, make yourself available for consultation to child and/or parents on an *as*

needed basis, so that the child may return for checkups and additional clinical help.

9. Identify signs for the child and parents to look for, which would indicate that a clinical booster might be useful.

Involvement of Child's Caregivers

Whoever provides the child with primary parenting care must become involved in the treatment process if the therapy is to be effective. The caregiver may be a parent, foster parent, childcare worker, or some other adult charged with the child's care. Their involvement is not a violation of the child's confidentiality, but a planned clinical intervention. Rarely do children expect confidentiality in a clinical relationship, and rarely is confidentiality needed to meet clinical objectives for a child's treatment.

The extent to which the adults become involved in treatment must be carefully assessed, with emphasis placed on the abilities of the caretaker and the needs of the child.

The reasons for caregiver involvement provide, in effect, a synopsis of the treatment program.

1. One or two hours of therapy per week is not sufficient in these cases. Guided parental involvement can significantly enhance the clinical work, directly and indirectly. One benefit is the ability to move forward more quickly, thus reducing feelings of despair for both parent and child, and minimizing the likelihood of the child's identifying with the victim role, a possible consequence of the healing process itself.

2. The involvement of others lessens secrecy and feelings of shame. The child is shown that his issues can be dealt with by others, implying that he, too, can deal with them.

3. Involvement of others also promotes the child's self-acceptance. Knowing that others have witnessed his expression of feelings related to the trauma and shown their acceptance, makes it easier for the child to accept himself.

4. The parents' initial and subsequent concerns can be identified and appropriately addressed. Parental resistance to the child's treatment is sometimes healthy and understandable. Providing the parents with ongoing information and support can greatly reduce any tendency on their part to sabotage treatment, consciously or unconsciously. Premature termination of the child's treatment is less likely when the parenting adults are part of the treatment team.

5. Treatment objectives for most child victims of trauma include strengthening or improving the child's attachment to a parent or caregiving adult, and this requires the adult's active involvement. Clinical focus on the attachment relationship is especially important when there has been a sudden,

unexplained, or prolonged disruption in that relationship; when the interactions have been dysfunctional; or when a child has internalized the parent as helpless or as not loving him or her because the parent did not prevent the traumatic event.

Parental involvement generally begins minimally and increases to a maximum level, where their position is essentially that of a cotherapist. How much and to what extent a parent can be involved is a complex clinical decision. If parents are particularly needy, intrusive, or immobilized because of their own problems, it would be best to involve them no more than minimally.

Minimal Involvement

The parent meets with the therapist alone for an hour each month to discuss the child's behavior at home and to be updated regarding treatment. The meeting provides a forum for discussing parental concerns. The parent also takes part in the last ten minutes of each clinical session with the child, so the child and therapist can explain what they have been doing.

Medium Involvement

The caregiver meets with the therapist bimonthly, to discuss the child's progress at home and to assist in developing plans for work to be done at home. The caregiver attends the child's clinical sessions regularly, and is present for up to half of each session.

Maximum Involvement

An adult who becomes maximally involved in the child's treatment devotes the same amount of time as caregivers in the previous category. In addition, the parent leads some parts of the clinical sessions, with the therapist providing ongoing guidance and feedback. The parent acts as liaison to the extended family and to the outside community. This can extend to the point where the parent, in consultation with the therapist, makes regular contact with others to discuss strategies, and follows through with specific treatment plans.

Caregivers often remove a child from needed treatment prematurely. Understanding their reasons for doing so will help clinicians engage in preventive work with these caregivers to reduce the possibility of early termination. Some of the more common reasons caregivers stop treatment before the clinician has recommended doing so are because

- They want to believe that the child is not damaged.
- They feel guilty for not having protected the child, and want the problem resolved quickly.

- They believe treatment is harmful to the child, since it is just a rehash of painful events.
- They believe treatment is harmful, since the child's behavior has worsened.
- They believe treatment is ineffective, because the child just plays with sand and toys.
- They cannot afford the time and/or money for treatment.
- They feel they are neglecting their other children.
- They are jealous of the child's treatment.
- The child's treatment triggers feelings related to the parents' own past or present trauma.
- The child's positive relationship with the therapist is experienced by the parent as a significant loss, and contributes to feelings of parental inadequacy.

Direct, Open Approach

Guided play, direct discussion, and an open, active approach are needed to assist children in acknowledging and integrating the traumatizing events they have experienced. Children cannot initiate discussions of matters that overwhelm them, or those they have hidden from themselves. The treating person can mistakenly reinforce the child's belief that the issue is too overwhelming to deal with by avoiding direct discussion.

Nondirective techniques are used extensively with these children to help them integrate feelings and experiences, but are insufficient for healing unless used in conjunction with directive techniques. An overall, straightforward approach can best serve the needs of the child for several reasons.

1. The trauma has probably resulted in both the child and caregiver losing trust in people and in the environment. A clear explanation of the therapist's role, with involvement by child and parent in planning and executing treatment objectives, demystifies the process and provides the child and the parent with a sense of control while they continue to perceive the therapist as experienced and powerful.

2. Many children believe permanent, negative change has been created by the event. This may be true in some instances, especially where there is somatic damage, and such lasting effect should not be dismissed. This is an especially big issue for children who have had repeated surgery or chemotherapy. Where actual physical scarring or disfigurement has occurred, the therapist helps the child accept the realities and limitations of the situation, while quietly teaching the child that her totality is more than just her body.

3. Children need direct intervention to best deal with their strong, internalized belief that they are emotionally disfigured, and therefore limited,

for life. It may be true that they are permanently damaged emotionally, and this, too, should be dealt with directly. For example, "Sally, it is true you have experienced a loss of innocence, and we need to grieve about that loss, but it does not mean that you can't be proud, strong, and a wonderful person." Because of the shame and intensity of these feelings, they are not likely to be readily available, nor are they apt to be influenced by clinical intervention unless brought into the open and dealt with directly.

4. Children are often confused by the mixed messages we give them, such as, "What happened is not your fault, but you will have to see the therapist every week because of it." This strongly reinforces the "I am bad" message. The therapist can place the traumatic event into a broader context of being one of many terrible things that can happen to children, and describe what work they have to do together in order to understand both what happened and how the child feels about it. Addressing this openly reduces confusion and stigmatization and gives a message of hope.

5. Children may be emotionally paralyzed when traditional child-therapy approaches are used because these approaches mirror the dynamics of some trauma. For example, sexual molestation usually involves an adult whom the child knows to be trustworthy who asked to be alone with the child. They played together and told secrets; the child eventually discovered the activity had another purpose and meaning. The child is therefore likely to be suspicious and unresponsive unless the clinician utilizes a direct, open approach.

6. A "worst possible" scenario might be the child's experiencing flashbacks and/or severe regressive behaviors before a working relationship has been established with the therapist. Such a situation would probably result in the child's identifying the therapist with the person or situation that caused the trauma, and thus make the development of a trusting relationship virtually impossible.

7. Most children figure out why they have been brought for treatment; not talking about it may be experienced as dishonesty or trickery.

8. When the child and therapist just play in sessions and do not talk about *it,* the message heard by the child is that the event is too scary for even the therapist to want to discuss. The child cannot master what is unspeakable, and is left asking, Why am I here?

9. Parents take their cues from the expert. If the causative matter is not directly addressed in treatment, it is not likely to be addressed at home.

10. An open, direct approach gives the child the sense of a firm foundation and some power. This, together with the message that the therapist is clearly in charge of the situation, is the needed base from which a child can venture out to capture, and then slay, dragons.

Intense, Fun Style

Traumatized children are usually well-defended emotionally, but locked inside them are powerful and terrifying beliefs that they are helpless, bad, and at fault. The messages the child receives from therapy must match the intensity of these negative messages in order to be heard, felt, and believed. It is fun that keeps the child emotionally receptive so that the intense positive messages can slip through her defenses.

This does not mean the clinician must dress up in a clown suit and have trumpets blare at his entrance. But it does mean he must maintain good eye contact and give genuine, clear messages.

"I like you."

"You are fun."

"It's not your fault."

"You can still play."

"You can still be a child."

"Your mom loves you."

"I won't let you hurt yourself."

"You can make friends."

"Your body belongs to you."

"I will teach you."

"I know everything that has happened to you and I like you, and respect you."

"You deserve to be cared for and to be treated well."

When the clinician uses a playful therapy style, the child not only gets great benefit from the message that he is a fun kid to be with, but also learns play-skills that often need to be part of the treatment plan. Many children who have lived in chronically traumatic situations may not have play-skills, or may feel so self-conscious and awkward that they are socially ignored or harassed by their peers.

An intense outreach of positivism is needed to get the message through the child's distorted, and usually negative, self-image. Direct verbal messages should be continually reinforced through therapeutic activities in clinical sessions and (with the therapist's providing guidance to the adults) in home, school, recreational, and church settings. The child is still held accountable for misbehavior, and it must be made clear that the behavior, not the child, is unacceptable. Some guidance and direction may be necessary to teach the adults in the child's life how to give this message.

Therapy with traumatized children is so intense and painful that strong elements of fun are required for both the child and the therapist to survive and be able to continue the hard work. Many children who have had terrible things happen to them or who have witnessed horror do not believe they should ever laugh or have fun again. Incorporating good times in the treatment process subverts that belief, and teaches the child and the family that it is all right to take time out to have fun, and that despite the pain, life actually can move on.

Multidimensional Strategy

Trauma may assault the child physically, cognitively, emotionally, and spiritually, and therefore treatment strategies must deal with each of these dimensions. Clinical intervention in just one area is usually not sufficient for achieving mastery and healing. For example, a child may be able to reach a cognitive understanding of the death of a sibling and rationally know the event was not her fault; but unless some work is directed toward her irrational emotional feelings of guilt and anger related to the death, or her experience of extreme body vulnerability and spiritual confusion, she will not experience relief and will not be able to master the traumatic event fully. It is equally true that if the child works through her emotional response but is unable to reach a cognitive understanding of the event, the experience will not be fully integrated.

Physical mastery is achieved through body work in clinical sessions or with active involvement in ballet, gymnastics, karate, soccer, or other physical activity; such activity should be a mandatory part of the therapeutic program for children who have experienced traumatic physical intrusion. Supportive instruction and modeling related to body boundaries are important therapeutic interventions needed in most treatment plans.

A child can achieve cognitive understanding of the event and related circumstances through direct teaching by the therapist. Storytelling, the use of metaphor, and direct discussion of reality at a level appropriate for the child helps achieve this understanding.

Emotional mastery comes from a variety of experiences that enable the child to feel safe enough to explore and to express feelings that were once seen as overwhelming or unacceptable. Art and play-therapy exercises help delineate, identify, and express myriad feelings.

Spiritual impact can have the most long-lasting effect on the child. Spirituality has especially important significance for children who have experienced profound losses over time. These children can be made to feel they have something of value within them that is beautiful and powerful and continuous, which cannot be taken away. They need to learn that their essence is not only their appearance, their behavior, their family, or what has happened to them, but something more. Spirituality can be approached through the excitement and wonders of nature, through music and poetry, or through the teachings of a specific religious affiliation, usually that which already exists in the child's family.

Hidden Trauma-Reactive Behaviors

Hidden trauma-reactive behaviors are important considerations for the therapist. Although they have a negative impact on the child, these behaviors are generally not discovered without detailed, skillful probing within the context of a trusting, safe relationship. If not dealt with, the behaviors become entrenched and more complex, and the child's feelings of guilt and alienation are likely to increase. Continuing research and clinical experience in the areas of post-traumatic stress disorder, dissociative behaviors (including multiple-personality disorders), and child sexual abuse have brought new understanding about children's secret, and sometimes compulsive, behaviors. Dissociative splitting and paraphilia behaviors must be assessed when traumatized children are evaluated or treated.

Dissociative Disorders

The genesis of dissociative disorders appears to lie in traumatic experiences during childhood. Current understanding indicates that children with a genetic predisposition to dissociate under stress, when experiencing what they perceive to be a life-threatening event, with no sense of having adult protection available to them, will react to the event by entering a dissociative state. Dissociation is used not only to cope with the initial trauma, but also to deal with subsequent events that stimulate memories of the original event or that appear to be threatening.

The possible involvement of dissociative states has a number of implications for the treatment of traumatized children:

1. Clinicians must recognize the indicators of dissociative behavior in children.
2. The diagnostic process must include an assessment of the possibility of dissociative responses by the child.

3. The treatment goals of mastery and integration of traumatic events will not be met if the child has isolated a part of his personality from awareness and from treatment.

4. The possibility of dissociative behaviors should be evaluated at the beginning of therapy and at different times during the course of treatment.

Dissociative disorders are complex in nature and not well understood; significant serious study is relatively new. Chapter 11 provides a more detailed examination of this phenomenon and discusses treatment techniques.

Paraphilia Behaviors

Terr's research (1981) has shown that traumatized children engage in post-traumatic play that is secret and ritualistic, with a driven quality to it. Clinicians who work with sexually abused children have learned that some victimized children engage in post-traumatic sexual behaviors that are generally considered deviant or inappropriate. These behaviors, referred to as paraphilia behaviors, include exhibitionism, obscene telephone calls, humiliating or dangerous self-stimulating sexual behaviors, sexual abuse of animals or younger children, and the pursuit of adult sexual contact. The behaviors may initially serve some emotional need, or be an attempt at achievement of mastery and conflict resolution. But because of the drama, excitement, and orgasmic reinforcement, the behavior eventually takes on a life of its own and can become part of an addictive cycle rather than just meeting a specific need. Left untouched by the treatment process, paraphilia behaviors can escalate until the victim becomes a victimizer of others.

Professionals and caregivers alike have enormous difficulty in dealing with children's sexual behavior. We deny what we are observing because we are not prepared to believe that children are sexual beings. We do not want to see evidence of the child's having been damaged, and are fearful that we will somehow make matters worse—if we ignore the behavior, maybe it will go away. We don't know what to do and consequently may ignore this aspect of treatment.

The clinician should consider the possibility that her client has been sexually assaulted if any paraphilia behaviors are reported or suspected. Sexual assault is not limited to overt molestation, but includes sexual overstimulation, threats of sexual abuse, child pornography, witnessing violent or aberrant sexual behaviors, and other related events or situations.

We now know that it is not uncommon for children who have been sexually assaulted to engage in paraphilia behaviors, and thus the therapist must consider the following:

1. Care should be taken to avoid clinical interactions that polarize the discussion of the child's sexual trauma into categorizations such as victim/good guys and perpetrator/bad guys. A child who has been secretly engaging in actual or fantasized paraphilia behaviors will not bring these issues into the treatment arena if he believes he will be perceived as bad.

2. Caregivers must be advised that such behaviors are not unusual in children who have been sexually traumatized. The adults should be made aware that this does not mean the child will mature into a sexually perverted grownup. This knowledge allows caregivers who have been blocked from volunteering information about such behavior because of fear and shame, to talk about what they have seen or suspected; it also alerts caregivers to such behaviors so they may be addressed clinically. Treatment, of course, should encompass the paraphilia behavior.

3. The therapist must develop the skill to directly address these issues with the child and know how to intervene clinically, should the child be engaging in such behaviors.

Identification and treatment of the eroticized child is given more detailed coverage in chapter 13.

Therapist's Responses to Children's Experiences

Therapy with any child involves dealing with his fears, loneliness, and other strong feelings. It is not unusual for us to become exasperated with parents whose ignorance or selfishness is harmful to the child. But working with traumatized children is far more intense for the clinician and may, in fact, traumatize the therapist. Understandably, overwhelming feelings of horror and disgust can arise from working with youngsters who have been sodomized and forced to eat feces by cult members, or who are permanently disfigured by fires started by drugged parents, or with emotionally crippled children who may never be able to sustain intimate relationships, or with children who are permanently disabled physically. The therapist's defenses can mirror those of the child. Denial and minimization can detour us, for instance, into focusing on a parent's issues rather than the child's experience of physical abuse. Or we may project, based on our own feelings, that the child is not yet ready to address the issues. This is not work for the fainthearted or for those who become therapists to make themselves feel good. This is work that is exhausting—emotionally, physically, morally, and spiritually.

A strong impulse to rescue the child, and an impulse to destroy those presumed responsible for the child's trauma, are other common responses which will significantly impair the treatment process. The therapist could be led to overprotection and thus focus on nurturing the child; the urge to rescue may be so great as to result in avoidance of such important tasks as limit-setting, and providing guidance.

A more serious problem that may arise from the therapist's desire to rescue the child is a conscious or unconscious resistance to working toward strengthening the parent-child attachment. Some children do need protection from their parents; in these cases the clinician has a legal and ethical obligation to insure that appropriate steps are taken to gain that protection. Unfortunately, those cases in which parenting is marginal, and in which the most parenting assistance is needed, are those situations where the clinician is most likely to resist engagement with the parents. The clinician commonly believes he could parent better if given the opportunity; while this may be true, it is not relevant. The child needs the best parenting he can obtain *from his available caregiver*.

A related reaction that blocks effective treatment is the angry feeling a therapist may develop toward parents or loved parental figures who have traumatized the child. These adults are often primary attachment figures, and maintaining this attachment relationship contributes to the child's emotional survival.

Abused children learn to "read" adults quickly. They often interpret the therapist's hatred of the perpetrator as directed toward themselves, since they secretly *know* the abuse was their fault. Believing (or realizing) that the therapist hates the person they love and upon whom they are emotionally and physically dependent leads to feelings of guilt and shame in the child, and creates a chasm between the child and the therapist.

Anger about an offending parent's behavior can be expressed by the therapist only after the following conditions have been met:

1. The child and therapist have formed a therapeutic bond;
2. Work has been done to acknowledge positive interactions between the child and the offending adult;
3. The child has learned to differentiate between feelings toward a person and feelings about a person's behavior;
4. There is a degree of acceptance by the child that what happened was not his fault.

As therapists, we must be brave enough to confront, acknowledge, and work through our own emotional responses, at the same time that we ask children to reveal themselves to us. Clinical supervision and consultation frequently provide invaluable support for the therapist.

Summary

Although there may be a specific treatment or approach unique to working with traumatized children, many of the practices that may not be commonly used in one's work become routine when dealing with these children. They are often without hope and afraid to trust others or their environment, yet must form a relationship with their therapists that will enable them to return to the painful events that overwhelmed them, and understand what happened. The practitioner needs to work openly, directly, intensely, and playfully, allowing the children to accept his or her past and present feelings and behaviors related to the trauma, and to change behaviors that are dysfunctional. A team approach is utilized, with the child's caregivers as an important part of the team. A variety of techniques are employed so that the child experiences cognitive, emotional, physical, and spiritual mastery. A developmentally sequenced treatment model anticipates, and provides for, return to therapy, as the child matures and relates to the traumatic experience with different perspectives. The return to therapy is conceptualized as new growth and understanding.

Parallels can easily be drawn between working with traumatized children and working with adult victims of trauma. Many of the same treatment requirements exist, and many of the techniques are similar.

In the following chapters we will attend to the specific impacts of trauma on children and the treatment techniques suitable for clinical use.

3
Traumagenic States to Be Considered in Treatment Planning

T raumagenic states are emotional conditions that have their origins in traumatic experiences. The concept of traumagenic states related to sexually abused children was developed by Finkelhor and Browne (1986). They identified four categories of emotional conditions, each with characteristic dynamics, psychological impact, and behavioral manifestations. I have expanded their concept to include the effects of virtually any traumatic event on a child, not just sexual abuse. This expansion is in the form of five additional categories, each with its own dynamics, psychological impact, and behavioral manifestations.

The traumagenic states presented in this chapter provide useful guidelines for evaluating the impact of trauma during the assessment phase of therapy, and for developing treatment plans. The therapist can compare the child's experiences and presenting problems against the characteristics of each of the traumagenic states. Not all identified characteristics are likely to be seen in any one child, and there may be characteristics other than those identified here.

A child's experience of an event can differ significantly from what the therapist may anticipate. For example, a strong and resourceful child who has undergone emergency surgery may not be emotionally traumatized but may perceive the event as just some negative experience. A three-year-old may experience oral copulation with an adult as interesting, while a ten-year-old is still terrified because her mother's boyfriend touched her once gently between her legs a year previously. A sixteen-year-old's primary concern about having cancer was that he might die a virgin. An event may or may not be experienced as traumatic by a particular child, and it may be traumatizing at one stage of a child's development and not at another.

Knowledge of the possible impact of specific negative events in children's lives (such as alcoholism, abuse, or life-threatening illness) can be helpful, but we must be careful not to adopt generic formulas for diagnosis and treatment. The concept of the traumagenic states of childhood allows the therapist to examine the specific dynamics of a child's situation and, if some or all of the listed conditions exist, the clinician can assess the likelihood of psychological impact and look for possible behavioral manifestations.

(Again, a word of caution. This is a guideline and, as such, may not cover all aspects of a child's state. I have found this framework useful in the evaluation of traumatized children and in developing treatment plans for them. I would appreciate comments from colleages suggesting additions, offering criticism, or otherwise reporting their use of this guideline.)

Following are the nine traumagenic states of children, representing an expansion of the concept presented by Finkelhor and Browne. For each state there is a short introduction and a list of the dynamics, psychological impact, and behavioral manifestations, along with references to one or more chapters where the states are discussed in more detail and where treatment interventions are suggested.

Self-Blame

It is important that the child truly believes that the traumatic event is not his fault—if, indeed, it is not. (There may be instances, such as starting a fire, in which a child's behavior did, in fact, lead to trauma. In such situations the clinical focus is on the child's *intent,* and the assignment of limited responsibility is dealt with in a delicate and realistic way.)

Children blame themselves for almost everything that happens to them. In treatment they quickly parrot, "It's not my fault," because they feel it is the expected response and because they wish to please the listening adult. Exploration in play easily reveals the youngster's deep-seated belief that all or part of the traumatic event is somehow his fault. Intelligent, insightful adults who were victimized as children often experience overwhelming shame in revealing childhood abuse, even in the privacy of the clinical setting, because of their childhood understanding that they were responsible for their own victimization.

This self-blame belief is embedded in the child's cognitive understanding and in his affective, sensory, and muscle memory. The cornerstone of treatment is to help the child understand—mind, heart, and soul—that it is not his fault! Specific clinical interventions are discussed in chapter 7.

Powerlessness

Many children hold on to the powerlessness they experienced when traumatized, and that feeling expands to become their self-image. The clinician needs to help them recognize that they have power and choices, and that their powerlessness as victims does not extend to other areas in their lives.

Dynamics:

Cognitive Development
A child thinks a person is good or bad. If a *good* adult does something bad to the child, the child blames himself.

Excitement
Child experiences part of trauma as physiologically thrilling and believes he must have wanted it to happen, so blames self.

Payoff
Child experiences material or emotional reward; believes he must have wanted event to happen.

Compliance
Child did not actively resist his aggressor, so blames self.

Purification
Child keeps image of aggressor positive and blames self so he can continue to have loving feelings toward the aggressor.

Role Reversal
The child is parentified, i.e., he assumes the caretaker role in the family, and blames himself when something goes wrong.

Identification With Aggressor
Child associates emotionally with role of aggressor and blames self as part of this identification.

Timing
Child associates something he did with onset of traumatizing event and blames self.

Control
Child blames self to create illusion he can stop the traumatizing event when he chooses.

Assignment
Child is told by others he is to blame, and believes it to be true.

Psychological impact:
    Guilt
    Shame
    Belief that self is bad

Behavioral manifestations:
    Isolation
    Attempts to rectify, remediate
    Self-punishing acts
    Self-mutilation
    Suicide
    Substance abuse
    Sabotaging achievements due to belief of self-unworthiness

Figure 3–1. Self-Blame

Dynamics:

Helpless
No one and nothing was able to protect the child or halt the event.

Fear
Experienced fear, often repeatedly.

Isolation
Assistance, support, and a different perspective from others are unavailable

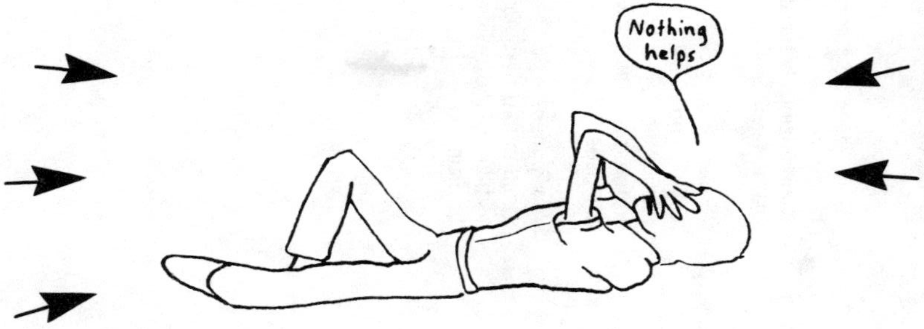

Psychological impact:
Anxiety
Fear
Depression
Lowered sense of efficacy
Perception of self as victim
Need to control
Identification with aggressor
Experiencing part of self as being split-off

Vulnerability
Child's personal boundaries invaded, often repeatedly.

Disbelief by Others
Child unable to make other believe his experience.

Nothing helps

Behavioral manifestations:
Nightmares
Phobias
Toileting problems
Delinquency
Pseudomaturation
Eating/sleeping disorders
Agitation
Withdrawal
Retreat to fantasy world
Running away
School problems
Vulnerability to subsequent victimization
Obsessive and age-inappropriate caretaking of others
Aggressiveness, bullying
Suicidal ideation and gestures

Figure 3–2. Powerlessness

As is true with many other childhood disturbances, behavior is manifested along a continuum for the child who finds himself in a traumagenic powerless state. Toward one extreme are children who exaggerate and maintain their roles as victims in order to gain protection from others. Toward the other end are children who become bullies to ward off potential aggressors or threatening events. Children move away from these behavioral extremes as they become empowered. The entire course of treatment can be an empowering experience for the child if the therapist makes him a partner in his treatment by offering choices and inviting active participation in the planning and implementation of treatment.

See chapter 8 for a detailed discussion of powerlessness.

Loss and Betrayal

The losses sustained by traumatized children are enormous, but are sometimes overlooked by the clinician who focuses on the more dramatic components of the trauma. A young child who engaged in ritualistic cult activities that involved eating feces and participating in sexual activities with adults, may not experience relief upon disclosure and rescue. She may instead experience loss—loss of the only attention she knew, loss of a loved parent, home, friends, school, identity, and everything familiar.

The child who experiences life-threatening illness or the death of a sibling or parent loses faith in the future and in the belief of his own invulnerability. He is forced to deal with realities for which he is unprepared.

Betrayal and the child's subsequent loss of trust disturbs the very foundation of her development. Betrayal by a loved caregiver is translated into "I am no good. I don't deserve better treatment. The world is threatening." If a child cannot trust her primary caregiver, she cannot help feeling that literally no one in the world can be trusted. When her energy is bound into trying to hide from the world, or into building emotional fortresses, she has little energy left with which to grow.

Throughout the course of treatment the child and the therapist work toward integrating the trauma (see chapter 14); it is in such mastery that the child learns to deal with loss and betrayal. Coping with loss includes grieving for what is now gone.

Fragmentation of Bodily Experience

People who have been physically traumatized appear to have encoded the event through sensory and muscular memory as well as affective memory. With specific stimuli such as an odor, or a certain touch to the body, they

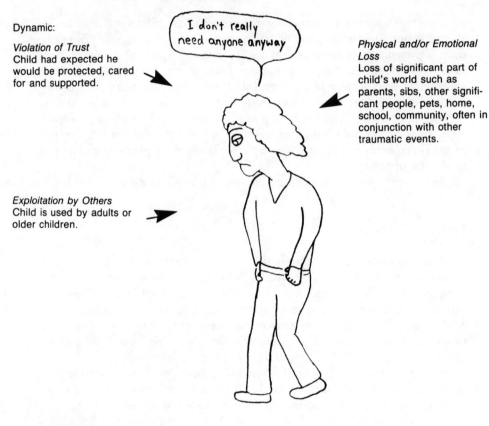

Dynamic:

Violation of Trust
Child had expected he
would be protected, cared
for and supported.

I don't really
need anyone anyway

*Physical and/or Emotional
Loss*
Loss of significant part of
child's world such as
parents, sibs, other significant people, pets, home,
school, community, often in
conjunction with other
traumatic events.

Exploitation by Others
Child is used by adults or
older children.

Psychological impact:
    Numbing of emotions
    Denial
    Suppressed longing
    Guilt
    Rage
    Distrust of self and others

Behavioral manifestations:
    Somatic reactions
    Recurrent anxiety dreams
    Regressive behaviors
    Withdrawal
    Inability to attend, leading to learning difficulties
    Emotional disconnecting
    Avoidance of intimacy
    Elective mutism
    Apathy
    Indiscriminate clinging
    Hoarding
    Explosive aggression

Figure 3–3. Loss and betrayal

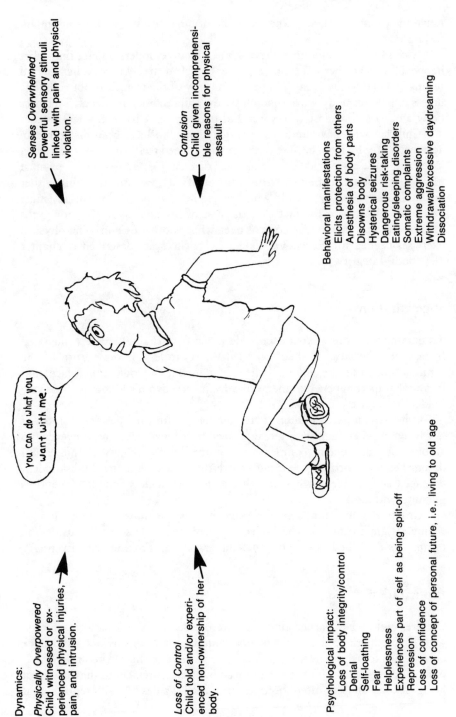

Figure 3–4. Fragmentation of bodily experience

relive the event and again experience the original trauma with its attendant feelings.

A child may be able to achieve some cognitive understanding that what happened was not her fault, and she may be able to freely express her myriad feelings related to the event. However, mastery of the trauma is not complete unless it includes body-work that allows the child to reclaim ownership of her body and to feel a sense of respect and mastery on a basic physical level.

Children who have undergone surgery, or who have been disfigured in accidents, or who have been sexually violated, need to learn respect, care for, love, and trust their bodies once again. For example, abused children must *physically* experience the successful warding off of unwanted touching, either in simulation or reality; a child who has had a leg amputated in surgery must *physically* experience the fact that the rest of his body is not up for grabs because he *does* have some control over what is done to him. The physical exercises needed for corrective healing experiences are described in chapter 10, "Body Integrity."

Stigmatization

Traumatized children experience a deep sense of shame and feel alienated from others because of their experiences, regardless of the nature of the trauma. Many of these children believe that anyone can look at their faces and know what has happened to them; they frequently avoid eye contact, and stay hidden in a variety of ways.

Other stigmatized children try to compensate for their perceived status of not being good enough with a driven need to achieve. Usually, however, no amount of achievement compensates for the child's feelings of shame and diminished self-worth, because the awards do not accrue to the child's hidden, damaged self. Achievements are ultimately meaningless, but the relentless pursuit continues.

Group therapy and conjoint peer therapy facilitate the reduction of shame. Stigmatization is eliminated or significantly lessened by using the techniques described in chapter 14, "Integration of Traumatizing Events."

Eroticization

Children who have learned that they are of special value as sexual objects, who have experienced control over an adult's sexual behaviors, who have been taught to behave in ways that are provocative to those who sexually exploit children, and who have experienced intense excitement in the process of being sexual abused often become eroticized. Yates (1987) reports that

Dynamics:

Blame
Child blamed, denigrated, humiliated.

Secrecy
Child pressured not to tell about traumatic event.

Shocked Reaction
Family and community respond to event with horror.

Damaged Goods
Child treated as if permanently damaged.

I'm sure everyone knows.

Psychological impact:
Guilt
Shame
Lowered self-esteem
Feels different from peers
Self-loathing

Behavioral manifestations
Isolation
Avoidance of achievement/success
Compulsive drive to achieve, but never experiences self as good enough
Substance abuse
Self-destructive behavior

Figure 3–5. Stigmatization

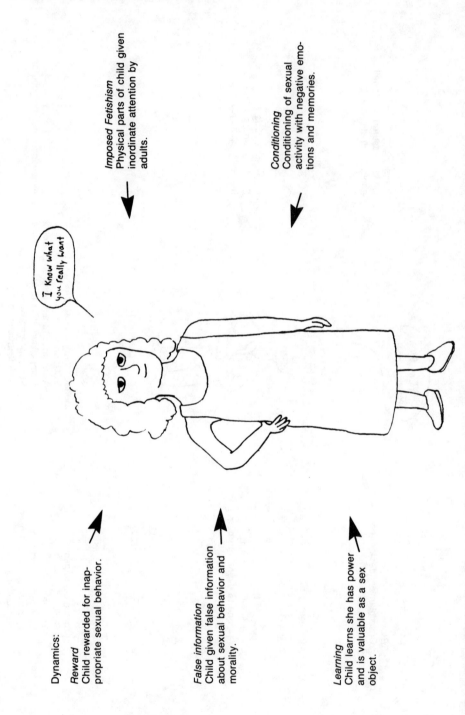

Psychological impact:
    Preoccupation with sexual issues
    Confusion about sexual identity
    Confusion about sexual norms
    Confusion of sex with love and caregiving or caregetting
    Negative association to sexual activities and arousal sensations
    Positive association to exploitative sexual activities

Behavioral manifestations:
    Sexualization of affection
    Sexual preoccupation
    Compulsive aggressive or sadistic sexual behavior
    Precocious sexual activity
    Sexual victimization of self or others
    Responds to neutral touching as a sexual approach

Figure 3–6. Eroticization

heightened eroticization occurs whether or not there has been coercion and whether or not the child initially perceives the experience as frightening or painful.

The entire persona of the eroticized child is wrapped around his view of himself as being valued only for his sexuality. In adulthood, these people may place themselves in high-risk sexual situations, reenacting the intensity of their early, forbidden experiences. Sexual excitement can become focused on or limited to objects, acts, or the body parts involved in the child's abusive history.

Living with these children presents special problems for their caregivers. Sexually explicit behavior in children can be frightening or can create feelings of disgust in others, often resulting in the child's being moved from placement to placement which, in turn, reinforces his belief that his badness overwhelms adults. This child may invite further abuse with his eroticized behavior or he may act out with other children, in which case he is deemed an abuser. Both responses further lock in the child's sense of sexual power and reaffirm his belief that his only value is as a sexual object.

Eroticized children frequently have had many of their early developmental needs met through sexual activity, and find both somatic and psychic pleasure in the behavior. It is very difficult to nullify that which has been good, and little is currently available to the clinician that would help this process. Specific approaches and techniques for treating eroticized children are presented in chapter 13, "Social Rehabilitation."

Destructiveness

Destructive children quietly or outrageously engage in a wide range of behaviors that result in others disliking and punishing them. The loss of impulse-control in some leads to frightening displays of their own rage. In the context of trauma-induced destructive behavior, our concerns are with the etiology of the behavior, that is, the nature of the traumatic event and how that event is experienced by the child.

Thorough assessment is the key for successful therapy with these children. A careful evaluation of the frequency, duration, and history of behavior, with special attention to recurrent suicidal themes and the risk of danger to others, is virtually mandatory. Neurological implications should not be overlooked.

Whether or not the caregivers can be taught to manage the destructive child's behavior in the home must be an important consideration. The caregivers will need adequate respite. Support available in the community, such as day treatment and special education, should be evaluated. The child may need the structure and control of residential treatment for his own protection as well as for that of other children. Therapy will not be effective until the behavior is brought under significant control.

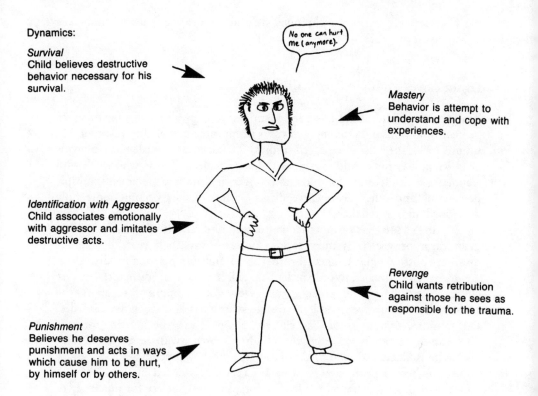

Dynamics:

Survival
Child believes destructive behavior necessary for his survival.

Mastery
Behavior is attempt to understand and cope with experiences.

Identification with Aggressor
Child associates emotionally with aggressor and imitates destructive acts.

Revenge
Child wants retribution against those he sees as responsible for the trauma.

Punishment
Believes he deserves punishment and acts in ways which cause him to be hurt, by himself or by others.

No one can hurt me (anymore).

Psychological impact:
Reinforces self-blame, guilt, shame
Frightening loss of impulse-control
Confusion regarding self-concept
Confusion regarding values, morals
Addictive cycle: destructive or abusive acts relieve tensions caused by destructive or abusive acts

Behavioral manifestations:
Child engages in destructive violent or sexualized behavior toward self, other people, animals, objects
Withdrawal
Preoccupation with revenge fantasies
Dangerous risk-taking
Ritualistic reenactment of all or part of traumatic events
Compulsive secret play
Elicits abuse from others

Figure 3–7. Destructiveness

Chapter 9 describes techniques helpful in dealing with traumagenic destructive behavior.

Dissociative/Multiple Personality Disorder

Traumatizing child abuse has been identified as a predisposing factor in 95 percent of a thousand documented cases of multiple personality disorder (see Braun, 1988, for a list of research studies). Dissociative disorders can provide an efficient way for a child to cope with his difficulties. Those who work with traumatized children are in a position to identify and treat incipient multiple personality and other dissociative disorders before they become more fully developed and entrenched.

Braun (1984b) has proposed a continuum of dissociative phenomena that includes, in progressively more serious order, normal behavior, dissociative disorder, post-traumatic stress disorder, and multiple personality disorder.

Identifying dissociative disorders in children can be difficult, because children's normal developmental behavior and temporary responses to extreme stress can appear similar to some symptoms of dissociative disorder. Furthermore, symptoms of dissociative behaviors may be hidden from the observation of others or from the children's own awareness. (See Dean's "Behavioral Checklist" and "Adolescent Inventory," appendix B.)

A number of professionals who are very experienced in working with dissociative disorders have founded the International Society for the Study of Multiple Personality and Dissociation, and publish *Dissociation,* a journal of current research, clinical findings, and reviews of professional writings (see Appendix A).

Further discussion of dissociative disorders and specific techniques which have been found to be effective in clinical work with children are discussed in chapter 11.

Attachment Disorder

Attachment may be defined as the tendency of a child to repeatedly seek the proximity of a specific person for tension reduction. Bowlby (1969) describes attachment as an enduring affectional bond with a vital biological function, indispensable for survival. The relationship between a child and his attachment figure can provide a secure base from which he can explore and master his world (Ainsworth & Wittig, 1969).

Attachment disorders in children can result from repeated traumatizing events which keep a secure attachment from forming, such as may happen with neglectful or abusive parenting, hospitalizations, or war. Alternatively,

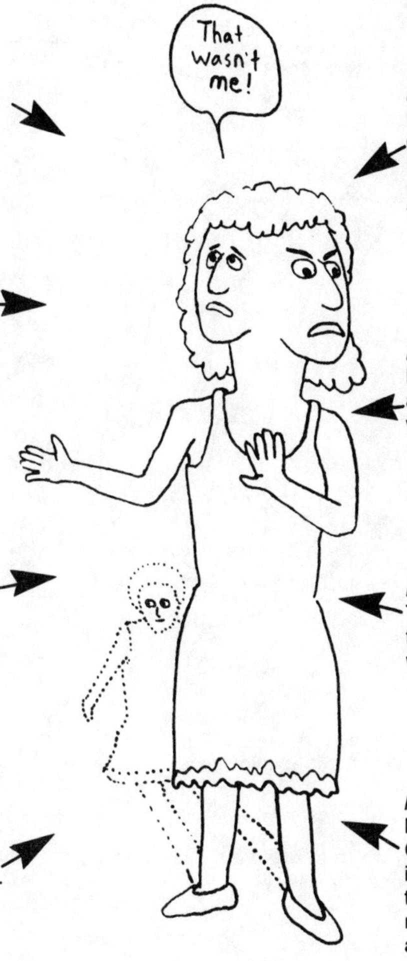

Dynamics:

Predisposition
Biopsychological capacity to
dissociate.

Insufficient Protection
Child experiences lack of
internal or external
resources to cope with
experience.

Overwhelming Terror
Environment chronically and
inconsistently infused with
traumatic events.

Programming
Child taught to self-divide
through constant reference,
e.g., "You are two people . .
Grandma lives inside you, "
etc.

That wasn't me!

Modeling
Behavior observed in several
generations.
Parents' dissociative
responses become models
for child.

Reinforcement
Dissociative splitting is
approved by others and provides relief from pain.

Pain Phobic
Thought of physical or emotional pain overwhelms child
with fear.

No Restorative Experience
Lack of soothing.
Child blocked from processing feelings related to
trauma by secrecy and/or
not being allowed to express
anger, fear, neediness, etc.

Psychological Impact:
    Fragmentation of personality
    Inconsistent and distorted development
    Depersonalization
    Feels alienated from others
    Encapsulates intense emotions

Behavioral Manifestations:
    Spontaneous trance states, sometimes associated with eye-roll
    Dual identity: uses more than one name, refers to self as "we," uses third-person form of
        address
    Denies witnessed behavior
    Peculiar forgetfulness patterns
    Odd variations in skills, schoolwork inconsistent
    Sudden mood and behavioral shifts
    Self-destructive

Figure 3–8. Dissociative disorder

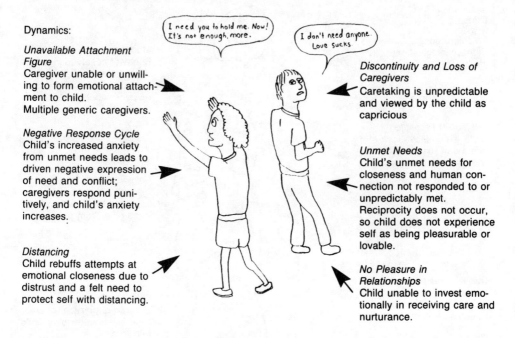

Dynamics:

Unavailable Attachment Figure
Caregiver unable or unwilling to form emotional attachment to child.
Multiple generic caregivers.

Negative Response Cycle
Child's increased anxiety from unmet needs leads to driven negative expression of need and conflict; caregivers respond punitively, and child's anxiety increases.

Distancing
Child rebuffs attempts at emotional closeness due to distrust and a felt need to protect self with distancing.

Discontinuity and Loss of Caregivers
Caretaking is unpredictable and viewed by the child as capricious

Unmet Needs
Child's unmet needs for closeness and human connection not responded to or unpredictably met.
Reciprocity does not occur, so child does not experience self as being pleasurable or lovable.

No Pleasure in Relationships
Child unable to invest emotionally in receiving care and nurturance.

Psychological Impact:
    Cannot trust needs will be met
    Cannot find comfort or security in relationships
    Isolated, lonely
    Depressed
    Low self-esteem
    Lacks secure base from which to explore the universe
    Unable to develop a sense of mastery

Behavioral Manifestations:
    Clingy
    Rage reactions
    Learning difficulties
    Overcontrolling with peers and adults
    Emotional detachment
    Lack of emotional reciprocity
    Engages in social interactions that block and avoid emotional closeness and vulnerability
    Will engage in relentless and repetitive demands for caregiver attention while not experiencing
        satisfaction or comfort from interactions
    Nonresponsive to affectionate caring
    Lack of spontaneity; rigid; lacking in warmth
    Does not turn to adult in times of need, rejects adult's efforts to soothe him
    Child suppresses own emotional responses and instead imitates behaviors of others
    Sabotages potentially gratifying situations

Figure 3–9. Attachment disorder

the traumatizing event can be a single event that threatens a child's attachment relationship, for example, parental abandonment or other sudden disruption of the family relationship, such as removal from the home.

Securely attached children go through dramatic displays of anger and protest when separated from the parents they love, and rebuff any attempts to soothe them. The behavior of attachment-impaired children can range from indiscriminate clinging to any adult to denying that anything is amiss (Bowlby, 1973). They can be demanding or overly compliant; a common factor is that they give their caregivers nothing back emotionally (Carson and Goodfield, 1988).

Even experienced foster parents who have successfully dealt with children with severe behavioral problems cannot identify the source of their discomfort when attachment-impaired children are involved—the foster parents just don't like these children. The children, in turn, often experience one failed placement after another, and the vague reasons given for the moves reinforce their view that no one is available who really cares about them.

As their neediness and tension mounts, attachment-impaired children behave in driven, negative ways—behavior which is perceived by others as volitional and manipulative. People respond to these children with anger, and only their negative behaviors get attention. They become further convinced that no one can meet their needs, and the cycle continues.

Clinical research by Carson and Goodfield (1988) reporting their experience within a family-model residential-treatment program, has demonstrated that attachment-impaired children are amenable to treatment, although it will be an arduous process. The adults providing care for these children, whether family members or professional caregivers, must be able to tolerate living with a child who will not attach easily; the adults must have considerable patience, and be able to stay emotionally engaged without immediate reward.

Treatment objectives for the attachment-impaired are complex, but if we do not intervene, these children will grow up to parent another generation of attachment-impaired children.

Techniques which provide corrective experiences, to facilitate healthier attachment possibilities for these children, are presented in chapter 12 and in the "Children's Garden Attachment Profile" developed by Carson and Goodfield (Appendix D).

Summary

The concept of traumagenic states can be of assistance to mental health practitioners when used to structure how to consider the impact of a traumatizing event on the child. For instance, given the child's makeup and the unique aspects of the event, is the child likely to blame himself, feel powerless, or feel betrayed? Are there dynamics that might lead to a fragmentation of bodily experience, or stigmatization? The behaviors that suggest the possibility of dissociative disorder, eroticization, destructiveness, or attachment impairment may not be spontaneously reported by a child or caregiver, and must be looked for by means of a careful history and behavioral observations in the home, at school, and during clinical sessions.

By considering possible traumagenic states when evaluating a child, the therapist may determine, for example, that the child has a significant attachment impairment, no dissociative disorder or destructive behaviors, but some degree of feeling powerless, feelings of loss/betrayal, and a significant amount of self-blame. This profile then becomes the framework that the clinician can use to develop a specific, detailed treatment plan.

4

Guidelines for Evaluation and Treatment Planning

E valuating traumatized children and assessing their treatment needs require thoroughness, reflection, and planning, all of which are time-intensive operations. The needed time is often not taken because of the pervasive sense of urgency that tends to surround these cases. We receive strong messages from both the environment and from within ourselves to do something—anything—and to do it quickly because there is a child in pain. Regardless of whether the pain is old or new, the pull is for the expert to provide "fast, fast, fast relief," probably in order to reduce the parents' or the therapist's anxieties relating to their inability to tolerate the child's difficulties. However, providing fast relief from pain is not the objective here. It is likely that numbing, repression, and denial have already relieved the child's immediate pain, thereby complicating the process of healing from within. For the child's sake, the wound will have to be reopened, examined, probed, and kept clean while it heals properly, so that minimal or no scarring remains.

Treatment objectives can be formulated only after careful examination of the child's past and present circumstances. The therapist must make a determination of the likely impact of the events on *this* child, given her experiences and the meaning she gives to the event, plus her unique strengths, vulnerabilities, and resources.

An assessment is made of available help. All known support resources, the skills and knowledge of the clinicians involved, and the interests and aims of involved parties (family, medical, legal, protective services, etc.), are considered. The result of this search is a unique situation for every youngster, and as each is unique, so, too, are the treatment objectives. Since the therapist will learn as she goes, she must be prepared to scrap or modify her treatment plan. Dashing in to help a child without going through this process can be likened to rushing off on a journey without knowing where you are going, how to get there, what you need to bring along, or who will be traveling with you. The flurry of action may be impressive, but will probably be meaningless ultimately.

The following guidelines for evaluation and treatment planning address the major areas that should be considered when working with a traumatized child.

Clarifying Needs, Expectations, and the Therapist's Role

The specific professional services sought must be clarified prior to initiating any treatment, preferably during the first contact with the referring or requesting party. It is not always exactly clear who wants what, and who makes the final decision as to what is to be done. It may be necessary to discuss the matter with parties other than the child's caretakers, such as attorneys, protective service workers, and previous therapists. Treatment may be requested, for instance, when what is really being sought is an expert opinion for court, or a second opinion. Clinical interviews that are not properly directed, due to misunderstandings of roles, are a disservice to the child and could negatively affect subsequent clinical relationships that the child may need to form with another therapist. Furthermore, a legal matter may be biased if the child is clinically interviewed, when what is required is a generic expert opinion given intentionally *without* knowledge of the specific facts of the case.

The therapist must describe his own evaluation process and style of working, mention any requirements for parental involvement, state his fees, and answer questions the involved parties may have prior to the evaluation. If the parents and the therapist decide to proceed with an evaluation to determine whether or not psychotherapy is indicated, the therapist should advise the caregivers how and when the child should be told.

A seven-year-old who has been physically abused can be told a day or so before the family meeting that the whole family

> will be going to a special meeting with Dr. X, a person who helps families who have all kinds of different problems. He has helped a lot of kids and their families when adults have hurt children. I have talked to Dr. X, and I think he is smart and could be helpful to all of us. After he talks to us all together, he will talk to you another time or two separately. He might also want to talk to the police officer and doctor, too. When he has a really good idea of how everyone, but especially you, is doing, he will meet with all of us again and let us know if we might need some help.

Physical Examination

A physical history will probably be readily available if the trauma is recent and somatic. A physical examination does more than just provide a reading on the youngster's state of body health: it can help the mental-health practitioner by ruling out organic causes of distress or other symptomology, and can provide assurance to the child that she is not brain damaged, does not have AIDS or venereal disease, is not pregnant, and so on. One caution, however: routine medical exams do not usually screen for brain tumors or other nervous-system disorders that may manifest themselves as "behavioral" problems. A pediatrician's diagnosis of a physically normal child should be construed as meaning normal only insofar as the physician examined the child. A biological basis for abnormal behavior must always be considered, and the clinician may wish to consider referral for a neurological consultation.

One area which seems to be gaining attention is the consideration of allergies and allergic reactions as etiologically responsible for behaviors which would typically be described as psychological in origin. A normally behaving child who suddenly, and for no apparent reason, becomes depressed, aggressive, uncoordinated, somnolent, or witless, or who exhibits any of a number of unexplainable behaviors should be considered for allergen sensitivities.

Doris Rapp (1986) has documented dramatic changes in children's behaviors, drawings, and handwriting when they have sensitivity reactions to certain foods, odors, and pollutants. The sudden onset of symptoms may lead to the mistaken belief that the children are responding to psychic traumas. This in turn leads to caregiver frustration, exhaustion, and loss of control because the children cannot tell why they are "misbehaving." Furthermore, Rapp reports the possibility of allergic reactions being exacerbated by stress, so the clinician should consider the effects of the stress of treatment on children who have allergies. Refer to appendix C, Rapp's checklist for recognizing possible allergic reactions.

Comprehensive Background Information

Review all case materials after obtaining written consent from appropriate parties. These materials may include hospital records, police reports, protective services investigations, immigration documents, physician's notes, school records, and notes from other therapists, among other items.

Parents or caretakers should submit written information that can serve as reminders to themselves during the assessment interviews and can, in most instances, remain as part of the therapist's record. In the case of separated parents who need to be interviewed individually, each should prepare material. If the initial contact is by telephone, the parents can be asked to have this material with them when they come to the initial appointment. Although a good deal of information is sought, the therapist should request something to serve primarily as a reminder, not a long, formal document describing every facet of the lives of all who may in any way be involved in the child's or parent's lives. The material to be submitted should include

1. Child's History—This should contain a brief description of the pregnancy, birth, infancy, toddlerhood, and early school years. The child's serious illnesses, accidents, general health, and developmental milestones should be noted. Significant childcare providers should be identified. Losses, separations, and other events believed to be of significance to the child's development are to be included. Special qualities and difficulties during the child's development should be stated. A brief comment with the parent's view of the child's present functioning should be part of this document.

2. Family History—This should include dates of courtship, marriage, household relocations, job changes, births, serious accidents, illnesses, losses, separations, and changes of people living in the household, and all other events in the family with positive or negative significance.

3. School Records—Parents may request that the school send records directly to the therapist. Teachers' written comments, grades, and identified problem areas are especially important.

4. Pictures—Up to ten or so pictures of the child and family, taken at different times, should be brought to the first session. These will be returned to the caregiver.

Parent Interviews

Information gained from parent interviews should be used to expand the family history list, including information about each parent's family of origin, as well as additional details related to the child's history and family history. Parents' perceptions of the child's sibling relationships and any other significant relationships should also be explored. Marital problems, problems with substance abuse, or any other negative areas should be discussed, along with details about the traumatic event leading to the referral, and any of the child's behaviors which are worrisome to the parents. Parental concerns and beliefs regarding the impact of the traumatic event on the child should also be explored.

Parents must be questioned carefully to help determine if the child is likely to hurt himself or others. A child's parents cannot be relied upon to volunteer information about a child's self-punishment or abusive behavior: they will often protect themselves from such realities, and must be asked directly about these possibilities. Day care providers, teachers, pediatricians, and others should be asked specific questions relating to destructive and abusive behaviors noted in the youngster.

Collateral Interviews

Collateral interviews can usually be conducted by telephone, and may include interviews with the child's physician, schoolteacher, childcare providers, and others whom the parents may suggest. The therapist explains his role as evaluator (and possibly treatment-provider) to these contacts, and asks for information which may help in the evaluation of the child, such as the child's functioning, strengths, problem areas, and interactions with others, both in the past and at the present. The interviewee should be asked about any concerns he or she may have regarding the child.

Child Assessment

The assessment should begin by seeing the child, usually together with those family members who live in the household, followed by a session with only the child and his parents. This provides the clinician with the opportunity to evaluate family and parent-child interactions, and helps prepare the child for individual sessions with the therapist.

Child with Family Interview

Interviewing the child with his family is a diagnostic technique used to help identify family styles of communication, values, alliances, perceptions of various family members regarding the child, and interactions that could help or impede the child's treatment. This meeting also provides an opportunity for the therapist to clarify possible misconceptions the child or family members may have regarding the need for professional help. Some situations may preclude an interview with child and family, such as when parents cannot be in each other's presence without being antagonistic or otherwise behaving in an unacceptable manner. In such instances the clinician may choose to forgo this part of the evaluation, relying instead on separate child/parent interviews, or she may decide to meet with only one parent and the children in the family. It may sometimes be useful to conduct an interview with the child and foster family in addition to, or in lieu of, the interview with the birth-parents.

The clinician directs the discussion to assure that the desired information is obtained. Who is in the family? What is dinnertime like? Who does chores? How is discipline carried out? What does each person like the best about each of the others—and what one thing would they change about each person? Questions such as these provide significant diagnostic material. All family members working together on a single large drawing of the family can illuminate dynamics as well as defuse the intensity of the session. Finally, asking each person to state what they think of the situation and what most worries them, can elicit support and identify trouble spots.

Child with Parent Interview

The child/parent interview allows the therapist to observe the child's interactions with each parent, orients the child with regard to the purpose and procedures of the meetings, and provides an opportunity for parents and therapist to answer questions the child may have. By this time the therapist should have a beginning sense of the child's developmental abilities and temperament. This session will include an introduction to the playroom, description of family relationships by means of "genogram" (see chapter 17), projective drawing techniques such as House-Tree-Person, direct discussion, and free play.

A useful and effective tool for evaluating child/parent interactions is Jernberg's (1982) adaptation of the Marschak International Method (MIM) for clinical purposes. The newly assigned tasks of the MIM are designed to elicit the following four clusters of behavior from adults and children:

1. Attachment
2. Purposive behavior
3. Alertness
4. Receptiveness to proffered help

Child Interviews

A young and fearful child should have a parent present during the first part of the interview. Some children's anxiety levels or developmental stages may require assurance that the parent is nearby during the session; thus it is good practice to advise parents to be available in the reception room for a possible sight-check by their child.

Some children who are anxious and hesitant to talk, or who object to being alone with the therapist, quickly change to more age-appropriate behavior after being gently separated from their parents. The "pitiful victim" role may have been invoked by the child to protect a parent perceived as fragile. By acting helpless, the child hopes to forestall further discussion of the traumatic events that are upsetting to the parent. Or, in contrast, the child may be responding to the parent's need to exaggerate the traumatic experience, expressed as, "My poor baby has to go through such painful experiences." These children gain needed respite—and visible relax—when their parents leave the therapy room.

In individual sessions, the therapist adds to his initial impressions of the child's functioning in the areas of assertiveness, initiative, curiosity, playfulness, aptitude for insight, and coping behaviors, among others. He can evaluate the child's ability to separate from the parent, as well as changes in the child's behavior when apart from the parent.

Activities during child assessment interviews include projective and directed play using such things as a sand tray, painting, dollhouses, storytelling, clay, and puppets. The therapist should also engage in direct discussion with the child about her talents, strengths, worries, and problem areas.

After two or three sessions the clinician and child should be able to explore the child's understanding of the traumatizing experience and its meaning for her.

Two areas of risk which must often be assessed are (1) undisclosed abuse to the child, and (2) destructive behaviors initiated by the child.

A comprehensive discussion of behavioral indicators of abuse will not be attempted here, but the behaviors to which the practitioner should be particularly alert, especially when the reported history does not appear to explain such behaviors, are

- extreme aggression or passivity
- sexual behaviors that are inappropriate for the child's developmental level, or that are coercive or hurtful to others
- self-destructive behavior
- dissociative behavior
- child relating instances of abuse

Further risk is seen in children's behaviors that are self-destructive or that pose a danger to others. Clues to these behaviors may emerge in two different ways. The child or her caregiver may describe such behavior or the child may present clues in art and play themes. This information should be carefully assessed and documented by the clinician.

Many children will honestly respond to direct questions about their thoughts, plans, or acts having to do with deliberately hurting themselves, but will rarely divulge that information spontaneously. During the evaluation period they are less likely to respond honestly about sadistic and sexually abusive behavior toward others, but can be asked about abusive behaviors in a manner which leaves the door open for future revelations.

> Sometimes kids who have things like this happen to them have strong and secret feelings. Sometimes they do things to other kids or animals that hurt them or that are not OK. I wondered if you remember hurting your _____ [therapist fills in the appropriate body part] or other kids or pets. Or maybe you did other things that weren't OK?

This type of questioning may result in a confession of normal behavior that should be labeled with a statement like "Lots of brothers and sisters fight. If you think of other hurting or secret things you may have done, will you tell me?" If the child says he would not tell the clinician, the clinician can say, "One of the things we need to work on is knowing each other better so we can feel more comfortable with each other. Most kids need help to stop doing things like that, and it's my job to help kids."

Should it appear that extraordinary supervision is needed to insure the child's safety or that of others, a determination must be made as to whether or not his caregivers, with guidance and direction from the clinician, can provide the requisite protection.

Assessment and recommendations related to a youngster's safety are difficult to make. The profound traumatizing effect of removal of the child from his home for the sake of his and others' safety must be weighed against potential danger to the child. When there are indications that the child might be at risk from abuse, or might engage in self-destructive behavior or abusive behavior, the assessment is not limited to the initial evaluation, but should become a continuous theme which the clinician must consider throughout the course of treatment.

In considering possible diagnostic categories for traumatized children, I have found Frederick's table, which includes the American Psychiatric Association's (1986) DSMIII numerical categories of mental disorders, to be very useful (see table 4–1).

Written Report

A written report with a summary of the findings is extremely helpful to both clinician and caretaker. I recommend that such a record be created and given to the parents as a reference, since there is a tendency to remember selectively whatever is presented orally. The written document also helps parents gain and maintain a more balanced, comprehensive perspective of the issues and treatment needs. The report should furthermore be a written validation of the strengths of both child and family, and should generate the feelings of hope and confidence needed for effective treatment. (These positive aspects are often overlooked as the parents worry and focus on problem areas.)

The written report should include the following information:

1. Family history and dynamics
2. Child assessment
   a. Development
   b. Health

Table 4–1
Common Psychiatric Disturbances Found among Children in Selected Catastrophic Situations, in Relative Frequency of Occurrences

	Disasters		Child Molestation		Physical Abuse
Rank	DSM-III Disorder	Rank	DSM-III Disorder	Rank	DSM-III Disorder
1	313.21 Anxiety disorder, avoidant disorder	1	308.20 Post-traumatic stress disorder, acute	1	313.00 Overanxious disorder
2	309.12 Anxiety disorder, separation-anxiety disorder	2	309.81 Post-traumatic stress disorder, Post-traumatic stress chronic	2	313.21 Anxiety disorder, avoidant disorder
3	307.46 Sleep-terror disorder	3	300.29 Simple phobia	3	307.46 Sleep-terror disorder
4	313.00 Overanxious disorder	4	313.82 Identity disorder	4	308.20 Post-traumatic stress disorder, acute
5	300.29 Simple phobia	5	313.81 Oppositional disorder	5	309.81 Post-traumatic stress disorder, chronic
6	300.22 Agophobia, without panic	6	300.02 Generalized anxiety	6	309.40 Adjustment disorder
7	308.20 Post-traumatic stress disorder, acute	7	309.24 Adjustment disorder with anxious mood	7	314.01 Attention-deficit disorder, with hyperactivity
8	309.81 Post-traumatic stress disorder, chronic	8	300.81 Somatization disorder	8	300.29 Simple phobia
9	314.01 Attention-deficit disorder with hyperactivity	9	300.22 Agoraphobia without	9	305.00 Functional neurosis
10	314.80 Attention-deficit disorder, residual type	10	309.00 Adjustment disorder, residual type	10	313.82 Identity disorder

Source: Frederick, C., Children traumatized by catastrophic situations. In Eth and Pynoos (1985a).

    c.   Intellectual and academic functioning
    d.   Emotional and social functioning
    e.   Strengths
    f.   Problem areas

3. Suggested treatment plan
    a.   Short-term objectives and strategies
    b.   Long-term treatment goals

The written record should be presented when it can be reviewed in the presence of the clinician so that questions and concerns, if any, can be addressed. It may be appropriate to have a professional case conference with all involved parties present when, for example, the child is in out-of-home care and there is a need for coordination, or a need to establish the child's primary caregiver as part of the treatment team.

A separate oral presentation should be made to the child with the parents present, and may be included as part of a therapy session. (Exceptions to this would be very young children and adolescents.) The presentation to a two- or three-year-old child might just be a clear statement about continuing to come to the playroom in the future.

It is usually clinically and developmentally appropriate for adolescents to have the findings presented without parents in attendance, and for the child to have a copy of the Adolescent Assessment and Treatment Recommendations sections of the report.

Summary

Careful and comprehensive evaluation is especially important when working with child victims of trauma, because formulating treatment objectives requires that the clinician have a clear picture of how child and family has functioned—before, during, and since the traumatic event. A written evaluation with specific treatment objectives that can be explained to the child and family helps to lessen their feelings of self-blame, hopelessness, and fear of trusting another person. Having clear treatment objectives provides the necessary clinical framework for the therapist, who can become overwhelmed by the intensity of the child's trauma and the pressure from himself and others to provide immediate relief to child and family.

5
Basic Treatment Process

The intensity of treatment and the amount of work needed to achieve a treatment goal will vary with each child. The variables, including the children's resiliencies, vulnerabilities, temperaments, available resources, what happened to them, and the meanings they assign to their experiences, can be likened to the myriad pieces of colored glass in a kaleidoscope: the basic pieces are the same, but a different pattern appears every time the kaleidoscope is moved. So, too, do we get a different pattern of treatment needs for each child.

Clinicians who provide corrective experiences for traumatized children and their families find themselves pulled and stretched cognitively, physically, spiritually, politically, and emotionally. They can be overwhelmed by the plight of their young patients or can become desensitized to the calamities that have befallen the youngsters; either reaction can impair treatment. The reward for the therapist is the rapid progress in healing, which is readily apparent. The immediate and long-range impact of good clinical work with the child and his family is profound.

The goal is to have traumatized children reach the point where they can say something like, "Yes, that happened to me. That's how I felt and how I behaved when it happened. This is how I understand it all now. I won't really forget it happened, but I don't always have to think about it either."

If the result of the therapist's work is only minimal—that the child believes the therapist genuinely cares about him, in spite of knowing all about the traumatic experience in the child's life—the treatment can still be considered a good piece of work. And if only one of the treatment goals can be met, the elimination of self-blame is usually the most important. It is not likely that the goals of mastery, social rehabilitation, and other life goals will be fully met if the child consciously or unconsciously feels responsible for having caused the problem.

Clinical work with traumatized children can generally be categorized into four major areas, namely, communication, sorting out, education, and perspective. As the child and therapist work and play together in each of these areas, they should pause to allow for stabilization, and take time to savor and celebrate the child's gains. As with most categorizations, these are not as neatly separated in practice as in theory, and overlapping of categories, with attendant confusion, will occur.

Communication

Traumatized children generally do not know how to express their complex and conflicting feelings and ideas, either to themselves or to others. This inability to communicate appears age-related to some degree, but not to the point where we can say that older traumatized children can express themselves but younger ones cannot. The inability seems to go with the trauma experienced, not with the age of the child.

Young children enter treatment with amorphous, undefined masses of negative feelings that they are unable to name. This is not necessarily because the children have repressed memories or are resistant to discussing their feelings. Whether or not repression and resistance are involved, at least three other elements may be at work.

1. Youngsters do not have the language skills needed to communicate their feelings accurately.
2. Their feelings and emotions are apt to be too varied and too complex for them to describe. Feelings and emotions new to the child may also be present, such as guilt, and consequently they can say no more than "It just doesn't feel good."
3. Children's feelings and emotions are often contradictory, such as is seen in a child who has been abused by a parent he loves. He cannot express coexistent feelings of love and hate.

It is usually best to begin by teaching a child to identify and distinguish the various feelings common to *all* children. He can then be helped to develop methods for communicating his own emotions to the clinician, although emotions related to the traumatizing events should not be explored until the child has developed some skills in communicating emotions, and feels confident that it is safe to do so. Having learned labels for various emotions, and ways to communicate them, the child is taught how to express simultaneous, conflicting feelings, and learns it is acceptable to do so.

The process typically involves interactions during which the practitioner establishes, through a combination of art, music, play, psychodrama, and direct discussion, a common language or outlet through which the child can express himself. He is taught directly and indirectly that he will not get into trouble for expressing feelings, that he will not overwhelm the therapist with his emotions or behaviors, and that the therapist can understand, control, and guide him.

The communication tools he learns in this phase will help him sort out his traumatizing experience in the next phase of treatment.

Sorting Out

A safe, "holding" environment (Winnicott, 1960) is established within the clinical setting so that the child and the therapist can, at a pace suitable for the child, sort out

the child's understanding of what happened;

the meaning of the event to the child;

the youngster's feelings before, during, and after the traumatic experience;

the child's behaviors before, during, and after the event;

the child's worries related to self, siblings, and family, in the present and in the future.

During this process of exploration the child learns that others who have been traumatized feel and do things that are hard for them and others to understand. The clinician, honoring and respecting the child's experience, facilitates her being able to acknowledge and accept her feelings and behaviors that are related to the traumatizing event.

Education

Direct and indirect teaching enables the child to understand, to the fullest extent possible, all the elements contributing to the traumatizing event, and the roles of the various persons involved. This education may focus on how bodies work, how hospital systems operate, the process of death and burial, how people can lose control of their actions and hurt those they care most about, how the court system operates, what daily life is like inside a prison, or how people live with paralysis. The process helps avoid misinformation and misconceptions.

Another part of the process is to have the youngster learn how to control his objectionable behaviors. When empowered as a part of the treatment team, he learns to identify the factors that stimulate the unwanted behavior, learns techniques that allow him to gain control of the behaviors, and finds alternative ways to express himself or to have his needs met. He also learns that he is responsible for his actions, that adults can help him control and protect himself, and that it is acceptable to ask for help.

Perspective

Through her relationship with the therapist, and through discussions and exercises, the child develops a sense of self in which she knows that she is more than her experiences, her body, her possessions, and her relationships. She learns that terrible things *do* happen to children, and that she is not the only little girl who has had the same horrible experience. She learns that other children survived and that she will too, and that she doesn't have to be a super person or a humble person because of what happened. She learns that it is not her job to try to make up for the experience. The child is helped to recognize and appreciate her present physical and emotional strengths, as well as her limitations, without minimizing or exaggerating reality. The traumatizing event thus becomes integrated and fully accepted as part of the child's history.

Basically, the therapist should appear to the young person as a gentle giant who clearly, and with unshakable strength, conveys a number of very important messages:

- I will protect you.
- I care about you.
- I will not let you hurt yourself or me.
- I am not overwhelmed by your experiences or your feelings.
- I know it is not your fault.
- I know we can face these issues together.
- I know you are going to be OK.
- I will help you to be OK.

The following diagrammatically illustrates the basic messages sent to the child by the clinician, and the messages that should be received by the child during their work together. The messages illustrated below flow along a time continuum—the longer the clinician and child work together, and the stronger the relationship becomes, the more closely the message sent will parallel the message received.

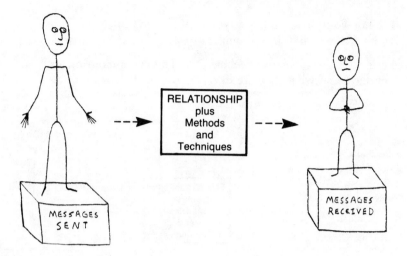

I respect you.

I like you.

You are interesting and fun.

I will be honest with you.

Kids come to therapy because of problems in the family or because of something that happened, like someone who is really sick or people fighting a lot or drugs or divorce or death or work problems or just kids having really mixed-up feelings.

Therapy is both play and work. Our job is to figure out worries, problems and mixed-up feelings.

I know what happened to you (or something about it) and I am not overwhelmed.
    You are OK now.
    You are still a child.
    I like you.
    I will keep you safe (if I can).

Maybe I am worthy of respect.

Maybe I am likable.

Maybe I am interesting and fun.

Maybe I can trust my therapist.

Oh, so that's why I'm here.

This sounds important, like a job. Maybe it's OK.

Uh-oh.

Maybe I'm OK.

Maybe if he knows and still likes me, I'm not so bad (damaged).

It's not your fault. I know you won't believe that for a while.

Let's see how many feelings you have and what they are like.

It is too my fault.

This is interesting and a little scary. This is fun.

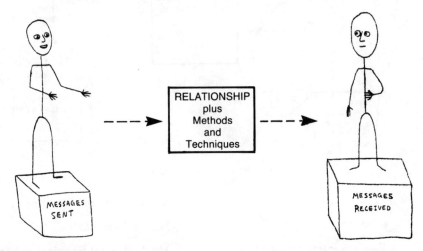

There are ways in which we are just like others and ways we are wonderfully special.

Let's slowly and carefully look at all the things that have happened to you. First I will explain why we are doing this, and how this will help us do our work.

Your experience (pain, loss, abuse, disfigurement, etc.) does not overwhelm, disgust, or frighten me or turn me on sexually.

Kids have lots of feelings about what has happened to them. The feelings are strong, mixed-up, and change back and forth. Our work now is to sort out how this was for you before and during what happened.

I'm just like others and also different in some ways—and that's OK.

Uh-oh. I don't know if I want to do that. It makes me scared.

It's important that we do this work, and I know why we need to talk about that stuff.

I guess I can do this work of discovering and telling. This really did happen to me. How come you still like me?

It's hard, interesting and not too awful, I guess, since others have felt this way too.

I really did feel this way.

I know about all these events and feelings, and I respect you and care about you.

I guess other people can like me and I can like myself.

It's not you fault! But you may still doubt that. Here are reasons why other kids used to believe it was their fault.

Well, I know at least part of what happened was my fault!

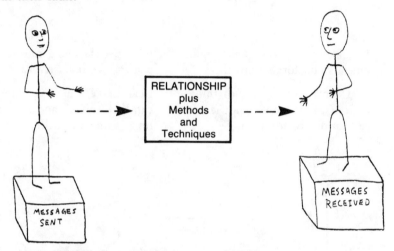

Because of what you did (in the playroom, office) I'm mad at you right now; but I won't hurt you or leave you, and I still like you.

Someone can be mad at what I've done and still like me. Someone can help me control my behavior without hurting or leaving me.

I get mad and control what I do about it. This is what I do.

This is how someone can have the feelings but not get into trouble.

You can be mean
        nasty
        really mad
        not perfect
        needy
        seductive
        soft and tender

I can act this way

and I won't hurt you
        trick you
        leave you
        use you

and be safe with my therapist and maybe others, too.

or let you hurt me
    hurt yourself
    hurt others
    parent me
    seduce me

My behavior can be controlled by my therapist. Maybe I can control it too.

and I will still respect you
    like you
    take care of
      you.

I am likable and worthy of care and respect even though I am not perfect.

I make mistakes and make amends and forgive myself.

Nice people make mistakes and can forgive themselves.

You can make a mess of things and, with acknowledgment and restitution, be forgiven.

I can make a mess of things and can be forgiven, and I can sometimes forgive myself.

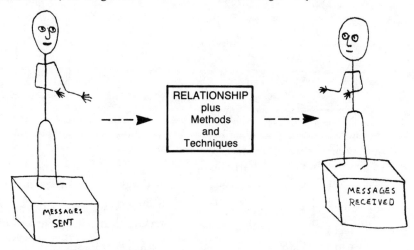

I like to take care of you
    do nice things for you
    tell you how pleased
    I am with your
    accomplishments
    celebrate with you.

I am worthy of nurturance.

This is how I nurture myself.

It's OK to nurture yourself, and this is how you do it.

Your body is yours
    valuable
    strong
    special
    worthy of
      respect
    worthy of care

I own my body and can control it and take care of it.

There are boundaries which I have set for my body.

It's OK to have personal boundaries, and this is how you keep them.

The spirit that resides within you is precious and powerful, and continues despite life's uncertainties.

The spirit inside me is precious, and strong and, lasts forever, no matter what.

I believe in you and value you.

I am valuable apart from anything else.

Let's explore all of the ideas, feelings, longings, and behaviors that you and other kids probably have which you haven't been ready to talk about yet—those things that began during or after the traumatic event.

Uh-oh. That part is scary (disgusting, perverted, etc.)

I guess I can talk about it a little bit.

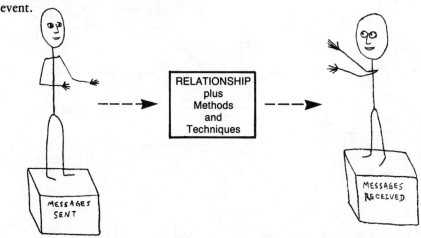

RELATIONSHIP
plus
Methods
and
Techniques

MESSAGES SENT

MESSAGES RECEIVED

I know all these things about you and I respect you and like you and will help you.

I can look clearly at what has happened, how I felt, and what I've done.

I witness your pain, pleasure, or humiliation and I am not overwhelmed. I respect you and care about you.

This happened to me and this is what I felt, thought, and did. I can still be respected and cared about.

Let's not blame.

Don't bother about blame.

There are some parts of the experience that may have benefited you. Let's explore what those might be, like strength, sensitivity, compassion, money, your own room, attention, a bicycle.

It's OK if I got some good things for what happened. I'm not afraid to know these things or to use them, just because they came from the event.

Let's understand what happened to you and how you responded.

I can understand.

Let's change your behaviors
  that are not respectful to your
  body, mind, or spirit
  make restitution where needed
  put this to rest
  move on.

I can do something about it.
I can let go.
I can move on.

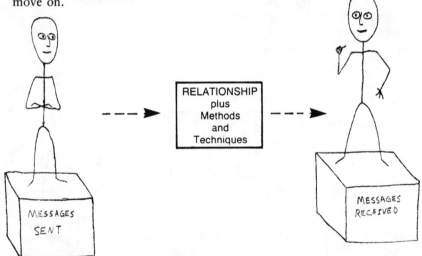

There are parts of you that are funny, heroic, strong, smart, warm, angry, gross, tender, weak, and tricky that make you wonderfully special. I like the whole, big, warm, smelly, alive package of you, and so do Mom, Dad, John, and Mary.

I'm OK.

Summary

The basic treatment process has been divided into four major categories:

1. Communication, in which the child learns how to delineate and express complex feelings

2. Sorting out, where he explores his understanding of what happened to him

3. Education, where he learns to understand the specific elements of the traumatizing experience

4. Perspective, where the child's experience is accepted as something that has happened to him, without the need for exaggeration or minimization of its impact.

An overview of the treatment process has been provided in terms of the clinical messages that need to be sent by the clinician—and how these messages are generally received by the child.

6
Explaining Therapy to the Child

I t is essential that the objectives of therapy be explained to the child victim as well as to the parents or other caregivers. Special care must be taken to ensure that the explanation is understood by *everyone*. Children often enter into treatment with the idea that there is something terribly wrong with them and that they are responsible for whatever event brought them to these circumstances. Furthermore, children who have been traumatized do not readily trust adults, and a careful explanation helps to reduce their anxieties about what is to happen. A straightforward approach is most likely to be the clinically appropriate method in virtually every instance.

It is useful to have both child and parents present during this explanation rather than explaining it to each separately. This reduces some of the parents' anxieties, gives them an opportunity to observe the therapist's approach, and assures the child that the process has parental approval. (See chapter 2 for a discussion of parental involvement in the child's treatment.)

A general caveat is in order: little children do not process ideas as quickly as adults, and the manner in which they do process is more concrete than that of an adult. Since a child communicates primarily through action and touch rather than words, it is important to pause after points are made or questions asked. Metaphor and graphic illustrations are very helpful, followed by sufficient time for mental processing.

Explanatory Metaphors

Following are three examples of explanatory statements which illustrate the previous comments.

The Helper and the Worker (for very young children)

"I help kids when there are problems in the family . . . "

Pause. (Many little ones will fill in here, describing exactly what happened, or at least their perception of what happened.) Then, slowly:

> problems like fighting, somebody being sick, horrible dreams, divorce, touches that are not okay, somebody dying, drugs, or drinking too much . . . "

Pause. Kids may volunteer their own problems. Many bring up issues that were not known to the therapist, thus providing information about the child's perceptions or primary concerns. By listing several family problems, including the reason for referral, the child is also given the message that other kids and families also have problems and that the therapist can handle it. Don't overwhelm them with too many items on the list.

> So my job is to be the helper. I help kids talk about what has been happening and talk about how they feel about it.

Pause. A response may or may not be forthcoming.

> Let me show you some things other kids have made (done) when they come to this playroom to talk about their problems . . .

This not only reinforces the concept that other children have problems and talk to the therapist about them, but it is a great icebreaker, conveying the notion that being in the office is not all drudgery.

> Your job is to be the worker. When you come here to see me we are going to play part of the time and work part of the time. Your job is to help me figure out what happened and how come it happened.

Pause.

> Another part of the work is for us to figure out how many different feelings you have about this, like maybe: scared, happy, excited, mixed-up.

Solidify learning with illustrations. For example,

> See these pictures? These were made by kids to show different feelings they have.

> Sometimes we can figure out ways to work on these problems.

Sometimes we will have Mom join us too. She can help us, or maybe we can tell her what we learned. Even if she doesn't join us she will know about what we're doing. There may be some things that we talk about in here that you are not ready to share with your parents right away, and we'll just tell them we will have something to say after we have done more work.

When secrecy has been part of the child's trauma, such as in ritual or sexual-abuse cases, it is best to declare clearly that no information will be kept from the parents, although some things may not be divulged for a few sessions—until the child has been strengthened enough to share the information.

The important thing is that we are going to be together every week. We will play and tell stories and talk about feelings and problems (or worries or what makes you sad, angry, or other things).

There are lots of ways we can talk about feelings. Let's look at our picture gallery. This picture John made is called the *Big, Bad Biting Dragon*. He told me sometimes this dragon got so mad he scared himself. And Jenny told a story on the tape recorder that she made for other kids to hear. It's about feeling all alone.

Would you like to make something now? I think we need to get to know each other better . . .

Your own judgment will determine the pacing, and how little or how much to say. It is important to give the child a sense of control while giving the strong message that the therapist is in charge.

The Coach and the Athlete (used with older children
and adults):

In our work together I will be like a coach and you will be like an athlete on the team. I'm strong, experienced, fun, smart, and I've worked with lots of kids, some just like you.

My job is to get to know you very well, and to help you figure out exactly what happened,
> what sense you made out of it,
> how you feel about it,
> what you did and thought about to help yourself, and

what you are doing now that might be causing bad feelings.

I do this by being a warrior who stands by protecting you so
    you can do your job without being bothered,
    being fun and playful so we can learn about each
        other and ourselves,
    being in charge and sometimes pushing you to do
        your work, and seeing that we get away from work when
        we need to,
    being gentle so that we can be quiet and thoughtful
        together, and
    being wise so that I can guide us on this journey
        together.

Your job is to be like an athlete in training who must come to the field
(office) regularly, even if:
    sometimes you don't feel like it,
    sometimes it seems like a waste of time,
    sometimes the work is hard.

You have to do the work. I can guide you, I may grouch at you, I'll
sometimes goof off with you, but you have to do the work, just as an
athlete has to do the work.

You get the payoffs. You will be a stronger, juicier, more real person,
and you will feel good about yourself.

I will never ask you to do anything that is not good for you.

It is important for you to give me information and ideas about what
will be helpful—what you think is useful, and what you think is a
waste of time.

The Detective (used with older kids and adults):

We will work together like the police detectives we often see on TV.
Although a few work alone, it is much better when they work as a
team, because then they can do more and they can help and protect
each other. [Discuss familiarity with detectives and anchor to child's
experience where possible.]

I'm like the old detective who has been doing this work for a long
time. I'm smart and can't be fooled. You're like the young detective

who is strong, smart, and likes to have fun, but you still don't know as much as I do. Our job is to figure things out together. One of the things we will have to figure out is how this big trouble happened in your family.

Now, like in any partnership, we need to get to know each other and get comfortable before we get started on our case. This means that when you come here, we will do a lot of fun things to get to feel easy together. Then when we're feeling like a team and ready to do some work, we'll start combining the work with the fun.

Some of the investigating we do will be hard, some of it will be interesting, there will be some surprises, and some of it will be fun. We will have to find out.

What we will be looking for is to understand exactly what happened, how you and everyone in the family feels about what happened, how your life is different now, and what plans you have for the future.

Summary

Children and their caregivers frequently have vague and sometimes erroneous ideas of why they are in therapy and how it is supposed to help, given that the traumatic event cannot be undone. Children who have not had the need for treatment explained to them are likely to make up their own self-defeating explanations, for example, that it is punishment, or that the reason for treatment is because they are to blame for what happened. A careful explanation of therapy not only dispels wrong ideas the child may have or might develop, but also can educate the child's caregivers, who may be inclined to remove a child from treatment prematurely, especially if they believe the process is useless or painful and not beneficial to the child.

7
Self-Blame

A common treatment objective is to have the child understand and accept that she is not to blame for the event which led to her present situation—assuming, of course, she was not actually responsible. The complex dynamics which foster this sort of deep-seated blame, and the resultant psychological impact, are described in chapter 3.

Self-blame is not easily dispelled. Clinicians regularly see adults who continue to harbor strong feelings of shame and guilt about events which took place during their childhood, for which they still feel responsible despite years of consideration and a more mature understanding, which could rationally absolve them of blame. Traumatizing occurrences tend to leave victims believing that they somehow could have or should have done something to prevent what happened to them, or that they somehow deserved what happened.

Responsibility

The child should be strongly and unequivocally told that the traumatizing event was not her fault, but that she, like other children before her, may not believe that for a while. The clinician represents reality, namely, It's not your fault. The child's need to hold on to her beliefs and express them is supported, while the clinician gently, relentlessly, directly, indirectly, and subliminally teaches the child that she is not to blame. She is also told she may have many feelings related to what happened—sad, mad, disappointed, lonely, and more—but her feelings of guilt or shame are based on wrong thinking or misunderstanding. If the child has actually been blamed by others, the clinician should tell her that it is not true and that the blaming person was in error.

Some of my colleagues disagree with this approach. They believe that the child will be compliant while secretly fostering feelings of self-blame, feeling misunderstood and discounted. And most importantly, they feel, the child may shield material from therapeutic intervention. Their preferred method is not to express a view to the child, but to remain neutral and allow the child full expression first.

I have given this criticism serious consideration, but maintain that it is essential to present the clear, emphatic, unequivocal view that the child is not responsible for the trauma unless it is true that she was responsible. (Examples of this latter situation would be fire-setting, mentioned earlier, or a six-year-old playing in the family car who releases the hand-brake, resulting in the car's rolling out of the driveway and maiming or killing the child's friend. In such instances, the clinician would explore intent and feelings, and gently and realistically help the child to accept her limited responsibility for the actions which led to the accident.)

Until the matter of responsibility is addressed, the child is likely to retain feelings of guilt and shame. Failure to propound the child's blamelessness may not only reinforce, but may actually encourage the child's perception of her responsibility. Not stating otherwise would be to agree by default.

A child who believes her feelings of self-blame are being discounted may shield material. But it is not likely that she will feel discounted and suppress genuine feelings if the therapist makes it acceptable for the child to disagree, encourages her to do so, and reinforces this position by giving examples of other children who initially blamed themselves. The therapist presents the facts of responsibility, but does not tell the child how she should feel.

The "It's not my fault," or INMF, work begins when therapy begins, and is a constant thread woven through the complex tapestry of treatment. This work is sometimes bold, sometimes barely visible, but always present. It does not stop when the youngster first says she knows she is not to blame; children will quickly mimic the stance of nonblame simply because they have learned to tell adults what adults want to hear. The clinician would do well to continue the work until he is certain that the child means what she says.

Creative Support for INMF

The use of storytelling is a wonderful way to teach and to learn for all of us. Stories can be created to address each dynamic that can foster feelings of self-blame in the child. Children readily make up their own learning stories when given some simple directions, such as, "Tell a story about a little skunk who did something wrong, and later lightning struck his den and he felt it must have been his fault." Linking the learning story to the child's own experience may or may not be needed. When personal creativity has been drained, friends, relatives, and colleagues can become good sources for stories.

During puppet play I said I wanted to direct the next scene, because I wanted the child to use her wonderful thinking ability to answer some questions. I set up the story by saying,

The scene involves a little girl who was very sick. When the parents brought her to the doctor, he said their daughter had diabetes, an illness that made her feel terrible whenever she ate anything with sugar in it, like candy and soda. The doctor told the parents they should be very careful and not allow their daughter to eat anything sweet. The parents questioned the doctor very carefully and really understood what he said. A week later, when they went shopping, the dad gave the little girl a candy bar. He knew it was wrong, but he did it anyway. The girl got very sick.

After we act this part out with fun and flair, I ask the child to think very hard and answer some questions.

Who did the wrong thing? What if the little girl didn't make the father stop? What if she enjoyed the candy? What if she really wanted it? What if she begged for it?

Depending on the age of the child, I might ham it up and say something like

I can't live another moment without a candy bar . . . please, please, even though you are my parent, let's forget that it's not good for me and do it anyway.

Puppets, of course, can say anything. And children as young as four can understand complexities such as these when the situation is understandable to them.

When work with children is directive, it should not be one-sided. The therapist and child can take turns deciding what to draw, or what theme the psychodrama will have. Opportunities to direct the play will build the child's sense of power and mastery, as well as giving his scary imagination a workout in a controlled setting.

Let's paint a picture together. I want us to make one character who is all good, one who is all bad, one who is basically good but does a bad thing, and one who is really bad but does one good thing. When we finish, we'll make up a story about these four characters.

This exercise is sufficiently complex for one session for most children. The process itself teaches and reinforces the notion that a good person, or one you need to love, is capable of doing something wrong without having to be viewed as totally bad. This exercise can enable a child to feel okay and not guilty about any affectionate feelings he may have toward an abusive parent.

In some instances I might ask the child to relate the characters to his own experience. Since the work takes a fair amount of time, it usually has to be continued to a later session, at which time the painting, which by now will be hanging on the wall, is the subject of reference.

When a child completes a painting and relates the painting's story, the therapist should visibly make written notes which the youngster sees attached to his painting. This notation establishes the importance of the story to the child, preserves the material as clinical notes, and serves as a refresher for possible use in later sessions. Collaterally, the story is seen by other children who come into the playroom and stimulates them to do likewise.

One of the children's favorite exercises is yelling out the window, with me, "It's not my fault!" I tell them that all the kids like to do this, that the firemen whose station is down the street know it's never the kid's fault when _____ happens (refer to the reason the child is there), and that they like to hear us, so we have to yell really loud. This is a very powerful exercise. Kids who will not say INMF, or who do so only halfheartedly, will readily, even avidly, say the words when they have a chance to yell out the window. Children who adamantly insisted that they were to blame for their parent's behavior (alcoholism, abuse) did not hesitate to join me in yelling INMF out the window. Rarely will a youngster refuse to join in this exercise, and I have not had any suggest that something other than INMF be yelled. Yelling freely to the general public seems to imprint the message and counteracts feelings of self-blame. The child first tells the universe and then learns to tell himself. It's like peeling an orange—one starts from the outside and moves inward.

I have been told by several young people that when self-blaming thoughts emerged, even years after the initial course of treatment, these thoughts were quickly and powerfully overlaid by remembrances of the intense, playful times in our work together, which would usually evoke a smile and feeling of security. And they remembered not only the laughter and fun parts of the therapy, but also the quiet, poignant talks we had in the "soft corner," exploring tender feelings relating to their beliefs of responsibility.

> Rob told his mother he was thinking about his dad's car accident and was remembering how we had a therapy session at the house when his dad came home from the hospital. That session had been especially notable because it ended with the whole family's making an "It's Not Robbie's Fault" banner that ran the length of their dining room. They invited the grandparents to dinner that night so they, too, could appreciate the family's artwork and affirm its meaning.
>
> The mother, who had been part of the treatment team for the

child, was a sensitive woman who remembered that the thrust of the home session had been on self-blame. She gently helped Rob explore his feelings about the accident and his father's resultant disability. She made a mental note of their talk, being particularly attuned to those things which might indicate a new concern from Rob about his responsibility, and called me the following day for a consultation.

That same night Rob had a menu-sized card propped up on the dinner table on which he had written, "Be it known to all ye who partake of food from this table . . . It stilleth is not my fault (about the accident) or anybody else's and the whole thing makes me MAD as helleth. Forsooth, Rob."

Rob came back for six sessions. We worked on some new issues related to his then-current developmental stage, that is, his embarrassment and resentment about having a paraplegic father, and his sense of shame and guilt for feeling as he did.

Children have made big posters on which they pasted their instant photographs and wrote, "It's not my fault." Some have made INMF badges to wear at home or on a supervised visit with an abusive parent. Others have written INMF prayers, or performed INMF dances.

Privacy versus Secrecy

The openness and direct expressions of feelings appropriate in a treatment setting must not be continued indiscriminately outside that arena. The therapist needs to remind the parents and the children to respect their own family privacy. Unfortunately, the negative reception with which such news is usually met outside the family more than offsets any benefit that might be gained from being able to speak freely and openly about the situation. Neighbors gossip; classmates can be mean; parents panic. The family should decide with whom the child may talk about the situation, remembering that adolescents need more flexibility in this than do younger kids.

I remind youngsters that their mother does not tell everyone how much money she carries in her purse, not because she is ashamed of the money or the amount, but because it is . . . (pause, and wait for the child to fill in that it is private, or nobody's business). The child is told emphatically, and can understand, that she is allowed to discuss the traumatizing events with ——— (have the parents come up with a list, such as the doctor, Grandma, BettyLou, children in the therapy group, whoever can and should be properly designated). As far as anyone else is concerned, the matter is private, not shameful, as is the money in Mom's purse.

Religious Support

The family's religious adviser may be encouraged to come to the therapist's office to take part in a therapy session. If the family has been looking to this person for support, it is even more important that the therapist and he be together during a session. His support can be very helpful. Or, contrariwise, he may be overly protective of the child and may be talking to the family and child in ways that need to be corrected. It is sometimes useful to include parents and siblings at the meeting with the religious adviser.

Prior to extending an invitation to a clergyman to join in a clinical session, the therapist should clarify the proposed objectives and format for the meeting. If he is unwilling or unable to abide by the rules established by the therapist, or if it appears through this initial contact that he may somehow sabotage the process, the clergyman should not be invited.

During the session the therapist should tell him, in the youngster's presence, that lots of children believe it is their fault no matter what others say, and ask the adviser for a religious perspective.

The religious adviser should reinforce the therapist's position that the child's job is to be a child, which means to grow, to learn, to play, to make mistakes, and sometimes to be naughty or rebellious. The child's job does *not* include being godlike, taking care of her parents, or doing things to make up for what happened. They should also explore notions the child may have about God's participation in the traumatizing event. For example, many children believe God was punishing them. The religious adviser should tell the child that God was not punishing her, that He loves her, and, furthermore, knows it's not her fault.

This session should be held in the therapist's office, which, by now, has been firmly established as a safe environment where powerful feelings can be contained. This location also gives more power to what the therapist says.

Summary

A key issue to explore and eliminate is the matter of self-blame. The clinician needs to balance the work in this arena between play statements and serious statements, both with the underlying message that responsibility for the trauma does not lie with the child. Time and permission is provided so that there is emotional space for the child to express contrary feelings. Even after a child has said he believes it is not his fault, the clinician needs to periodically check in with the child, by asking something like, "On a scale of 1 to 100, how close are you to really believing in your bone marrow that it is truly not your fault?" Many of the techniques that reduce self-blame can be dramatic, fun, and well-remembered by the child in case self-doubt about responsibility arises in the future.

8
Powerlessness

A sense of powerlessness, which causes an inability to act or perform effectively, often becomes part of a child's concept of himself following a trauma. His perception of the experience (which may be a reality) is that there was nothing he or his parents could do to stop the event. Not uncommonly, adults who have been unable to integrate the traumatizing events of childhood perceive themselves as ineffectual people, and respond to situations that are reminders of the early trauma with feelings of helplessness.

Empowering Process

Empowering a child who has been traumatized is a constant, vital activity, like a heartbeat, that must be present throughout treatment. Clinicians can create specific exercises and play sequences that help a child experience power, but it is more effective to be constantly alert to any opportunity to give the child choices, to provide opportunities for him or her to behave effectively, to highlight those times when the child is acting and performing well, and to teach others in the child's environment to support and enhance developing power in the child.

It is likely there will be times during the course of treatment when medical or legal procedures require the child to be cajoled, coerced, or forced into doing things against his wishes. This cannot be avoided, but even in these situations there may be opportunities for the youngster to make choices, such as the time of the meeting or appointment, who will accompany the child, what he can bring with him, and what they will do afterward. Hospitalized children can be empowered, for instance, by guaranteeing them that specific playtimes will not be interrupted for medical procedures. These children can have some decision-making power over medical procedures by stating where and when blood samples are to be drawn, and they can be taught to do some procedures for themselves, such as suctioning.

From Victim to Survivor

In everyday play, as well as in play therapy, children commonly take on the role of aggressor, vanquisher, or super hero. Those who have been traumatized can get stuck in a limited play theme such as killing and burying everything so that the event is over, but do not seem to feel strengthened, comforted, or relieved by the enactments. They appear addicted to the helpless victim role.

There is a striking similarity between these children and adults who become bogged down in purging emotions related to childhood trauma, and who do not move on in their lives. There is also a resemblance to attachment-impaired children who constantly cling to their caregivers without appearing to gain anything from the interaction. The repetitiveness of the behavior and the lack of reward can elicit antagonism from those who want to help. Children recognize the antagonism, which then affirms their view that the world is a hostile place.

Young people need to know that there is life beyond victimization. They should be clearly told and shown what it will be like to transcend the traumatic experience, exactly how to achieve the next step, how they will be guided and helped, and how they will know when they are successful. This can be accomplished (1) by direct discussion of treatment objectives and planning with the child, (2) through direct meetings with other children who have successfully integrated similar experiences, or by viewing videotapes made by those children in which they discuss their progress through a successful treatment program, and (3) through learning and rehearsing the move from powerlessness to effectiveness via nondirective play and direct practice.

It is particularly important to work closely with the caregivers because (1) they need a clear understanding of how the child can be empowered, (2) they find it very difficult to know when to respect the child's limitations and when to urge the child to try harder, and (3) they may consciously or unconsciously reinforce powerlessness in the child.

Children's repetitive play themes can reflect their entrenched feelings of powerlessness. The following example illustrates how a child was helped to gain a sense of power over what happened to him.

Six-year-old Billy spent a part of every therapy session creating a war in the sand tray. He divided the tray in half, with all the monsters, powerful animals, and weapons on the side he claimed was his, and directed me to place the human figures and vulnerable animals on my side. He then proceeded to annihilate all the figures in my territory. There was no progress and no deviation from this theme after six months of therapy. Being concerned that Billy was locked into a process that was not helpful—and from sheer boredom—I began to nudge him into changing the drama. I created wise allies who taught people to use invisible shields and poison gas that kept monsters away. My human figures had fun times and pizza-parties, to which they invited Billy's monsters.

Billy gradually added creative twists to his play sequence. Without letting down his guard in play, he began to expand beyond the kill versus be killed theme. His monsters still "wiped out" my figures, but Billy insisted they were not dead now but could still get up and have a good time; a few of his monsters would join the party while the rest stood by ready to destroy everything at his command. Over the next months Billy began to place some of the human figures on his side and gave some of the monsters to me. He directed that they form an alliance and join forces to defend against a specific villain, a small human figure he identified as "Steve" (the name of the adolescent who had in reality terrorized Billy). Billy led the therapist, all the monsters, the weapons, and the soldiers against Steve.

A breakthrough occurred when Billy demonstrated his tension and feelings of powerlessness, by stopping the action after less than a minute into a "war," filling the playroom baby bottle with water, and nursing. I acknowledged his regressive behavior by asking him how old he was feeling at that moment. His response was "Three," the age when he was terrorized. I gently pressed him to continue by saying, "If we had this Steve guy securely tied up so he couldn't possibly get loose, and had all our people and animals standing guard, how would a three-year-old show Steve his feelings? What would he say? What would he do? What noises might he make? You can sit here drinking your bottle, but just tell me what I should do and say to Steve." Billy directed the action while holding on to the baby bottle, drinking from it when his tension mounted. He had me make a clay penis for the doll and paint it with "blood," because Steve had hurt someone with it. He directed me to fill a disposable syringe with "blood" and repeatedly inject the doll's clay penis.

At my suggestion, Billy also verbalized some feelings by directing the monsters to tell Steve what a stupid, rotten, mean, bad guy he was, and how he was going to be punished.

After several sessions Billy was able to overpower Steve by himself. He had advanced to a place where he could vanquish his foe without having his therapist or the monsters do it for him. Using the Clay Bomb exercise described in chapter 17, he directly expressed his rage and fears as a three-year-old, then as a four-year-old, until he progressed to expressing his feelings at his present six-year age. Billy's parents, siblings, and the child's attorney came to a subsequent session in which Billy directed them in the Clay Bomb exercise, so he could see how angry each of them felt about what had happened to him.

His sense of mastery was evident in subsequent clinical sessions. He twice acted out a sand-tray drama in which the violent intruder came on the scene, Billy got help from others, overpowered Steve, placed him in a cage with a monster as guard, and then continued playing, having pizza parties, and racing cars with the sand tray figures. Basically, he learned that bad guys exist, they can be dealt with, and life goes on.

I was then able to have quiet discussions with Billy about what had happened to him, his past powerlessness, his present abilities, and how there might be future times when the traumatic incident would have to be brought out and reexamined, like an old photo album, so he could understand it as an older boy, and then put it away again while he went on doing what he needed to do.

This example illustrates the clinical nudging sometimes needed to guide and direct a child into moving forward into a position of power. Traumatized children are often so overwhelmed by their feelings, including their worries about loyalties and retaliation, that they require the safety and guidance of their therapists to enable them to engage in play. Symbolic play provides safe opportunities for reenactment, rehearsal, the practice needed to strengthen the child, and prepares them for dealing directly with the traumatizing events.

Summary

The powerlessness experienced subsequent to trauma often extends to other areas of the child's life, leaving him feeling powerless in everything. For some, the powerless role is reinforced by parents' overprotectiveness. Corrective experiences are needed in the clinical setting and in the child's home, school, and recreation environments; this shows the youngster that he can make choices and take actions, including asking for help when necessary. Therapists sensitive to this clinical objective will find many opportunities to empower the child during the course of treatment.

9
Destructive/Abusive Behaviors

S elf-destructive behaviors range from suicide to a victim's subtle sabotage of her own achievements, and includes everything in between. The
child may be dedicated, at significant psychological and physical cost
to herself, to attempts to remedy what happened to the family. Children who
have been abused often create situations in which abuse is elicited from caregivers who are not the original abusers. The self-hurting can be direct, as with
the child who makes secret, ritualistic cuts on her skin, or more subtle, like
the youngster who always appears battle-scarred from chronic "accidents" in-
curred during driven, high risk play. Some children create situations in which
they are begging to be hurt or punished, such as provoking the school bully
into a fight, or breaking into a house when they know someone is home.

Behaviors destructive to other children, animals, and property also range
from overt, such as the child whose apparent lack of impulse-control results
in explosive physical rages, to the boy who "accidentally" injures an infant
sibling. Many children who have been sexually exploited or overstimulated,
sexually assault other children in turn.

Protection

The most immediate objectives of treatment are the most obvious, namely, to
protect the child from himself and to keep him from hurting others. The risk
of destructive and abusive behavior must be immediately and directly
assessed, and the possibility of risk must be borne in the mind of the therapist
throughout her association with the child. In these cases, the therapist will
probably have to provide guidance and support to the adults caring for the
child. They, in turn, have to provide strict supervision to insure the safety of
the child and his environment.

If the needed protection cannot be provided in the home, it may be
necessary to place the child in a hospital or residential treatment setting where
such supervision is available. This complex clinical decision requires weighing

the psychological impact of placing the young person in out-of-home care against the psychological consequences for the child should he harm himself, others, or property.

Control

The next focus of treatment is to bring the destructive and abusive behavior under control. Eliminating objectionable behavior is not usually an immediate occurrence. Most practitioners recognize that change occurs slowly and is brought about by direct behavioral intervention, environmental control when needed, and psychodynamic interventions that deal with the issues and conflicts leading to the behavior. Many clinicians unrealistically seek a solution or technique that will immediately stop or change the child's behavior when it is frightening or upsetting to the clinician, such as sexual behaviors. This attitude is readily picked up by the caregivers and the child, and then all parties, including the therapist, become discouraged when quick results are not forthcoming. The desire for immediate cessation is often based on the adult's fears and embarrassment about the exhibited behavior.

Destructive and abusive actions, like other conduct which originates in traumatic events, serve the child in some way. The practitioner should consider the following as some of the more common needs being accommodated by these behaviors:

- Survival
- Gaining understanding of his own victimization
- Gaining mastery by reenactment, this time as the aggressor
- Addiction to the sensation (power/excitement/fear/other)
- Attempting to hold on to a positive image of his own abuser
- Revenge
- Power
- Reinforcement of self-blame, guilt, shame
- Need to be punished, hurt, killed by another
- Reenacting learned behavior
- Need for affection and emotional closeness

The child's destructive or abusive conduct is, initially, often a conscious or unconscious attempt to meet an emotional need or to resolve an emotional conflict. She then finds that the acts do more than relieve tension: they are experienced as powerful and exciting, and take on a life of their own. The behaviors strongly reinforce themselves. For example, setting a fire may meet a child's need to express rage related to having been tortured. She experiences such power and relief of tension in the act of fire-setting that the behavior is repeated.

Another example is the child who sexually abuses someone much younger to meet the need for mastery of his own victimization. He finds his orgasmic response and relief of tension so powerful that he repeats the behavior.

Stimuli perceived as threatening often engender reflexive rage in destructive children; this behavior can become habitual. One treatment objective is to teach these children to slow down their reaction time, first for a second, and then for longer periods. They are taught to think and to feel and to decide on a course of action during the gradually increasing period.

John, age seven, often defined ambiguous or negative interactions as threatening or rejecting, and he responded with extreme aggression. A child bumping into him during a schoolyard game would be viciously attacked. John kicked a hole in the wall in response to his foster mother's enforcement of a "time-out" consequence. Through direct discussion and with the help of metaphor imbedded in story-telling and dramatic play, the therapist and John came to the conclusion that his life might be better if he were not always in trouble. They enlisted the aid of the foster mother and John's teacher as members of a treatment team whose goal was to work out and implement a plan to help John win personal control over his rageful actions. The boy was told he need not work on gaining personal control until his team had worked out a plan of behavior. This took pressure off the boy, reinforced the idea of team support, and gave needed time for the development of a workable plan.

The first phase was designated a "time of clarification" during which the team, with John as the leader and the therapist as the coach, worked on describing exactly what was meant by personal control. This was done during several short meetings over a ten-day period. The group discussed and wrote brief, illustrated descriptions of "no control," "minimal control," "regular control," and "super control." Each group member gave examples of incidents in their own lives in which they responded with each level of control. The group agreed that the best goal for John, at that time, was to have more minimal- and regular-control incidents in a week than no-control or super-control components.

The second phase of work was called "monitoring." John kept records of the times that he did not maintain minimal or regular control. Using a tape recorder, he described briefly what happened and how he responded. He recorded, as best he could, his feelings and thoughts just before the event, during the event, and what he told himself and how he felt afterward. His foster mother assisted him in condensing the material produced about two incidents. His teacher helped him do the same for another incident. The tape recordings and brief written report were presented at the next team meeting.

John and the therapist spent time during individual sessions and during team meetings discussing "red flags," signals they had identified which indicated a probable loss of personal control. These red flags included times when John thought about his mother and not living with her at home, which made him angry, and those times he felt other kids did not want to play with him and he got mad. The team developed a plan which included identifying a number of "mad behaviors" acceptable for John to use when he became angry. These included jumping up and down or yelling in the yard at home (no profanity), writing mad or bad or dirty words on toilet paper and flushing them down the toilet at home or at school, hitting a pillow or his bed, making fierce, growling noises in the boys' bathroom at school, telling the person he was mad at that he was mad, and asking someone on the treatment team for a fifteen-minute appointment to say or show how mad he really was about something. The written plan of action was as follows:

1. John would be on the alert for red flags and when he felt mad, would exercise one or more of the allowable mad behaviors

2. In order to strengthen personal control, he would train himself in the following areas as if preparing for the Olympics:
   a. talking to himself, saying he was right to feel mad, and has personal control over what he does when he feels mad. He is to say this before brushing his teeth, before getting on the school bus, before recesses, and before each regular meal on Saturday. Sunday is a day off!
   b. practicing the Ocean Exercise (five-minute relax-action exercise) once a day;
   c. spending part of each therapy session for the following two months learning and practicing how to recognize and show many different feelings so he would have more to choose from than just mad, sad, and OK;
   d. keeping a Personal Control Chart to show his progress. He was to be in charge of the chart, keeping it up-to-date and bringing it to therapy sessions.

3. During those weeks in which John *won* a medal in his Personal Control Olympics (that is, he exhibited minimal or regular con-

trol more often than no control or super control), he could either pick out a video at the store for the family to watch, or he could have a dollar to spend on video games.

Underlying Issues

The clinician parallels his behavioral therapy with psychodynamic therapy, conducting both at a pace the child is able to tolerate. A decision will have to be made as to the usefulness of, and degree to which, the child needs to make conscious connections between the dynamics of the trauma and subsequent destructive or abusive behavior. Whether or not the child's developing insight is a goal, the practitioner should go through the following steps to diminish the behavior:

1. identify the needs being met by the behaviors.
2. help the child meet those needs in an appropriate way.
3. identify possible underlying conflicts.
4. help the child achieve some degree of resolution of those conflicts.

The underlying issue for John in the case mentioned was his profound sense of abandonment by his mother. His tender feelings for her were intertwined with feelings of ambivalence and anger toward her. The focus of the psychodynamic work was to assist John in identifying, acknowledging, and owning these conflicting emotions.

A base of strength and understanding needed to be established, before exploring the more tender feelings. To accomplish this, John and his therapist had to spend some solid time talking about all of the boy's memories of his mother, focusing first on the good times he remembered—so he would not be utterly bereft when they talked about the hard times. Acknowledging his longings for her, mourning his losses, and coping with the uncertainty of whether or not she would ever get her life sufficiently together to take him home, were pieces to be dealt with during John's therapy.

John needed to have his behavior brought under control just as much as he needed to work on the deep, underlying issues. Dealing with one and not the other would have been a disservice to the child, and would not have gotten the job done. The boy's academic learning was impaired, he was not involved in social relationships, and nobody liked him. His destructive behaviors were strongly self-reinforcing because they made him feel powerful, brought him attention, made people afraid of him and, perhaps most importantly, supported his belief that he was not worthy of being liked and cared about and that no one could control him, not even himself.

The example of John's treatment demonstrates how a clinician can work simultaneously on underlying issues while dealing directly with urgent behavioral matters.

Community Members as Clinical Helpers

Friends, associates, clergy, and others from the local community who are known to the child, can be incorporated as clinical helpers in a structured and limited way for virtually any trauma treatment.

The next example is of a technique I learned from Felix Polk, a clinical psychologist in Berkeley. It is a powerful intervention for use where there has been a suicide attempt.

> Mark was a fifteen-year-old who saw an assailant shoot his mother. He was overwhelmed with feelings, including guilt at not being able to protect her. He became the "man of the family," who tried to fill the role of father at home and through his driven academic work, tried also to be a superstar son. He was tough, straight, and cool, an emotionally rigid teenager who had friends, but who kept relationships emotionally distant. He had no insight into the impossible demands he placed on himself.
>
> There was a family history of suicide. A paternal uncle had killed himself five years earlier, and it appeared to Mark's therapist that the family tended not only to idealize the uncle but in some ways, to support his action as having been a viable solution. While exploring the lethality of the current situation, the therapist learned that Mark had stolen a gun from a relative "for my protection," and that he fantasized killing himself. He had fired the pistol "to see if it worked."
>
> The therapist and three clinical colleagues whom he pressed into service called a meeting of people who knew Mark. Prior to the meeting each person was told that Mark and his guardian had given their consent for the meeting, and that its purpose was to utilize their collective caring and skills in problem-solving to help Mark.
>
> The group, in Mark's presence, heard a talk from his therapist, again explaining that their assistance was needed to help Mark solve his problem. They were then divided into their respective groups: church people, teachers, relatives, neighbors, friends from school, friends from the neighborhood, and the distributor and two customers from his paper route. With the four clinicians circulating amongst them to facilitate the process, and with Mark observing, the seven groups spent two hours working on suggestions that might help the young man.

After a break, the groups reconvened and verbally reported their concrete offers of help. Written copies of their offers were given to Mark at the end of the meeting. These included offers for dinner, offers to tutor Mark's younger siblings (thereby lessening his worries about them), and an offer to join the basketball team. Most important, however, was the clear and convincing message that people cared about him, that he was not alone, and that people could and would help him in many ways.

The impact on Mark reduced the potential for self-harm immediately and gave an enormous boost toward his being able to more realistically examine the traumatic event in the family, to look more closely at his assumptions about his own life, and to begin to plan a future direction for himself.

Dual Focus for Victim-Victimizing Child

A child who is both a victim and a victimizer requires exquisite treatment interventions that simultaneously address both issues. One cannot teach a child to understand that he is a victim (not responsible for what happened) while, at the same time, dismissing his own assaultive behavior and the effect of that behavior on his own victims. Likewise, one cannot address only the child's assaultive behaviors, but must deal with the underlying issues that acknowledge his own victimization.

Some clinicians elect to work only with victims. These practitioners may well miss the victimizer present in the same child, since that behavior is likely to remain undisclosed unless its presence is specifically sought.

Other clinicians will work with the victimizer aspect, but only superficially and tentatively, while emphasizing the child's own victimization. Children treated that way quickly learn to admit their assaultive behavior and apologize in order to avoid exploration of what is difficult for them to deal with. In communities where resources to help troubled children are limited or nonexistent, children often end up in short-term peer therapy groups where they learn to say, "I did it, it's totally my fault, and I feel bad." The unwary therapist may then look no further, and in fact may applaud the disclosure and begin the process of terminating treatment.

Children who assault others often do so by engaging in behaviors they know to be powerful as an attempt to escape their own state of helplessness and terror. These children must learn that there are ways to feel freedom from helplessness other than by dominating and abusing others. The following example demonstrates the use of metaphor, developed and used as a reference repeatedly during the course of treatment of a young female victim/offender.

Anna, nine, had been terrorized, abused, and forced to engage in sadistic rituals by members of a cult. A primary treatment goal was to eliminate her violent sexual assaults on other children. To accomplish this, Anna had to learn that there were places for her in life other than as extremely powerful (as the victimizer) or extremely powerless (as the victim). She needed to learn cognitively, emotionally, physically, and spiritually that power could be exercised without domination, abuse, or pain, and that she could be powerful.

The therapist, with Anna's help, created a story using known characters from *Star Wars*.

To summarize, Princess Leah was captured by the powerful, evil, and slimy Prince Zanox. His intent was to marry her and so consolidate their respective empires, with himself as ruler. The Zanoxans supported their leader and helped in Princess Leah's "education." They drugged her and tortured her and forced her to watch and then participate in all manner of disgusting things. Slimy Prince Zanox consulted with all his magicians and all his scientists to think of ways he could make the Princess become one of them. She fought hard, but was outnumbered and overpowered. She began to despair. Her body weakened, her heart ached, and she began to think that the evil prince would win.

When she felt totally helpless and was ready to succumb to Zanox, a greenish fog appeared in her cell and materialized into Yoda. This strange little gnome emanated great power, although only three feet high. He spoke to Leah gently but powerfully, explaining that she had deep within her a force, a power equal to that of Prince Zanox. He told her the force could be used for good as well as evil.

Princess Leah escaped, taking with her two young boys and an adult man who had been held captive for years. In the following adventures, Princess Leah used her bravery, intelligence, innovativeness, etc., to help all of them.

Yoda reappeared at the end, when Leah was frightened. He dramatically explained that, although she was afraid, she did not lose the force within her. He told her that those who learned to control the force within them did so despite their fears. "Fear," he said, "is to be respected, and one must honor the ability to experience fear. Fear is a powerful fuel for humans, even for princesses. It accelerates the brave heart, sharpens the clever mind, feeds determination, and allows one to use the power within."

The princess, despite her fears, overcame the final obstacles and led them to safety. There was a major celebration. Leah had learned the lesson well—that even a princess is sometimes frightened, but that does not mean she loses power. The force was within her and would always be there. Princess Leah could use the force silently or in a glorious display of fury; it was hers to be used for goodness and forever.

The framework was provided by the therapist; the colorful, juicy details by both the therapist and Anna over the course of several clinical sessions. The story was embellished with the use of paintings, clay sculptures, and psychodrama. Anna strongly identified with the princess and the Force—and the therapist, of course, became the hairy little gnome.

Using metaphor is fun. The clinician can, through metaphor, bypass protective barriers and slip important messages to the child. Creating meaningful stories encourages creativity in fearful and constricted children. Excellent descriptions of the clinical use of metaphor can be found in the work of Mills and Crowley (1986) and Bettelheim (1977).

Summary

Children may react to traumatic experiences with destructive and abusive behaviors. The practitioner's first step is to carefully evaluate the need to protect the child from hurting himself and others. The assessment will include looking at the ability of the child's caregivers to control the destructive/abusive behavior and to provide adequate and proper supervision. Placement in out-of-home care, or in a restrictive environment, is the result of a clinical decision arrived at only after extremely careful and thorough consideration of the consequences of such action.

Children who are both victims and abusive/destructive need to have both issues powerfully addressed in treatment. The clinical stance is to be simultaneously tough and tender. The child learns tenderness toward himself through the modeling of the therapist, and learns that hurting behavior is unacceptable regardless of his past learning or experiences. Therapists who focus primarily or entirely on only one aspect because of their own fears, comfort level, skills, or sympathies, are not likely to be effective with their therapy.

10
Body Integrity

E stablishing a sense of body integrity should be a treatment goal for most traumatized children. It is specifically indicated when the traumatic events led to the young victims feeling physically vulnerable, ugly, powerless, having no control over what is done to their bodies, or believing their bodies are toxic—that is, that their bodies can cause fear, lust, or loss of control in adults. These are children who have been subjected to serious illness, disfigurement, or intrusive medical procedures, who have witnessed violence or the death of loved ones, or those who have been severely abused.

Trauma is experienced in the body, and so the treatment needs to provide corrective experiences that impact upon the child physically and psychologically. Van der Kolk and Greenberg (1987) reviewed studies conducted to determine how people organize their experiences, and note that some victims of trauma may be without the symbolic and linguistic representations necessary to place the trauma in its historical context. This suggests that a verbal approach alone may be ineffective. The same authors also present and summarize recent studies of physiological arousal resulting from trauma, and suggest that a physiological addiction to trauma may develop under certain conditions, becoming an adaptive, automatic response to stimuli. This possibility suggests that body therapy, which teaches a child to modify and control physiological responses, can assist in reducing the addictive components of the child's functioning.

Movement, music, body-awareness exercises, self-calming techniques, and sensorimotor play provide the most effective therapy for children who experience extreme physical vulnerability and/or who have distorted body concepts. The reader is directed to chapter 17 for exercises in each of these categories. Other therapy techniques will also be needed, but experiencing physical power, pride, and mastery helps most children to balance their negative physical experiences and leads to feelings of body integrity.

Treatment is maximized by having the youngster participate in structured, regular physical activity as part of the treatment plan. Gymnastics; soccer, and other team sports; ballet; or other physical activity that leads to a concerted use of the body's large muscles can provide a powerful positive experience. Intense, positive physical experiences help to counterbalance the negative physical ordeals in the child's memory; the child who attains some success in gymnastics will probably develop a powerful sense of body control and pride. The attendance of adults at gymnastic demonstrations reinforces the child's positive feelings and helps to neutralize strong adult-associated negative memories, such as having been sexually abused. The child will remember the abuse, but will not be as likely to feel physically repulsive or helpless.

The therapist may need to begin work in a slow or minimally intrusive manner, due to the child's inhibitions, physical handicaps, or environmental limitations (such as hospital rules), but as the child's comfort level increases, the therapist should move just a little ahead in order to create a stretch for the youngster. As with other therapeutic approaches, the therapist should actively join with the child.

A severely burned three-year-old girl avoided adult contact. The therapist started by blowing bubbles where the child could see them. When the child began to maintain attention, the therapist introduced music on a tape recorder; this addition resulted in the little girl's making longer and more frequent eye contact. The therapist then began singing children's songs and playing one-sided child games. After two months of bubble blowing, music and games, the child started to engage interactionally by making continuous eye contact and wiggling her toes on cue.

A diabetic child who resisted emotional connections with others was given a rubber baby doll and "hospital equipment" that included syringes without needles. She eventually allowed the therapist to assist her in giving the doll countless injections. Music was played in the background. They began to make dolls move to the music, and then the child and therapist moved to the music. The music became increasingly energetic, and eventually the child assumed the role of a military commander, barking out orders to the therapist, dolls, and toys, all to the sounds of stirring march music.

Body Awareness

Many traumatized children behave as though alienated from all or part of their bodies—as though parts of them were anesthetized or did not belong to them. The clinician's task is to create a safe and fun environment in which the child can shift from a negative to a positive position, such as from unawareness or awkwardness in the physical self to awareness and confidence; from rigid or chaotic movement to fluid and integrated movement; from being physically fearful to being physically relaxed.

The following exercises and examples provide some general ideas on which the reader can build to create specific exercises for each unique client.

Singing with Movement

Singing and moving with the child serve several beneficial functions. A closer relationship, a joining, is established; the clinician does not appear as another intimidating, demanding adult; the child learns new words and a new vehicle for expressing herself; shame is lessened; there is greater freedom for expression; everyone has a better time.

Peter Alsop has written many songs that delight children and which can be particularly helpful in therapy. A few lines from his song, "My Body," follow. The words to the entire song are in appendix G. This song is wonderful when working on body awareness.

> My nose was made to sniff and to sneeze;
> To smell what I want, and to pick when I please!
> (chorus) My body's nobody's body but mine!
> You run your own body; let me run mine!
> My lungs were made to hold air when I breathe.
> I am in charge of just how much. . . . I need!

An "oldie but goodie" that is effective for desensitizing children about their bodies and helping them learn to enjoy moving is "The Hokey Poky."

> You put your right hand in. You put your right hand out.
> You put your right hand in and you shake it all about.
> You do the Hokey Poky and you turn yourself about.
> And that's what it's all about!
> [repeat for other body parts]

Movement and Music

It is fun and beneficial for both child and therapist to move creatively to music, including classical, new age, environmental sounds, and Sesame Street music. They can pretend they are climbing mountains, trekking through the jungle, exploring underwater, or being a snowflake in a storm. The movements are high and low, fast and slow, smooth and jerky. Gradually, the child becomes less afraid of his own physical expression and gains mastery of his body.

Normalizing the Genital Area

The child needs to learn that his genitals are a normal part of his body and that everyone else has genitals, which are normal parts of their bodies. He needs to learn that there is no need to behave as if his genitals will disappear or explode if given attention.

The sexually traumatized child has probably never discussed the problem with an adult other than in a very serious, matter-of-fact manner. Once a secure working relationship has been established, the child can be helped, and the relationship bettered, by getting away from serious discussions of the genitalia and approaching the subject in a manner that is both playful and straightforward. (Playfulness does not include teasing, which can be hurtful and confusing.)

> Your mother used your private parts for sexual reasons and we've talked about how you felt about that. I notice that when we've done some exercises, or some drawing, you act uncomfortable when we mention those parts. I thought it would be kind of interesting to talk about why we have those parts of our bodies and what life would be like without them.

The clinician should use the child's words for body parts, unless the clinician finds them so objectionable she cannot hear them or use them without a noticeable negative reaction. In that situation, she must find a way to allow the child expression while creating a comfortable environment for herself.

> I know that you and your mom use the words "pussy" and "prick" when you are together, and that your social worker and the district attorney wanted you to use those words to describe what happened. I don't feel comfortable using those words with children. Your mom's words were for grown-ups, not for young people. So, while she's learning not to do that anymore, you and I are going to learn to use child words. Children your age who live in this neighborhood call boys' body parts "penis," or "pee-pee," or "wiener." Have you heard these names used before? Have you used any of them? Which one would you choose for us to try for a while? Girls' parts are usually called "gina" or "vagina" or "pee-pee" or "privates." Have you used any of these? Which name should we try using?
>
> First of all, let's take "butts." Do you realize that everyone in the world has a butt? What good is a butt? You're right, it's good for sitting on. What would it be like if people didn't have a butt? They couldn't sit down. There'd be no chairs in the world. Everyone would lie down a lot. What would cars look like? What else is the

butt good for? What comes out of the butt? If we didn't have a butt, then poop would have to come out somewhere else. Where could that be? What would that be like? What would bathrooms be like?

A similar process would continue for "vagina" and "penis." The message to be left with the child is that all humans have these things, they are efficiently designed for their unique functions, and they are neither glorious nor shameful, that is, "Parts are parts."

Clowning

Children allow themselves some emotional freedom and more range or movement in the assumed role of a clown then when they have to be themselves.

A clown is a very funny person whose job is to use his whole body to make people laugh. You and I are going to get our clown bodies ready. First, let's wiggle our toes. Now let's turn our ankles. See how we can make our ankles move round and round this way? Now let's reverse and move the other way. Let's see what we can do with our knees. . .

This continues until most of the major body joints have been moved, twisted, turned, examined, and explored. The therapist and child then try all kinds of clown walks—tiptoe, long and low strides, floppy and loose, rigid and robotic, and so forth. This can be followed by creating and acting out a skit that puts together the movements they have practiced. See further discussion in chapter 17.

Emotions Related to Body Trauma

Children need to express their feelings about their bodies and their bodily functions, and about what has happened to them. They may spontaneously express intense feelings when emotions are released during movement or body exercises. It is important to make them comfortable about any such release. The clinician can reassure them by letting the children know that such expression is a natural phenomenon, that the muscles hold tight for protection and then release when it seems safe, with feelings and memories usually emerging during the release. The clinician and child can play with tightening muscles as much as possible while saying something appropriate such as, "You can't hurt me. You can't hurt me," and then letting go. They then examine how it feels when the tightness lets up, and talk about associations the child may make during the exercise.

Young boys and girls should be taught that emotions are wonderful and necessary parts of being human. The therapist can discuss creative ways feelings are expressed, such as by writing, poetry, song, and drama. Simply telling someone how you feel is an important release, and the expressed feeling can be explored. This can be followed by an examination of destructive expressions of feelings that can hurt others. The child and therapist can then focus on their job of having the child examine her feelings with the assurance that creative, not destructive, expression will be allowed, and that the therapist will help the child directly express what is necessary for others to understand when the child is truly ready.

Seriously ill children are sometimes blocked from expressing feelings because they may equate their required compliance in the treatment of their illness with the need to suppress strong feelings of fear, anger, or helplessness. A strong father telling his young son that he knows he will be brave and not be afraid of his necessary, second bone-marrow transplant, places the child in a bind—the child needs to express his fear and helplessness, but is blocked from doing so by the father's attitude.

Children in these predicaments often block expressions of feelings because they do not wish to burden their parents, or because they believe they will be rejected if they do so. This may simply be misinterpretation by the youngster of his parents' desires or strengths, in which case parental discussion and demonstration may be all that is needed. However, if the child's assessment is correct, the clinician must educate and gain the cooperation of the caregivers. To avoid further conflict in the child, such barriers to the expression of emotion need to be eliminated. Only then can the child be taught that expressing emotion is both proper and satisfying.

Children are acutely aware of what is fair and what is not fair. They need to have validated that what happened to them is just not fair. As Miller (1984a) reminds us, they need to have their plan witnessed. Showing and telling others (who can be accepting of their experience) what the event was like for them validates their experience, and assists them in accepting what has happened so that they can grieve and mourn their losses. Expressing feelings about trauma can be accomplished through discussion, story, puppets, song, and drama. Some of these may later be repeated in a therapy session for an audience of loved ones.

It's Just Not Fair!

The clinician tells the child directly that most traumatized children feel that what happened to them was just not fair, and affirms that what happened to this specific child was not fair. The youngster can be encouraged to demonstrate with her body how an infant who could not yet speak might express feelings of rage or confusion. The youngster is then asked to show

how a two-year-old would do so, and then a three-year-old, etc. This structured permission-giving allows the child to engage in regressive behaviors that she is likely to feel but reluctant to express because of the shame or worry usually attendant upon such expression. When the child responds to the therapist's request for a demonstration, the regressive acting out is, in a sense, itself an experience of mastery.

The child can make five-minute audio tapes at home, in which she talks, cries, or yells about her feelings, and then have the therapist listen to the tape during the next session.

The therapist and youngster can make a videotape to show others how really rotten it is to have had "it" happen.

If the child spends ten minutes each day really paying attention to her feelings, and spends another ten writing or drawing about "it" in her *It's Just Not Fair!* book, she receives messages that her feelings are respected and justified and that they can be consciously concentrated so that they do not permeate all facets of her life. She learns that attention to feelings about "it" are OK and can be controlled.

Feelings: Inside and Outside

The therapist folds a letter-sized piece of paper in half and places it in front of the child so it opens like a greeting card. He says,

> I want you to draw a picture of yourself on the outside of this card the way you think everyone sees you. It should show the way the world thinks you are. Then I want you to open up the paper and draw a picture of yourself the way you feel on the inside. This inside picture should show what is *really* happening, not just what people see.

I have had children as young as five draw a smiling, compliant outside image and a depressed or chaotic inside image. The portrayal need not be given further attention or it can be used as a vehicle for discussion. The picture can also help the child express feelings to caregivers during a later session, and can be saved to compare with later drawings.

Feelings: Where are they in my body?

The child is asked to draw an outline of his body or, if he is small, he can lie on the paper and an actual outline of his body can be made by the therapist. The child is then directed to make a legend on the side of the picture in which he writes (or has the therapist write) a feeling he sometimes has, such as "mad," and a color he wants to represent the feeling, such as red. When the legend is complete, the therapist says, "Now, your job is to think carefully about one of those feelings, and to remember where you feel it in your body when you feel that way. Then mark those places on your body outline with the right colored marker." The process aids the child in delineating feelings. As with other exercises, the art product can be used in a variety of ways.

Significant insight was gained when a not quite four-year-old boy colored the genital area green for "scared." Further discussion confirmed that the child was accurately describing his experience and emotion. The father had earlier asked the clinician for guidance in dealing with the problem of his young son's waking him during the night and asking to sleep with him. The child, sexually abused in the past, would then masturbate frantically. The father, afraid that attempts to stop the boy's behavior might be harmful, pretended not to notice. (Ironically, pretending not to notice is a common child's response to being confronted with adult sexual behavior.)

The father was brought into a session and his son proudly displayed his life-sized picture showing where he felt his feelings in his body. The son, father, and therapist talked about the boy's feelings of being scared, and the father was able to view the masturbatory behavior in a different perspective. Thereafter he responded to the boy's behavior by providing verbal assurances that the child was safe and protected. The behavior diminished considerably.

Making a Friend of the Scar (Bald Head, Wheelchair, etc.)

After grieving, the child must come to terms with the damage, especially if it has resulted in physical evidence, permanent or transient, such as a scar which will remain throughout life, or loss of hair from chemotherapy. Using metaphor in story, a child can be shown that having a "friend" around, even one who is ugly or different, can be better than always having "someone" around who is hated. This proposition can then be joined to the child's physical evidence by pointing out, for instance, that since she must live with the scar, it might be best for her to make friends with it. The process of getting acquainted can become a game. Name the scar. Get to know it. Take it to the pool for an outing. Make it do things by flexing the underlying muscles. Introduce it to friends. Compare it to the scars of other people.

The scar can be personified through story, puppets, drawings, or by means of other devices. An elaborate story can be told, for example, using as a theme a mother cat with a yucky-looking kitten. She didn't want the cat and just wished it would disappear. But it didn't. It was with her every day and every day she fed it and licked it and groomed it and got to know it, and finally she came to love it more than anything. The kitten did not change (as did the ugly duckling), but after a while it just didn't matter to either of them that the kitten was yucky-looking.

The therapist can initiate discussions with the child's scar directly or by using puppets, with the child joining in. A dialogue might begin with the therapist talking to the scar.

> I know you didn't ask to be on Sharon's leg. It must not be very nice to have her hate you so much. Sharon, have you ever hated anything so much as you've hated your scar?
>
> You (scar) have to understand that this was unexpected for Sharon and it just wasn't fair for her. But I guess you could be lonely. Sharon, could you be your scar for a while and talk to me about how it is for you?
>
> Sharon's doctor said you healed very nicely. I guess you have done an important job. I think it will take a while for Sharon to make friends with you. How would it be for you if she spent just a few minutes each morning and each night talking to you and stroking you gently?

The child could draw pictures of the scar. She could design announcements about her scar to send to people who are especially close. To avoid inappropriate responses, the announcement should clearly set out the response wanted, for example,

> My therapist and I know that some people will wonder what to do when they read this special announcement. We do not expect you to do anything, but you could send me a card if you want, because I enjoy getting mail.

She can make up a song about her scar, or create a play that will be attended by friends and relatives during a session and that will be videotaped, so she has a record of the event to take home and share with others if she likes.

Throughout these exercises the child is encouraged to fully express feelings and to gain mastery by claiming reality.

Education Related to Body Trauma

Educating children about what has happened to their bodies can demystify the event, can dispel misconceptions and in many cases can reduce fear. Children's unasked and unanswered questions often harbor secret fears that block healing.

Negative body concepts most often arise in children who have been sexually molested or those who have severe medical problems. This section deals with the specific body worries of these two groups.

Sexually abused children harbor many concerns and misconceptions about which they are afraid to ask. They often believe that their bodies are damaged or that they have AIDS or that they are pregnant, even if the girl is too immature and the sexual acts were such that they could not result in pregnancy. These children are typically confused and ashamed of their sexual arousal during the abusive acts. Most are unable to express their worries, even when asked to do so directly by the clinician or a parent. Waiting for the child to demonstrate a need for education may be a disservice. Education can be sensitively provided, either individually, in family sessions, or in group therapy.

Guess What Other Sexually Abused Kids Worry About

Educational information is generally best received when the child and therapist are relaxed and engaged in quiet, parallel play, such as kneading clay or painting side-by-side. The activity lessens intensity and allows the child to distract the therapist easily and naturally if necessary. As things quiet down, the therapist begins a dialogue.

> We've had our lively, jumping-around time, so now it's time to do something easy and quiet with clay. I thought I would use this time to talk to you about what other sexually abused children worry about, and what I tell them. You can make guesses about those worries if you like, or ask questions, or you can just enjoy being quiet and relaxed and listen to what I tell these other kids.
>
> Lots of kids worry about their bodies being damaged in some way, and they are afraid that if someone looks at their body they will know that they have had an adult sexually touch them. There are some children who have been bruised, some who get sore, and some who have tearing of the skin so that there is bleeding. It's kind of like when you fall and hurt yourself: sometimes the skin is broken and bleeds, other times it's a scrape or a bruise. All of it feels bad and we wish it had never happened.
>
> Cindy, it's important that children really understand what has happened to them, and that they feel comfortable asking questions. Even if an adult has explained this to them before, they may need to have a few more explanations. The kind of molestation that was done to you caused a little bleeding from the vagina, as I remember. I don't know if you remember what your doctor told you the day that you were examined, but I know that the last time I talked to her she said that your body was absolutely fine. She said no one could ever tell you had been sexually abused by looking at you or touching you, unless that person were an experienced doctor doing a very

special examination. A doctor might be able to spot a little scar in the vagina, but your private parts are just like any other ten-year-old girl's. I thought I'd just let you know, in case you ever wondered or worried about that.

At this point Cindy asked if she was still a virgin, volunteering that friends of her brother had been asking him that question after reading about the abuse in the newspaper. She was told she was a virgin and that it was up to her to tell people that, or, if she chose, not to talk about such private matters. The clinician asked Cindy if she wanted to talk more about talking to other people or if she would rather continue with the lesson, and she chose the latter course.

Now, I don't know if you've had these other concerns, but some girls worry about being pregnant or having AIDS from what happened to them. Those are very big worries! It is important that therapists like me carefully answer these questions for children. Sometimes these things can happen. Some children I have worked with did get pregnant from being abused. So far, none of them have had AIDS. In your case, you could not get pregnant or have AIDS from the kind of sexual touching that happened. Did you know that? Did you ever have any worries about that?

Let's see. The last thing I can remember right now is that lots of boys and girls feel confused or embarrassed because their bodies felt excited by the sexual experience. I tell kids that sex is *supposed* to feel good—that's the way our bodies are made. If something flies toward the eye, you blink; if something startles you, you jump; and if something rubs your private parts in a certain way, you'll feel excited, whether it's a person or an orangutan doing the rubbing. That's the way things work.

The child should periodically be invited to respond to the therapist's discussion, because a casual and matter-of-fact invitation, as well as reference to what happened to the child, assists in defusing the abuse of its mystery and drama. The child should *not* be led or pressured into deeper discussions and expressions of feelings during this exercise. The exercise contract is to discuss other children's worries, not to probe youngster's emotions. To probe intensely would be unfair, and could be experienced by the child as trickery, consequently defeating the educational purpose of the exercise.

Children who have medical problems with significant attendant physical changes may not readily express their concerns. They may be afraid of the answers they might receive, they may not know how to translate their amorphous worries into questions, or, having already been given explanations, may not believe they have a right to continue asking questions. Bodily processes and medical procedures should be explained to them concretely. Drawings, movies, and demonstrations on models are helpful; afterward, the child can be asked to repeat his understanding of what is happening.

The young trauma victim should not be asked *if* he has a concern, but rather asked to state his three biggest body worries. These, of course, should be honored by being taken seriously and addressed. A hospitalized child's three biggest worries about his body can, by arrangement, be written in his medical chart and thus honored and dealt with by hospital personnel, or shown on a poster displayed in his room.

It is helpful for a child to know that wetting his pants, shaking, vomiting, and crying are what kids, teenagers, policemen, Olympic champions, and doctors sometimes do when they are scared or in pain. When a child's physical response to a problem includes any of the above, he experiences it as *further* loss of physical control or betrayal by his own body. I have found that a child feels less out of control and more accepting of what his body does when he has had a chance to talk and play out these reactions.

What People's Bodies Do When They Are Scared

Part One. The child and therapist write a column of physical reactions likely to occur when a person is scared about something. "Yes/No", "How Old", and "Event" columns are added. Ten copies are made and the child is told he can have more if he wishes. He is instructed to interview people of varying ages (such as other kids his age, teenagers, and adults), and to fill out one copy for each interview, with the results of his research to be completed by the next session. His approach to people and his interview techniques are rehearsed prior to his leaving the office.

Reaction	*Yes*	*No*	*How Old*	*Event*
Shaking				
Wet Pants				
Cried				

This exercise provides important education, contributes to mastery, helps normalize the child's response, and puts the behavior into a more healthy perspective by showing it to be a normal reaction to an abnormal situation.

Part Two. The child and therapist use the information gathered to play out scenarios of fear and pain reactions in contexts different from the child's.

Although this can be nicely done in the sand tray, by painting, and by means of puppets, I find it best to have the child act out the scenarios with me in psychodrama, so he has more opportunity to use his body in acting.

Young people require accurate information about what is happening to their bodies. When the adults are uncertain about a diagnosis or procedure, the child should be told about the uncertainty and helped to cope with it. Children usually know when they are not being told everything, or when they are being misled or "protected," and commonly respond by weaving their own convoluted idea of reality, made from bits and pieces of information (often misinformation), sensory impressions, wishes, and their worst fears.

Adults who care for children frequently avoid discussing the child's specific physical concerns, either because they, too, have difficulty coping with uncertainty or because of their mistaken belief that a child can be put on emotional "hold" while the adults wait for final, definite information, so that their response to the child can be accurate.

Advising the child of the current state of his body should addresss the body parts that work, as well as those parts that may be temporarily or permanently limited in function.

The child must submit to certain medical procedures, and this process does take away his power over his body. Some of that power can—and should—be returned to him, by allowing him to make choices about his treatment whenever possible. For example, a child may be able to decide which part of his body can be used to draw blood, or whether he will have an oral or rectal temperature taken, or if something can be done before or after a meal. This must be coordinated with the medical team, and may require that the clinician educate the medical practitioner and medical staff about the child's psychic needs.

Child's Perspective of Body Trauma

The reality of the child's negative experiences must be acknowledged by the clinician and put into perspective as being just a part, not the whole, of her life experience. The child should be reassured that she is more than just her body, and, as is true of all people, that she has strengths as well as limitations. The "Mean, Rotten Things That Can Happen to Kids" exercise described in chapter 14 can be useful in helping youngsters develop the knowledge that a variety of negative things happen to children, and yet they survive.

Letting the injured victims help other youngsters is a very effective way of helping them solidify what they have accomplished in therapy. It also helps them gain a broader perspective of the circumstances that were traumatizing for them. The clinician can make them "child graduate assistants," as described in chapter 14, or by having them make a short videotape to be shown to another child. In both instances the child describes her initial concerns related to the traumatic event and reviews how, with time and work, she gained mastery.

Summary

Helping children reestablish feelings of power and confidence in bodies they experience as ugly, vulnerable, and toxic requires a multiple treatment focus. The children need to actually experience, at the muscle level, that their bodies are powerful, that their bodies belong to them, and that they have some level of physical mastery. Misconceptions need to be dispelled and questions answered. The children need to understand exactly what happened to their bodies, and be able to fully express their emotional experiences related to the event. Meeting these treatment objectives will enable the youngsters to accept their realities and move on in their lives.

11
The Dissociatively Disordered Child

Dissociative Disorders

Professionals are still very much in the early phases of understanding dissociative phenomena and multiple personality disorders, particularly in children. We must therefore be tentative in our theoretical conclusions, and flexible in our clinical approach.

Dissociation is an involuntary, natural mechanism present in infancy and continuing through adulthood. The child who becomes so absorbed in a story that conscious awareness of the environment is lost, has dissociated. So, too, does the automobile driver who becomes so enrapt in her thoughts that for a time she loses conscious awareness of driving her vehicle. The dissociative process is a sudden, temporary alteration in the integrative functions of consciousness and/or identity, whereby one's experience is separated from one's conscious awareness. The trauma victim who does not remember parts of what happened to him and the person with multiple personalities has also dissociated, but more intensely and with more potentially severe consequences.

The primary area with which we will deal is defensive dissociation, which protects children from conscious awareness of overwhelming emotions, thoughts, sensations, and other negative behaviors. This loss of awareness enables youngsters to perform in their respective environments: they would be overwhelmed and handicapped in their daily activities if they had to deal continually with their frightening emotions and with other negative psychic situations. As with many defense mechanisms, the use of defensive dissociation may become so extreme it interferes with the child's functioning and development. Dissociation can become habitual, and, under certain conditions, can result in separate, distinct personality states within an individual.

Braun (1984b) has conceptualized dissociation as a continuum of increased loss of awareness, starting with daydreaming and extending to the incorporation of fully developed multiple personalities. Between these extremes we find intermediate conditions such as depersonalization, repression, and psychogenic amnesia. Not all dissociative episodes are disordered states. Most are benign and pass unremarkably.

When a child's behaviors and subjective experiences include the symptoms enumerated below, a dissociative disorder should be considered. These symptoms may appear as transient phenomena following any trauma; it is their *continued* presence which creates concern.

1. entering into trance states in response to trauma-related stimuli;

2. perception of surroundings as being unreal;

3. depersonalization—a change in one's perception or experience that results in a feeling of being alien, unreal, mechanical, or otherwise not one's self;

4. repression—an inability to recall important events, or periods when memory of a specific event is not consciously available, although memories surrounding the event in time are recollectable;

5. psychogenic amnesia—the inability to recall important personal information related to identity;

5. dissociative splitting—the perception that a separate part of the self has been "preserved" and has not experienced the actual traumatizing event, or, conversely, that a separate part of the self was traumatized, but not the true self. Unacceptable emotions are assigned to be experienced only by the split-off part, for example, hatred or love for a terrorizing parent (or both);

7. multiple personality disorder—the existence of two or more separate and distinct personalities or personality states, each with its own relatively enduring pattern of perceiving, relating to, and thinking about the environment and self. At least two of these personalities or personality states take full control of the person's behavior recurrently (DSM III-R, 1987).

Clinicians can become confused and immobilized in their efforts to accurately diagnose dissociative disorders in young clients. It is difficult to categorize both children's complex voluntary and involuntary behaviors, many of which are often hidden, and their internal experiences, which are sometimes impossible for them to describe. The task is made even more complicated because these behaviors and experiences evolve over time and may appear and disappear with apparently random frequency. A youngster's functioning and clinical presentation can change, for instance, in response to ongoing environmental influences, for example, changes of caretaker, changes in parental functioning, home or school relocation, required painful medical procedures (such as bone-marrow testing), having to testify in court, or any fear-producing situation.

Uncertainty relating to a child's specific diagnostic label should not undermine the clinician's confidence regarding therapy. The clinician must remember that diagnosis and treatment, while intimately related, are not the same. Even when the diagnosis is unclear, a clinician can still build a relationship with the child, assess the child's strengths and problem areas, formulate specific treatment objectives, and provide corrective experiences.

Multiple Personality Disorder

Children diagnosed as having a multiple personality disorder (MPD) commonly have histories which include severe repeated trauma experienced by the child as life-threatening, habitual dissociative responses to stress, and a lack of healing experiences. Two independently derived and similar models for understanding the etiology of multiple personality disorders were developed by Kluft, and by Braun and Sachs.

Four Factor Theory—Kluft (1984)

The Four Factor Theory postulates that every person who develops an MPD has the following four factors in his or her constitution, experience, intrapsychic organization, and interpersonal environment:

- the biological capacity to dissociate
- a life experience of severe trauma
- an established foundation and continuing shaping influences that determine the form taken by the dissociative defenses, such as internalizations, introjections, or identification with an MPD caregiver
- inadequate provision of stimulus-barriers and restorative experiences

3-P Model of Multiple Personality Disorder—
Braun and Sachs (1985)

Focuses on the factors associated with the development of the MPD syndrome.

- predisposing factors, including the child's biopsychological capacity to dissociate, and repeated exposure to an inconsistently stressful environment
- precipitating events that are repeated, traumatizing, and linked by a common affective theme and/or neurophysiological state
- perpetuating occurrences such as interactive child/abuser behaviors.

In the latter model, separate memories (for example, pleasant and unpleasant) are established after continuous inconsistent behavior, and are linked to the respective behaviors on which they are founded. The separate memories, in turn, become the bases for separate histories, each of which develops its own affective response to similar traumatic experiences. These adapative responses eventually become functionally separated by an amnestic barrier, leading to the development of different personality states; each state functions independently when confronted with the appropriate stimulus.

Braun (1988) reports that a compilation of various studies of MPD patients (a total of a thousand individuals) shows severe childhood abuse to be a predisposing factor in ninety-five to ninety-eight percent of the reported cases. It follows that practitioners working with abused children need to be aware of the clinical manifestations of the disorder and its treatment. Vigorous attention to the diagnosis and treatment of MPD can prevent prolonged entrenchment of the disorder and years of suffering.

Successful work with dissociative behavior begins with the practitioner's becoming comfortable enough to ask the right questions during history-taking and interviews. Two documents which can aid in the process are the "Behavioral Checklist to Help Aid Identification of MPD in Children and Adolescents" and the "Adolescent Inventory Scale," both developed by Dean (appendix B).

Diagnosing Dissociative Disorders

Although many symptoms found in dissociatively disordered children are also found in other traumatized children—and in children with other problems—those symptoms that are more specific to dissociatively disordered children include

- spontaneous trance states, when the child "spaces out" or stares off into space
- use of another name
- a claim not to be himself or a claim of dual indentity
- refering to self as "we"
- change in ability to perform tasks
- denial of behavior that has been observed by others
- changes in vision, handwriting, style of dress
- drastic changes in behavior, unexplained outbursts, disorientation
- hearing voices
- loss of time

- drawing self as multiple persons
- describing self as "unreal at times, feels like an alien (a mild form of this is not uncommon in typical adolescent experience)
- describing surroundings as becoming altered, feels remote from his environment
- getting lost coming home from school or from friend's house

A number of factors and disturbances can resemble the behaviors seen in the dissociatively disordered, thereby complicating diagnosis. These conditions, which include the following, should be considered and ruled out before a final determination is made.

1. reactions to foods, chemicals and other allergic substances. Allergic children are sometimes described by caregivers as suddenly changing behavior for no apparent reason, showing significant changes in handwriting, attention span, and learning abilities.

2. organic disorders that are not related to stress, including a clouding of consciousness and memory difficulties as symptoms.

3. drug use that can present dramatic behavioral changes, blackouts, and failure to recall events. Clinicians working with children who are under medical care should consult with the supervising medical person to learn of any drug use and the effects of any prescribed medications. Drug use can also be recreational, even in young children, or may be deliberately administered to a child by ignorant or abusive parents. Drugs are often implicated in cult abuse.

4. other psychic disorders that have features resembling the symptoms found in dissociative children, such as attention deficit, conduct disorder, and eating disorder. An MPD child may have a personality state which manifests symptoms of emotional disorder, while her other personality states do not show such disorder.

The dissociatively disordered children with whom I have worked progressed along the dissociation continuum to the point of incipient or early multiple personality development. Some had "pretend friends," as is commonly found in childhood development, and their pretend friends served the typical functions of providing support, comfort, acceptance, companionship, and consistent availability. But their pretend friends also became split-off parts that helped the children preserve intact images of themselves, and provided hiding places for unacceptable feelings. The children did not *become* their pretend friends, but did identify intensely with them and in some instances kept them into adolescence.

Others of my child clients switched, that is, *became* different identities, appearing to do so involuntarily in response to trauma-related stimuli. They were consciously aware of the change, knew of their other identities, and did not demonstrate evidence of an amnestic barrier. Young children do not typically experience the existence of their split-off parts as crazy and shameful. They simply and comfortably say, "It wasn't me." As they mature they learn that people do not magically change into other people, and know that those who claim to do so will be subjected to ridicule or punishment. Thus, untreated, a child will hide these other selves from the world, and perhaps from himself, as he matures. Maturity increases the likelihood that the dissociated parts will grow in complexity and importance.

The split-off parts of the children with whom I have worked have assisted them in managing their ambivalent feelings, and protected them by

- preserving part of themselves as intact, that is, the way they were before the traumatizing event. For example, their pretend friend was not assaulted, or the pretend friend's father was very sick but did not die violently as did the *real* child's father;
- hiding unacceptable powerful feelings that gave them a sense of hope and strength. The children believed that these feelings were not permissible, and that revealing them could be dangerous to the children themselves or to their families, as, for example, rage toward a terrorizing adult or love for a parent the child was told she should hate;
- hiding unacceptable vulnerable feelings that the children perceived as possibly placing them at risk if revealed. Such feelings included sadness, hunger for nurturance, and longings for physical or emotional needs to be met. An eight-year-old may have intense regressive yearnings and behaviors that she keeps hidden through dissociative splitting. By doing so, she protects herself in two ways. First, she is safe from an abusive mother who cannot tolerate dependencies, ridicules such behavior, and becomes violent when such behavior is exhibited. Secondly, the child is able to maintain the image of herself as capable and a good girl because she is not needy.

Although some of my young clients have claimed that a part of themselves did *not* experience the trauma, none have claimed the reverse, that is, that only the split-off part was traumatized. Nor have I had a child identify a split-off part that was self-destructive, although I have had that experience with adult clients. This may simply be my lack of discovery, or because it was not part of the dynamics of the children in my sample.

Treating the Dissociatively Disordered

Children with dissociative disorders require specialized treatment intervention in addition to those interventions set out in chapter 5. As much as possible within a given child's capability, dissociated experiences and disowned parts of their identity and consciousness must be brought into the treatment environment, where they can be safely contained, while the therapist assists the child toward integration. Experiences and feelings which remain hidden behind amnestic or dissociative barriers are interpreted by the child as too overwhelming or too dangerous to acknowledge. Treatment progress may become undone when the child believes that if the therapist knew *all* about what happened—or the way she feels—or what she did—everything would be different: the therapist would be disgusted, would know it was her fault, and would not like her.

It is important that the clinician identify the child's awareness, understanding, and attachment to dissociative behavior early on. The child's own terms for dissociation should be used.

> Whenever something is said about your accident, I notice that you stop what you're doing and kind of stare, but it seems as if you don't see anything. Do you know that you do that? One time in the playroom your mom called that being "spacey." Does she say that you're spacey at home? What do *you* call it, or what words do *you* use to think about it?

If the child does not identify a personal label, the clinician needs to continue.

> We need to call it by the name that seems best to you. Other kids call it "going away" or "being someplace else" or "being spacey"—or we can use your own words. What words should we use to talk about this?

The child can then be helped to examine the advantages and disadvantages of "going away." If he can be convinced that there are more disadvantages, work can progress toward controlling and lessening defensive dissociative responses. The child and therapist become co-detectives and together monitor, clarify, and identify the elements or conditions which trigger dissociative responses. They create a treatment plan to gain control of the behavior (the chapter 9 description of John's participation in his treatment plan is a helpful model). Concurrently, the child and therapist work on conflicts and ways in which he can cope with his environment, so that his need for dissociative defense will lessen.

The treatment exercises most useful for dealing with dissociatively disordered youngsters are those which help them

- identify and sort out feelings such as sadness, fear, anger, loneliness, longing, alienation, or discouragement;
- accept the premise that one person can have a multitude of feelings that often may be conflictual, for example, liking a friend a lot, although hating it when it picks his nose and eats the "boogers";
- recognize that thoughts and feelings are not actions. For example, people can be very angry and still not behave in ways that are hurtful;
- foster the belief they will not be punished or rejected for their feelings and thoughts. Children should experience this in their relationship with their therapists, and caregivers can declare this clearly during therapy sessions.

A Basket of Feelings:

This exercise has been very useful in helping children express ambivalent and contradictory feelings. More important, it teaches them that it is all right to experience such feelings. As with most exercises for children, demonstration is better than verbal explanation alone.

> This basket has about fifty marking pens in it. What would we usually use these for, Lori? Right, making pictures. But today we are going to call this a "Basket of Feelings." First, we are going to write down on this paper a feeling that children often have. Can you tell me one? Good, "mad." I'm going to write "mad" really large on this one piece of paper. Now, another paper for the next feeling. "Happy," good. OK, I've got one. "Mean." Remember last week when you talked about feeling really mean sometimes? This is for when you feel just like that. Now, another one.

When the child is a nonreader, it is best to limit the number of feelings to what the child can remember. (Simple face drawings may help.) The therapist should volunteer a feeling or two, even if the child gives many examples, so that there is a sense of joining. It is best for the therapist to do the writing to insure that it is large, clear, and that the procedure moves quickly. The therapist should avoid the temptation to use a "packaged" set of feelings, or papers prepared in advance; using feelings actually named by the child will keep the exercise fresher and more fun, and will often provide clinical insight. The therapist might not think of some words a child will suggest, such as "disgusted," "stingy," "grossed out," or "surprised."

Now it's my turn. I'm going to hold this Basket of Feelings and look at all these pieces of paper with feelings written on them. There are sixteen of them. I'm going to think about the time I went to the parking lot and saw that someone had made a dent in the side of my car. Now, I'm going to show you how I felt then. I'm putting a big bunch of these pens on "mad," about a handful of feelings (pens) on "sad," and a bunch on "surprised." Let me think, I guess that's all there ʋere. Wait—I think I want to put some on "worried," because I thought I would have to pay money and be without my car for a while. Now, let me see. I want to add a few more to "mad," that seems better. That's it. That's how I felt about it that day. If I were to show you how I felt about it a week later, I would probably have a different number of pens in each pile.

Now, it's your turn, Lori. Show me how you felt when everyone first found out your dad was touching you sexually.

Lori looked at all the feelings we had written and said the one she needed wasn't there: "confusion." This not only validated that she understood the exercise, but reminded me that there is value in not having all the feelings listed initially.

The great flexibility of this technique can be demonstrated by the number of ways it was used over several sessions with this same child. I asked her to show how she felt about Dad's sexual touching after she had been in her therapy group for a year, how she felt when she went to court, then how she felt during the time it was happening, when nobody else knew. Lori also used the Basket of Feelings to demonstrate how she guessed she would feel if she were to have a supervised visit with her father: a lot of pens were put on "excited" and some on "embarrassed." Then she guessed how her mother would feel if she, the child, were to have a supervised visit with the father. She indicated mostly "angry" and "feels like smashing." Last she showed how she feels when her mother has those feelings toward her father.

Lori then agreed to have her mother join us in the session, to show her some of the things we were doing. Her mother used the same technique to demonstrate her feelings about Lori's abuse. We shared some of Lori's speculations about her mother's feelings toward her father; Lori's mother was surprised with Lori's accuracy because she thought she had hidden her rage. The mother was dismayed to learn that Lori suspected that if her mother felt that way toward the father, she must be angry with her as well.

This exercise provided the mother with a concrete way of showing the child exactly how she felt about the father, and then exactly how she felt about her. The young girl directly, and through demonstration, received the clear message that it was acceptable for mother and daughter to have different feelings.

The characteristics of dissociation are such that treatment requires some modifications of typical therapy as well as some specialized approaches.

1.   Assist the child in delineating and identifying feelings that *all* children have, as well as the feelings the child acknowledges as his. Do the same with the feelings of the split-off "parts" which he has identified. Then examine together how the split-off feelings differ from his own feelings, and what would happen if they were to be claimed by him.

2.   Discuss together the function of the split-off part, perhaps using simile or metaphor, for example, cartoon characters who are heroes and never fearful, or a pretend friend who was molested, but not by her father. Demonstrate acceptance of the child's dissociative behavior and enable him to claim ownership of these behaviors eventually, by assisting him to understand the positive aspects of this other part of himself. Tell him, for example, that he has protected himself, and possibly others, in a creative, inventive, courageous, and caring way.

3.   Establish the child's ownership of the split-off part, and his power over the splitting process, by acceptance and gradual reference to the dissociative split as being *his* creation and being *part of him.*

4.   Investigate thoroughly the child's dissociative process, taking care not to further reinforce the mechanism. Do not, for instance, question in ways that encourage the development of a more complex identity for a personality fragment than already exists.

Direct questioning can be tricky because children feel obliged to respond to adult questions. Some children who have been traumatized are afraid *not* to come up with an answer, and will do so even if they have to make one up. We must therefore control our natural clinical curiosity and formulate questions that are not leading, and that are directed toward useful information and integration. For example, it would be more useful to ask a child, "Would you tell me about that part of you that is called 'Mary'?" rather than, "Describe Mary's hair and her clothes, and tell me what she likes to eat."

The therapist will have to help caregivers, teachers, and others by guiding them to behave in ways that are accepting of, but do not promote, dissociation.

The adults in close contact with the child should be sufficiently familiar with the dissociative process and its appearances so that any fascination is defused. As examples, they can be reminded that we all dissociate to some degree when watching a movie, or driving a long, straight, boring road.

The adults should be advised to deal with this issue matter-of-factly, quietly monitor how the child is progressing, and come to the therapist with questions and concerns. They should not discuss the child's behavior with others.

Without guidance and some monitoring, we may find the child's behaviors cause him to be the center of attention for those who are curious or mean, who are attempting to prove or disprove the diagnosis, who want to see for themselves, or who want to help cure the child by ridicule or some other inappropriate method.

It is important to restate two general principles to be applied when working with traumatized children, namely, to be active, and to approach issues directly. It is unlikely that an overwhelmed child will voluntarily bring forth frightening experiences. Nondirective and projective techniques in play, art, psychodrama, body movement, and music should be a part of the healing process, as these techniques provide some protective distancing for the child while working through issues which have been brought up directly.

Symptoms of a dissociative process may not be discovered until the child relives a traumatizing event in treatment and evidence of another personality or fragment emerges. Some children may not be diagnosed as dissociatively disordered until a new identity is created to deal with a current problem, for example, threats by a parent during the child's visit home from a foster placement, or removal from a placement he believed to be secure. Or the child may simply not be ready to reveal a dissociated part until he believes it is safe to do so. Dean writes in a personal communication that in her work with MPD preadolescents, there is always a "holdout" personality that discloses much later in treatment, often months after integration was believed to have been accomplished.

Following is a summary of the therapist's part of a dialogue that came about when, five months into therapy, the child's drawings suggested she may have dissociated parts of her experience. Other behaviors that supported this possibility had been observed during the course of therapy, although the young girl had denied indicative behaviors when questioned directly during her initial evaluation.

> You've drawn a picture of yourself that has two other figures, one behind this one, and another little figure. What can you tell me about this one? Has she been part of your life for a while? Does she have a name? What is she like? What does she do? How is she different from you? What do you like about her? Is there something about her you don't like? Does she get you into trouble? Does she help you? How old is she? When is the first time you can remember her in your life?

Being cognizant of how easy it is to become fascinated and probe too deeply in one session, the therapist carefully paced the questioning and respectfully acknowledged the trust and sharing of the child. The subject was reopened during a later session.

If it feels OK to you, I would like to talk to "Mary" [part previously identified by the child] for a while. May we do that? Are all your parts listening right now? Are you the part of Helen called "Mary"? Tell me about yourself. How old are you? [A split-off part is often a younger, regressed self, and the clinician must adjust vocabulary and timing for that developmental level.] What are your thoughts about coming here to my playroom? Can you tell me how you are different from Helen? And how are you the same? I'm really happy that we can talk. I'd like to tell you what we're doing in therapy to make sure you understand about working and playing to help with troubles. It's very important for kids to understand exactly what we do here, because they have a lot of power in deciding things in therapy. I, of course, am the one who is very strong and protects children who come here, and makes sure they are safe. I also make sure the few rules we have here are enforced. And I make sure that we have fun and snacks, too. You are an important part of what we are doing here. How do you think Helen is doing? Are there some things you are worried about?

Timing is crucial in this work, and a balance needs to be found between stretching treatment out for too long (which could lead to reinforcement or the creation of new split-off parts), and moving too quickly—not giving the youngster time to fully integrate the dissociative parts of herself.

Some therapists find it useful to negotiate a contract with children wherein they agree not to create new parts of themselves during treatment— and should they feel the urge to do so, they will discuss the matter with the therapist. This intervention minimizes the likelihood that new split-off parts will be created by the child to please or interest the therapist.

Some children experience such great horrors that even the strongest clinical alliance and most secure environment are not sufficient to reduce their stress when examining the past. In these cases the therapeutic process itself can evoke dissociation. When this occurs, the clinician should help the youngster create tough boundaries around the past events, which are then dealt with by taking one small step at a time (see, for example, the Garbage Bag exercise, chapter 14).

The integration of dissociated parts can be facilitated by the use of metaphor in stories, where separate parts can come together to create a wondrous whole that is appreciated by all, with no one losing. Examples might include a rainbow whose colors are all right separately, but especially beautiful, powerful, and appreciated when joined together. Or the clinician can speak of the separate ingredients of a cookie, pointing out that each ingredient can stand alone, and each has a function, but the totality produces a wonderful chocolate-chip cookie.

Dissociation should be presented as a protection that was once needed but is now superfluous, since the child is no longer at risk and able to do other things when feeling really frightened. This concept should not be presented to the child prematurely, since it may then be experienced as criticism.

Children will have to work through what integration, the uniting of split-off parts, will mean to them. Therapists will have to deal with the loss the child will experience in giving up separateness, as well as the therapists' own initial feelings of loss related to this process. Hope and strength can be fostered in the child by having him recall and reexperience a time when he successfully coped with loss, such as when he gave up a baby bottle or a favorite blanket. It helps if the child and therapist can engage in quiet recollections of how these things once provided comfort, the way splitting does, but are no longer needed, although they were missed for a while. The practitioner must know in advance that the examples of coping with loss that he uses were successful and not overwhelming to the child.

It is best not to force integration for the same reason that clinicians do not force a person to give up any defense, namely, that the defense probably serves as a needed protective device. Additionally, some of the child's experiences may not have been fully dealt with, which will make this integrative process more difficult. Spontaneous integration may occur in a child after a release of strong feelings related to traumatic events. However, this should not be interpreted as a spontaneous healing, since hidden material may still exist within the child. The therapist should gradually and carefully determine through play themes, directed play, and direct discussion, whether additional experiences or feelings about those events remain hidden.

Integration occurs with the reduction or resolution of conflicts and the learning of new coping skills. The child's desire for normalcy, together with a healing environment, allows integration to occur as a natural process. The process can be given a boost, and reinforced, with a meaningful ritual exercise such as having the child close his eyes and, through vivid imagery, bring together the separated parts of self. Each part, for example, can be a separate color that comes together as the rainbow of self. The child and therapist can formalize the process by having the child's caregiver, teacher, or whoever else has been part of the clinical team, present for the reunification ritual. The few days following integration should be fairly low-key for the child, allowing quiet, strengthening reinforcement.

As Braun (1986) and Kluft (1984) so wisely advise, work is not over with the occurrence of integration. The clinician must help the child solidify gains and support him in using his more recently acquired coping skills as he hits bumps along the developmental road. This stage of treatment is a most appropriate time in which to utilize the developmentally sequenced model described in chapter 2.

Braun's comprehensive general therapy plan (1986) should be very helpful to clinicians who work with dissociative and multiple personality disorders. Many of the factors listed in Braun's thirteen aspects have already been discussed as necessary for the treatment of traumatized children in general, or have been included under specific approaches in this chapter. Those not already mentioned are listed below; they are used primarily with older children and adults.

- contracting with each personality or with each part that can speak (as a therapist would in working in a family system) to meet all therapy goals, to avoid suicide and homicide, and for special uses as helper personalities;
- working with the problems of each personality, as well as providing limit-setting and focusing for each, when appropriate; and
- mapping and understanding the structure of the system.

Kluft (1984) thoroughly addresses treatment factors to be considered in working with childhood MPD. Two of his factors which deserve attention and have not yet been addressed in this discussion are:

- the need to be sensitive to forensic difficulties which may arise if hypnosis is used for assessment purposes (steps should be taken to protect the evidence, such as videotaping the process);
- the expectation that much work may be necessary to assure a child's safety, when the source of his traumatizing experience has not been clearly identified. Kluft reminds clinicians that it is a disservice to the child to work in any way other than in a supportive manner until such time as the environment is safe and the clinician has control of the case.

Spiegel (1984) conceptualizes MPD as a post-traumatic stress disorder. This has been extremely useful to me, and fits into my clinical experience. Among other things, he postulates that those who identify extreme dysfunctional family interactions (double-bind communication, enmeshed family systems, pseudomutuality) as contributing to the etiology of schizophrenia may have applied the correct dynamics to the wrong disorder. Spiegel feels that these dynamics are more properly identified with MPD families.

Summary

Dissociative disorders, including childhood multiple personality disorder, can be difficult to diagnose. Treatment is complex, and few practitioners have developed mastery in this arena. For these reasons, therapists may consciously or unconsciously avoid this very important aspect of patient care. Those who do recognize a dissociative disorder may become so fascinated by what they are dealing with that they lose their clinical timing and pacing. Although various clinical styles can be used to meet the treatment objectives for children with dissociative and multiple personality disorders, specialized treatment is needed. The treating therapist should be aware of current research, be willing to seek consultation, and refer out when needed.

The study of dissociation and multiple personality disorders has grown significantly over the past eight years. The International Society for the Study of Multiple Personality and Dissociation, a professional organization, provides interested professionals with current information, by means of conferences, newsletters, and the Dissociation Journal (see appendix A).

12
Attachment Disturbance

Disturbances to an attachment relationship can be traumatizing to a child *regardless of the quality of the relationship between child and caregiver.* Attachment disturbances are often uncovered while working with traumatized children; they are commonly caused by loss, threat of loss, disruption, and reunification. Traumatized children whose parental attachment is impaired continue their dysfunctional styles of interacting with caregivers when placed in out-of-home care, often resulting in placement failures which further traumatize the youngsters.

Clinicians who work with these children are likely to become deeply involved in evaluating and treating their clients' attachment relationships, whether or not the disturbances are presented as primary issues. This chapter addresses attachment disturbances by causative factors.

1. Loss and Disruption—typified by such situations as the death of a parent, or a parent's life-threatening illness or threats of suicide (which represent a frightening loss for children); also abandonment, sudden loss of parental contact, hospitalization of the child, or out-of-home placement.

2. Reunification—the actual or suggested renewal of contact with a parent after extended separation can be traumatizing to a child for a number of reasons. He may feel helpless and overwhelmed by intensified loyalty conflicts toward his current caregivers; may experience a restimulation of guilt and self-blame related to earlier trauma, separation, or reunification; or may fear bodily harm when the reunification is with a parent who has hurt or threatened him in the past.

3. Impairment—a persistent pattern of anxious or distorted parental attachment behaviors that interferes with the youngster's ability to form satisfactory relationships with others.

In the Children's Garden Attachment Model developed by Carson and Goodfield (1988), who built upon the work of attachment theorists including

Bowlby (1958, 1969, 1973, 1980), Ainsworth (1964, 1973). Ainsworth and Wittig (1969), and Rutter (1980), attachment is defined as a reciprocal, profound, emotional, and physical relationship between a child and his parent that sets the stage for all future intimate, trusting relationships. Attachment is described within this model as secure or impaired.

In a secure attachment the child normally and regularly turns to his parents for help, comfort, and nurturance. Simple physical proximity to the parent reassures a stressed child. He enjoys and responds to the mutual, intimate, loving relationship. The child develops curiosity about his environment, and the desire and ability to explore. During exploration, he acquires a sense of competence and mastery, returning to the security provided by the parent when the stress of exploration becomes too great.

Two distinctly identifiable styles of dysfunctional attachment are seen in attachment-impaired children, namely, anxious and distorted behaviors.

The anxiously attached child is unwilling to risk the separation from the parent that is necessary for successful exploration. Her determination to remain physically close to her parent, while intense, actually provides her little satisfaction and does not relieve or reassure her. As the parent is unable to provide comfort, the child's anxious and angry behaviors escalate. Exploration and play are restricted, and the child does not gain competency and mastery. Erratic, abusive, or neglectful parenting can usually be identified in the history of an anxiously attached child.

Distorted attachments appear to develop in children whose primary caregivers have been physically or emotionally unavailable for attachment, or in children who have had to deal with frequent changes of caregivers and have received minimal gratification from human interactions. With no parent to whom he can predictably turn for comfort, the child looks to possessions rather than to relationships for satisfaction, receiving little gratification from interactions with his caregivers. Attempts at intervention by adults do not provide him with comfort or solace, and are not valued. When he does behave in an affectionate manner, his displays seem shallow and imitative, and generate little response. Such a child can be socially skilled, but only superficially responsive in his relationships. Exploration and play are fleeting, random, and without pleasure.

According to Bowlby (1977), the representational models of attachment figures and self built up during childhood and adolescence tend to persist relatively unchanged throughout adult life. Recent clinical research by Carson and Goodfield (1988) shows that some change in these representational models can be achieved, although the process is laborious. Treatment recommendations for children related to parenting needs should be assessed in the context of their attachment relationship. For example, certain relatives or foster parents may be unable to cope with detached or clingy behavior, resulting in the child's experiencing negative parenting, or possibly a failed placement.

Clinicians may find it useful to have an attachment profile of the children with whom they are working. The Children's Garden Attachment Profile (appendix D) is a useful thirteen-question diagnostic guideline.

Loss and Disruption

The loss, threat of loss, or disruption of an attachment relationship, whether past or present, should be carefully explored in terms of its meaning to the child. The child's concerns are frequently different from what is assumed by an adult, who looks at the situation from an adult point of view. This is a dangerous trap for psychotherapists as well as for those not trained as mental health practitioners. For example, a child may feel punished or rejected when placed in foster care, and not consider that his parents are unable or unwilling to be responsible for him. Or he may be most worried about who is caring for his pet dog, or what his friends will think about his absence. He may have vivid fantasies about missing parents being tortured, or worse. Such concerns have to be addressed in both the clinical and home environments.

The approach should be to tell the child the truth about any loss or disruption, and to do so in a manner appropriate to the youngster's developmental level, making certain that it is understandable. Sparing the child the true facts may cause further trauma since he will feel betrayed and lose trust when he discovers what really happened.

Caregivers should be helped to anticipate and understand behaviors the child is likely to manifest. Ongoing consultations with the clinician can assist caregivers in recognizing when a child needs to be encouraged to protest or to express feelings of despair. Caregivers can inadvertently block the child from going through the necessary grieving process by congratulating the youngster for his cooperation, for being good, and for his swift adjustment. Children may block their feelings, numbing themselves emotionally, because they are fearful of behaving badly, believing that worse may happen.

The impact of loss and separation is influenced by the quality of the attachment before disruption, the nature of the disruption, the quality of the substitute parenting, and, when applicable, the nature of the reunion. Following are short discussions of the behavioral responses and treatment needs of children with secure, anxious, or distorted attachments who encounter loss or disruption in an attachment relationship.

Secure Attachment

Securely attached children usually respond to the loss or disruption of a significant relationship with anger and acute distress. The therapist can expect to encounter tearfulness, anxiety, and oppositional behavior. The children may rebuff attempts to soothe them, will engage in searching behavior for the "lost" parent, and experience intense longing. They often become withdrawn and lethargic, and the intensity of these behaviors increases with time. Securely attached children who have suffered loss or separation can be told, for example,

> I know it's terrible to be without your mom. You have every right to be as mad as you can be. It *is* unfair. I know that having me around doesn't stop the loneliness you feel, but I'm here when you want to talk, or just want to be with someone. You can scream if you want, or smash pillows or throw rocks in the river or run around the yard. But I won't allow you to hurt yourself or your brother. You can refuse to talk to anyone if you want—that's your right—but you are required to do some things, such as eating and bathing yourself and not hurting others.

A severed primary attachment for a securely attached child may result in an anxious attachment to subsequent figures.

Anxious Attachment

Anxiously attached children will intensify their anxious behavior, becoming more and more clinging, whimpering, and demanding. They will gobble up nurturing attention and only feel minimally satisfied or comforted. These children may not verbalize their worries about the absent parent or about who will be taking care of them, but express their anxieties more through their behavior. In either case, they need to be constantly and repeatedly advised of the status of the absent parent and be assured and reassured that they will be taken care of, and told who will take care of them, and perhaps how that person will take care of them. Transitions are especially difficult for these children and it helps them when they are told in advance of any changes in routine related to their care.

Anxiously attached youngsters must also be dealt with in a manner that allows expression of feelings while maintaining some control of behaviors. It is very important that their caregivers set limits on the clingy and demanding behavior to prevent the caregiver's emotional exhaustion, which may ultimately lead to burnout and negative response to the child. The clinician should be responsive in helping the parenting person develop appropriate limits, and should provide this guidance and information to the caretaker at the earliest opportunity.

The treatment approaches that best help a child reduce objectionable behaviors are those that include specific identification of the behavior, acknowledge its value to the child, and provide for specific times during which the child is allowed to exhibit the behavior (or some modified, acceptable version of it). Working in small, incremental steps to reduce objectionable behavior can make the task manageable and help everyone feel a sense of hope. It is unrealistic, and often unfair, to expect a child's negative behaviors to be totally eliminated.

> Donny, I'm going to hold you, and we'll rock in this chair for fifteen minutes. I'll set the timer and when it goes off, we will rock seven more strokes. You'll count them, and after you count them it will be time to stop. Then, while I work in the kitchen, you can draw or play with your toys at the kitchen table and you can watch me from there. I enjoy holding you, but there are special times for that. Tonight when we watch TV, I'll hold you during a half-hour program.

At a different time, when the child is relaxed and attentive:

> Donny, I don't like it when you jump up and suddenly grab me by the neck for a hug. I want to hug you—sometimes I want to hug you a lot. But when you just grab me, I feel grouchy and want to push you away. I'll show you the way we give hugs in our family. Let me have your arms. See, like this. Kind of easy and not so tight. It will take a while to practice and get it right, but probably not nearly as long as it took you to learn how to ride your bike. Let's see, how long did that take? For now, I would like you to *ask* for a hug instead of just grabbing. Do you think you can remember to ask for hugs, or do you need to have some help remembering?

The therapist may observe a child's clingy interactions with a parent during a session and deal with it directly.

> I notice that when Alicia climbs onto your lap, she moves her feet around a lot and puts her hands all over your face when you're talking. Then you seem to have trouble breathing and look really uncomfortable. I wonder if this behavior has been going on for a long time, or if she's just been doing this since her accident? Some dads feel worn out by behaviors like this, but they feel the child really needs to do it, or they don't know how to stop it without the child feeling badly. Some are afraid the child will become more clingy and whiny if they try to stop the behavior. I wonder how you feel about Alicia's behavior?

Should the parent or caregiver deny discomfort, the therapist can focus on the negative aspects of the behavior, pointing out, for instance, that people generally do not like children who engage in aggressive, uncontrolled clinging, or that such behavior has a negative impact on other children in the home. The therapist works with the parent and the child to deal both with the underlying needs and with the behavior by structuring physical closeness in a manner which literally allows some breathing space.

Distorted Attachment

Children with distorted attachments tend to respond to loss and disruption of attachment relationships with a "Big deal, so what" attitude. They are often contemptuous of sentiment and used to parental rejection. Their experience of attempts at closeness were painful and unproductive. Those who take care of children with distorted attachments must constantly remind themselves that they will not get emotional rewards from the child, and that this lack of feedback is not due to their immediate style of parenting, but is rather a symptom of an attachment disorder. Caring for a child who gives nothing in return is very difficult emotionally, but acceptance of this condition is necessary for a "successful" relationship. There is a strong temptation to reject these children, and we often deny to ourselves that our discomfort is due to the absence of a return on our own emotional investment.

As with anxiously attached children, these children need to be advised of the status of absent parents and be given specific information about who will care for them. Their hostile and/or apathetic responses should be overlooked, for they often act most contemptuous when feeling uncertain and vulnerable. If we do not provide these assurances and reassurances, their negative view that no one cares about them will only be reinforced.

> Alex, I read you loud and clear. I know you think talking with me is a bunch of bullshit, but that's what I'm getting paid for, so I'm going to talk. You can listen or not, but I'm here for you, and this is our time. Other guys have had parents who were more into drugs and themselves than they were into their families—and you know what? Even though these kids didn't get much from their parents, they still felt that it was a bad deal to have to live away from them. Most kids who have to live in a foster home or someplace away from their parents feel uneasy. At least at home they knew what to expect. You know and I know that your parents are not coming back for a long time. One thing you can do is to be cool and keep saying you don't give a shit—that's understandable.
>
> It looks to me like you've been taking care of yourself for a real long time now, and for a kid who's got a year to go before he's a teenager, that's pretty remarkable.
>
> I care about the kids who come here and I hang in there with them. Sometimes they get to like seeing and talking to me and some-

times they don't. No one is going to insist that you get friendly or close or trusting. No one is going to insist that you spill your guts about anything. There are a few simple rules, and there are consequences for breaking them that you need to know about. I also want to tell you how things work here about clothes, food, playing video games, spending money, and the time set aside just for us.

Regardless of which developmental pathway the attachment process has taken, children must be assisted in mourning their loss and separation from loved ones. For many this means going back and reexperiencing the traumatic events. The clinician needs to help the caregiver refrain from helping the child by protecting him from the painful process. For others, it means teaching the caregiver how to give the child permission to feel angry or ripped-off, and how to deal with his aching sadness. The clinician may need to sensitively probe for feelings the child had hidden from himself, and then teach the child various ways in which feelings can be expressed.

Many creative ways can be found to assist children in holding on to their parents emotionally while they adjust to letting go of their parents' physical presence. Children can take family pictures with them to foster care or to the hospital. They can conduct audio- or videotape interviews with various relatives to record memories of the lost parent. Scrapbooks documenting the child's relationship with a separated caregiver can be assembled. Various art, play, and drama techniques can be employed to help the therapist symbolically address the child's longings for his parent. Movies like *My Life as a Dog,* and books such as *Heidi* and *The Accident,* deal with the issue of parental death in ways that help children gain some comfort by reminding them that this happens to other young people too.

Reunification

Reunification with a parent after an extended absence is an additional stress with which many traumatized children must deal. This can be a difficult process, and sometimes further traumatizes the child even though the reunification is in the youngster's best interest and is the child's expressed wish. The situation can, for instance, create loyalty conflicts for a child who perceives the action as objectionable or unfair to the custodial parent or current caregiver. The resumption of contact with an absent parent can stimulate feelings of helplessness and fear in the child because of what he has been told about that parent during the separation period, what he has imagined, or what he has actually experienced in the past. Reunification may present an actual threat to the child's well-being in instances where the parent abused the child in the past.

There has been a significant increase in the number of voluntary and involuntary parent-child separations in the United States, and the separations appear to be associated primarily with abuse, custody disputes, parental abduction, or parental abandonment. In many of these cases, parents appeal to the courts for an order allowing them to resume contact with the child from whom they have been isolated. This in turn has led to an upswing in contacts from legal professionals seeking advice from the clinical community as to if, when, and how the parental relationship should be resumed. The issues to be assessed are complex and, as each situation is unique, preconceived formulas for making recommendations are never in order.

Reunification Evaluation

This example illustrates some of the complexities of court-ordered evaluations when the issues include childhood trauma as well as traumatic attachment disruption.

> Tanya's father petitioned the court to reinstate his right to resume contact with his ten-year-old daughter. He had not had contact with the child since she was five years old, at which time she reported that her father had been orally copulating her since her parents had separated three months earlier. The father denied the abuse until after a preliminary legal hearing, when he changed his plea to no contest, was found guilty, and was sentenced to five years probation. He was required to be actively involved in a sex offender's treatment program, and was not allowed to have contact with the child during that period.
>
> The evaluating clinician verified that the child had been actively involved in both individual and group therapy for three years following the disclosure of abuse. The child's mother had been in individual therapy continuously since the disclosure. The father had been in an offenders' therapy group continuously during his five-year probation, in addition to two years of individual therapy which overlapped the group work.
>
> A superficial look at the situation could reasonably have led an evaluator to recommend a gradual resumption of parental contact. After all, the molestation was restricted to a time of parental stress, did not involve penetration, and all therapists involved expressed the opinion that each of their clients was well-functioning.
>
> Despite the father's well-rehearsed display of openness, assumption of responsibility for the abuse, and tears of remorse, the evaluator concluded that the father had an obsessive romantic and sexual attraction to his daughter and did not have a concept of her

as a child with needs and feelings separate from his own. Much of this conclusion was based on a letter that the evaluator asked the father to write, in which he apologized to Tanya for his behavior. The letter, written by this well-educated professional man who had just concluded his mandated treatment, included remembrances of their "good times in the past watching sunsets" and stated "We both knew what we did was wrong." He also surreptitiously attempted to cue the child to recall past sexual interactions with him during a joint evaluation session.

At this point in the evaluation, it might seem that a recommendation that the father not have contact would have been in order, since he was not accepting complete responsibility, appeared still to be romantically and sexually attracted to Tanya, and, in her mother's presence the child said she did not want to see him.

The evaluator then explored the issues of the child's trauma and her attachment to her father.

Prior to the marital separation, Tanya's father had been her primary caregiver. The mother's involvement with Tanya had always been peripheral: her profession was very demanding of her time and she perceived the father's taking care of the child, including taking a year's leave of absence from his professional work, as evidence that he was an excellent father and that her presence was not crucial to the child's welfare. Tanya had a secure attachment to her father and a distorted attachment to her mother.

The child was traumatized by the sudden disruption and subsequent loss of her relationship with her father. To this was added her emotional inability to mourn his loss. Her mother, now representing survival to Tanya, was emotionally unavailable to her because of her unrelenting rage toward the father. Many authority figures in Tanya's life, including several therapists, told her she was a good girl for telling so that her father could be out of her life. But Tanya secretly longed for her father and, given the intense and continuous reinforcement of those in her environment, his memory became fused with sexual thoughts and feelings. The child was literally unable to think of him without thinking of sex.

The evaluator discussed her findings with the child's mother, acknowledging that it was understandable that the mother did not want Tanya to have contact with her father. But she also pointed out that the child would be left with powerful memories and longings for him, and that these memories would be based on what had transpired—that is, an abnormal and probably shameful (in later years) relationship.

The evaluator believed that more therapy for Tanya was contraindicated at the time. It appeared that Tanya needed supervised visits with her father that would give her memory options, so she could love, hate, or feel indifferent toward him without fusing her feelings for him with feelings about sexuality. The contact needed to be intensely ordinary and defused by having him bring his new wife to the visits and, on some occasions, Tanya's girlfriends. They needed to go to McDonald's and to Disney movies and to ride bicycles—no sunsets or mountaintops. The treatment needed was safe, normal parental contact, with the objective being to give the girl a father she could experience as ordinary, and even boring.

The mother was advised that any contact with the father would be extremely stressful for Tanya unless her mother endorsed such contact. The mother literally screamed her way through some of her feelings about this, and finally agreed to support the therapist's recommendations.

Tanya did not find the abuse traumatizing at the time it occurred, but the attachment disruption had been devastating to her: her primary attachment figure, her father, had been taken away, leaving her with a mother to whom she had little emotional commitment. She feared the loss of her remaining parent and in order to protect against this loss, and maintain the relationship, she kept hidden the positive feelings she had for her father. Having to keep these feelings secret strengthened Tanya's belief that loving and missing her father was shameful.

Reunification was equally traumatizing. There had been no contact with her father for five years. Her desire to see him increased her feelings of guilt because (1) she now had a mature understanding of what had happened five years earlier, (2) she blamed herself for what had happened, and (3) she had lied to her mother about her feelings toward her father.

Although we may wish it otherwise, children are sometimes nourished by the damnedest parental relationships, and we need to deal with what we have, not pretend that the situation is something else.

The Treating Clinician's Involvement in Reunification

Clinicians may feel they are being placed in an untenable position when asked to use their skills to facilitate a reunification that they believe will be harmful for a child. The professional response is often to stop treating the child, or to ignore the mandate of the department of social services or the court. Either response can compound problems for the youngster, for not only will she lose another significant adult in her life, her therapist, but she will not be prepared to deal with the reunification, which will probably be forced upon her whether or not she has seen a therapist.

Clinicians should avoid limiting their participation to recommending whether or not a reunification should occur, and they need not perceive themselves as helpless when carrying out the orders of a court. A written clinical evaluation, whether or not requested by the decision-makers, can be submitted to the empowering agency. An objective report clearly outlining the positive and negative consequences of a proposed reunification can be a powerful instrument that is difficult to ignore. The clinician must specifically cite the basis for her opinion, including observations, experience, and current related professional research. She may suggest an alternate, detailed plan of action that would insure the likelihood of a successful reunification, giving sound clinical reasons for the alternative. The clinician may need to request a consultation with the judge and social services supervisor, and/or insist that the child have legal representation.

Clinical work should focus on helping the youngster and current caregiver deal with the proposed changes. The child needs to identify and express feelings related to these changes and, as much as possible, the issue of conflicting loyalties should be addressed. Emotional and safety supports should be discussed, planned for, and, when appropriate, rehearsed.

The child's feelings and concerns about contact and reunification need to be explored and worked through. In many situations it is helpful to have the first reunification contact be a letter written by the absent parent to the child and delivered through the therapist, who can then work with it in the treatment setting. After the child responds, additional contact can include the use of audio- and videotapes, but these should still be filtered through the therapist until he determines that physical visitation is appropriate. The parent's first contacts with the child can be held in the therapist's office or on an outing, with the therapist present to provide guidance. If it appears that further parent-child contact is in order but requires supervision, very specific guidelines must be given to all parties. A list of parent-child supervision guidelines can be found in appendix F.

The adult who has been left out of a child's life needs to be apprised by the therapist of the child's need for a transition period of gradually increased contact, and of the importance of not overstimulating the child with presents, activities, and people. It is not unusual for a parent to be so intent on his rights and positive intentions toward the child that he does not consider the child's feelings, and needs reminders that the child has also had difficulties with the separation. Parents must often be advised that they will have to develop their relationship anew, and may need to join in the child's therapy sessions for a time in order to facilitate the process.

Custodial caregivers who are resistant to a child's reunification with a separated parent need to be assured that the child will be emotionally and physically protected during the reunification process. These caretakers have developed their own attachments to the youngster, and may consciously or unconsciously create more conflict for the child unless they are satisfied that the youngster will be well treated during the process. It is also important for them to know that the child may temporarily exhibit some stress symptoms, such as sleeping and eating problems, bed-wetting, and babyish and/or oppositional behavior. Although difficult to live with, these behaviors do not necessarily mean the child is in serious trouble and that the plan to reunify should be abandoned, or that the child is being abused in some manner. The caregivers may need to be told that stress is inevitable, given the particular family's circumstances, and that not all stress stems from negative experiences. As a comparison, it can be pointed out that many individuals exhibit signs of stress under positive circumstances, such as adults planning a wedding, or children at holiday times.

Impaired Attachment

Children who were unable to securely attach to a parent figure early in their lives develop styles of coping which help them to get along through childhood, but which can be detrimental in their later lives as they adopt this model for all significant relationships. Attachment requires the physical and emotional availability of both the child and his object of attachment. Barriers to the formation of attachments include such things as a child's physical disabilities and/or early and prolonged hospitalization; poor parenting due to such things as ignorance, lack of motivation, substance abuse, or physical or emotional dysfunction; or environmental circumstances such as war, or multiple or inadequate caregivers.

Restructuring attachment-impaired relationships in children is possible, but can be glacial in progress (Carson and Goodfield 1988). The hour or two per week that a child spends with the therapist, and the relationship that develops between them, is significant but does not provide the needed corrective experience. No matter how genuine and intense, love is not enough to overcome what these children have learned early in their lives, that is, that they cannot depend on others to meet their needs.

The primary treatment for attachment-impaired children is to have them live in an environment in which they experience therapeutic parenting. This could be in the home of their birth parents, adoptive parents, or foster parents, if the parents have the abilities and motivation and are willing to be part of the child's treatment team. Therapeutic parenting can also be experienced in a group home or institutional setting where staffing patterns are designed to maximize continuity in the child-caregiver relationship, and the primary childcare workers are part of the treatment team.

Basically, caregivers need to interact with these impaired children with solid parenting, in reliable, predictable, and consistent ways, while firmly managing the youngster's behavior nonpunitively. Caregivers need to provide nurturance and reassurance, despite a child's minimal or negative response to these attentions, and continue to do so for far longer than they imagined they could, or that would be necessary before some change was observable.

This parenting is therapeutic, because the caregivers will probably be teaching or retraining the child in life-skills such as communicating with others, manners, hygiene, playing, sharing, studying, and behavior control. The parenting adults will learn to identify the child's negative patterns as well as the underlying dynamics of objectionable behaviors that often appear volitional. They will also learn to intervene without indulgence or punitiveness. The caregivers need significant strength and dedication, and have to be able to curb some of their impulses in relation to the particular child, such as losing control or giving up on him.

When the situation finally improves to the point where the child experiences deepening pleasure in the relationship, feelings of vulnerability and loss of boundaries will emerge along with the feeling of pleasure, the child will experience an attachment crisis, and the whole process will shatter. Then the child and caretaker must start over, and the process repeats itself again and again. The child believes he does not deserve the good feelings that are coincident with a reciprocal attachment, and that it is just a matter of time before he is disappointed or abandoned anyway; his negative behavior escalates to precipitate a crisis and break the tension. There are parenting persons and clinicians with the ability to remain with these children on a long-term basis and assist them in restructuring their patterns of attachment; also, there are some children who can change.

The paradigm for parent-child interaction just described is exactly what is needed in the therapist-caretaker relationship: the professional feeds the parents with support, skill-training, patience, and a determination not to give up on them; the parents, in turn, feed the child the same menu.

Since we know things are easier to face when they have names, I have identified for myself a number of clusters of attachment-impaired behaviors and named them Clingy-Demanding, Rebellious, Parentified, Super Star, Compliant Robot and Kid Cool. These are more than the transient, worrisome behaviors found in both normal and disturbed children; they are entrenched styles of interacting in significant relationships that the child has developed to meet his attachment needs for safety, comfort, intimacy, nurturance, and mutuality. Basically, this is how the child interacts with the world around him.

Clingy-Demanding Child

These anxiously attached children are afraid their parents will disappear. Many have parents who have threatened suicide or abandonment. The caregivers consistently tell the child, "You make me sick," or, "I'll send you where they can teach you a lesson," conveying the message that the parent may leave or send the child away. The children cling to these parents; their demands for attention often trigger the parental behavior which frightens them, which in turn increases the clinginess. Fatigue, illness, and other stresses will also cause these behaviors, which can appear manipulative, to escalate. Soothing does not satisfy the youngsters, because their basic fears have not been allayed.

In addition to the basic therapeutic parenting necessary to address their insecurities, the caregivers and clinician can help the child sort out and express hidden feelings. The initial approach can be indirect, with art-play techniques, then when the child has gained some emotional strength, he can work directly with the issues.

In some sense, identifying the child's fears is anxiety-producing because the process initially makes his fears seem more real. But this is preferable to his experiencing unnamed panic because of a mass of amorphous, unidentified feelings. The child experiences being able to identify and share feelings through discussion as being a bit more in control. Some fears can be allayed with accurate information, some will need to be worked on in sessions individually or with the parents, and others will require that the child accept the reality of his life and learn skills in therapy to cope with his circumstances.

The Worry Wall. (Similar versions are the Anger Wall, the Happiness Wall) A section of wall in the playroom has been designated as the "Worry Wall," and a sign so signifies.

> Helen, I'd like you to look at the Worry Wall for a few minutes. Do you remember the first day you came here, and we spent time getting to know the playroom? What do you remember hearing about the Worry Wall? I know you've been reading some of the cards, and I remember that one day you stood on the chair to read Beth's card when it was way up there. Today, if you would like, you can join in.
>
> This is how it works. I want you to take a little time to think about the biggest worry in your life right now. When you're ready I'll give you one of my business cards, and you can write your worry on the back and sign it. Then I want you to look at that wall and think about how big your worry is today. Consider how much time you spend feeling bad, how much time you spend thinking about your worry, whether it's every day or lots of times during the day. Think about whether you have dreams about it. Is it a *little* worry, so that the card would be tacked down low near the floor, or is it a really, really *big* worry, so the card should be put up near the ceiling? Or should it be somewhere in between? When you've figured out your very biggest worry today and decided how big it is, then you can write it on the card and tack it up.

Each week when you come to see me, we'll check in with each other and see how you're doing with your worry. You'll need to move your card when there have been changes. Perhaps it will have gotten bigger or smaller or gone away. If you'd like some help with the worry, the two of us will make that a part of our work together.

This exercise helps children communicate the amount of their worry to the therapist, reminds them that other children have worries, defuses the worry through sharing thoughts about it, shows that worries can increase and decrease but that we have some control over them, and provides a nonverbal way to signal trouble. For example, if a child moves her card's position from the middle to near the ceiling when she enters the playroom, or asks for a new card because she needs to add a worry, the clinician is alerted and can investigate further.

The Worry Wall is useful with children who present various clinical problems. The intriguing nature of the exercise nudges many of them past their resistance. In fact, some children will use this exercise to write what they have found unspeakable. Sometimes a child will name a worry unrelated to the work he has been doing in treatment, which provides important additional information. For example, "I worry about Daddy dying because he takes drugs with his friends."

An expressed worry may appear mundane, such as, "I don't like to clean up the dog poop." But this provides the clinician with an opportunity to be empathic about another issue which *is* important to the child.

Sometimes the expressed worry can be a vehicle for practicing problem-solving. What is learned can be used at a later time to deal with more emotion-laden problems. Finally, helping the child deal with her concerns strengthens the clinical partnership between child and therapist.

And for all these reasons, this is also a good exercise for a class of anxiety-laden graduate students!

Teaching parents how to help clingy children control their behavior has been described earlier in this chapter, under "Loss and Disruption." Structuring and providing times when the child is allowed and encouraged to engage in clingy behavior can reduce the child's anxiety, and acknowledge that change is difficult.

Structuring Clingy Behavior

Susan, let's talk about the behavior that Gramma said is driving her crazy. First of all, is there a word you can think of to describe how you act? Let's see, "Hanging all over Gramma." "Asking for everything and being mean and bratty." Gramma, does that describe pretty well what's going on? Just to make it simpler, Susan, could we use your word "bratty" to mean all those things? How old do you feel inside when you do those things? Hmmm, that's about three years younger, about your brother's age. Gramma says it mostly happens after you have a visit with your mom. Is that how you remember it? Could you show me, right here and now, three minutes of bratty behavior? O yeah, whining, that's good. Do you ever whine louder than that? You do? Let's hear it just as loud as you do at home. Good.

Thank you, that was certainly a fine demonstration of seven-year-old bratty behavior. Now, Gramma, I'm going to ask you a tough question. I don't want you to answer right away, because this is hard and I want you to really think about your answer. I think it's very hard for Susan to see her mom, even though she's glad to see her and she loves her and all that. I think that she really, deeply feels like a seven-year-old brat, and it will take a while before she can stop these behaviors totally. So, here's your question. If we could make this behavior safe so no one or nothing gets hurt, how long could you deal with Susan's seven-year-old bratty behavior before you go crazy? Let's start with fifteen minutes: could you handle that? OK, how about twenty? Now Susan, let's say that for this week, Gramma can handle twenty minutes of your being a seven-year-old brat. Do you think that you can do it? The bargain is this: she'll let you be bratty for twenty minutes, and you have to keep it up for the whole twenty minutes, no short cuts. There are some other ground rules. You may not be bratty with your brother—he has his own uptight feelings about Mom's visiting. You may not do anything that is disrespectful to your Gramma, and you may not hurt anyone or destroy anything.

Gramma, are there some other things we should add to this list? Yes, that sounds reasonable: swearwords will not be spoken in the house. Gramma, is there a place Susan can say swearwords? How about in the garage? OK, Susan, you can say or yell swearwords, but it has to be in the garage, not in the house. Susan, is there anything you would like to add to the ground rules? Do you think you can keep the bargain? We need to make a nice poster for your room with the ground rules, and a place on it to mark off each day.

Gramma's hard part of the bargain is not to go crazy. She will also make sure you keep it up for twenty minutes and do not break the ground rules. Gramma, you'll probably want to rest up before Susan gets home. And, just a suggestion, you may want to get some of those earplugs they have in the drugstore for swimmers, just to use for this once-a-week time. When Susan starts to feel closer to being ten years old again after these visits, and we teach her some ways that older girls express feelings, you may not need the earplugs any more.

FTX
FOLLETT TEXTBOOK EXCHANGE
3139 NORTH OAKLAND AVE. • MILWAUKEE, WI 53211-3049

PHONE	STORE
414/332-2665	NO. 363

Customer's Order No.				Date 1/18 19 97			
Sold to							
Address							
City							

Sold by	Cash	C.O.D.	Charge	On Acct.	Mdse. Ret.	Paid Out	

Quantity	Description					Price	Amount
							41 13
	James						
	Peterson						27 98
						Tax	
Thank You In case of claims or returned goods please present this bill.						**Total**	69 11

No. 315609 Received by

Parenting Susan these days is a very difficult job, and you need to keep in training the same way athletes do. You need rest, exercise, perhaps some vitamins, relaxing time away from her, and earplugs to keep up with this girl. She's a great kid and a big handful.

Susan, let's get back to this bargain. How will you know when your twenty-minute bratty time is up? Do you have a timer? No, it's not OK for Gramma to tell you when to stop, this is your behavior and Gramma will monitor, but that's all. You are in charge of how you act. Could you arrange to have a timer of some kind before your Mom's next visit? I would like both of you to write a few notes on this paper about how the bargain went, so we can talk about it a little next week.

Rebellious Child

The rebellious child is angry and frustrated. He can be stereotyped as the kid who likes to kick over big, noisy trash cans or walk along a wall between two barking dogs. His secret message is "I need you." He is feeling frustrated, angry, and vulnerable. He both needs and distrusts caring relationships. While wanting closeness, he rejects or misinterprets attempts to provide him with comfort and security. This youngster lives in a condition of unrelieved tension and worry.

Rebellious behavior as a manifestation of an anxious attachment is a different presentation of the same dynamics seen in the Clingy-Demanding Child. Children in both categories are particularly difficult to parent because their neediness is obvious and yet they do not take in nurturing. These are the "empty bucket" children—it seems that no matter how hard one works to fill them up, they remain empty.

Therapeutic parenting can eventually enable these children to trust enough in the relationship to begin to absorb the positive caring they are given. Rebellious children must be firmly managed in a reliable and predictable manner. The adults who come into their lives must all send the message, "I will help you to be in control." They also need to validate the child's worth, provide safety, and teach new behaviors.

Clinical sessions are an extension of therapeutic parenting. The adults need to help these children to identify and express their anxious and fearful emotions, both at home and in therapy. Many feel unlovable and useless, and believe that their futures are bleak. Techniques which focus on building confidence and self-esteem, and give the message, "You are a fun kid and I like you" are essential. A goodly number of these children are starving for the primitive nurturance they have been unable to experience, but do not allow themselves to admit this neediness, because they then experience a sense of enormous vulnerability. Boys particularly, beginning at about age nine, feel too old for affection, and mightily resist affectionate touching for its own sake. Sensorimotor play in clinical sessions is very effective because it can provide nurturing closeness in the nonthreatening guise of being fun and silly.

Any nonthreatening activity that enables the clinician to meet the child's early needs for holding, stroking, cuddling, eye contact, and touching can provide therapeutic nurturing. Caution must be exercised in using these interventions with children who have been sexually exploited, because activity that appears to be just play but is, in fact, disguised touching, usually mirrors the sexual abuse. When treating such children, the clinician must truthfully state exactly what is happening, why it is being done, and remind them that they have the right to object.

Applying and removing face paint and clown makeup allows for physical closeness, eye contact, and gentle touches. Rebellious boys can enjoy having their faces painted to look like fierce wrestlers or monsters, while being gently tended as they are cleaned up and have their hair combed. Doing this in front of a mirror and with others present amplifies the experience, and adds to the child's feeling of safety.

Messy activities, such as painting the soles of a child's feet to make foot paintings, can naturally lead to the clinician's carrying the child to a washing place, and turns the washing, drying, and powdering of feet, and the putting on of shoes and socks, into a satisfying, nurturing experience.

Psychodrama presents numerous opportunities. A child could be a dangerous dragon tied up in a cave. A good person from the village finds him, and although she is too afraid to untie him because he is so fierce, she slowly feeds him cookies and milk. She talks to him during this feeding, and tells him that even though he does mean things, she knows he has a good heart.

The child's rebellious behavior is best dealt with in a direct, efficient, and matter-of-fact manner. For example, "These are the rules and these are the consequences. You can choose whether or not you want to be in trouble." Caregivers must be cautioned against allowing themselves to be drawn into power struggles with these children, which would most likely result in escalation of the child's negative behavior and feelings of guilt and frustration for the caregiver.

Jernberg's work (1979) provides the clinician with methods and dynamic, effective techniques to meet the clinical needs of rebellious children, among others, and promotes attachment between children and their caregivers.

Parentified Child

The Parentified Child believes that her parent is vulnerable and in need of protection, so does not look to that parent to have her own needs met. Rather, she acts as her own parent in this distorted attachment. She will often sacrifice herself in order to spare the parent hurt feelings that she believes will somehow destroy the parent and leave herself abandoned. A parentified child commonly feels responsible for the parent's welfare, and blames herself if the parent is unhappy, unsuccessful, or in any way has problems.

This dynamic has been clearly identified in the relationships found in many substance-abusing families, as well as in many sexually abusive families. It develops when a parent is emotionally dependent, perceives his or her environment as hostile, has had significant losses in life, and turns to the child to have emotional needs met. The young person will meet these needs as best she can, in order to maintain the relationship which, to her, represents survival.

Many parentified children are not identified as traumatized, because they are so wonderfully adept at meeting adult needs and hiding their own fears and deprivations. They mature into compulsive caregivers who give until it hurts, and become silently angry because their own needs are not recognized or met. They believe that if they give a lot, they will enjoy some reciprocal behavior without having to ask for it, for they have learned to savor crumbs and not ask for more. Asking directly for oneself invites the intolerable risk of rejection.

Children can disengage from this role and learn other styles of interacting; they must first be recognized and honored for the responsibilities they have assumed in the family, and then led to understand and accept the reasons for changing.

Unhooking the Child from the Parenting Role

We've talked about the trouble in your family and all the things you've been doing to help. Today I want us to talk about you being ready to give up your job as worrier and to let someone else be mostly in charge of that. I want us to begin by talking about kittens.

You have a cat at home. Do you remember how she acted when she was a kitten? She did? Would you show me with your body how she did some of those things? Let me show you some things my two kittens do. Mom, do you remember anything you've seen kittens do? OK. What the kittens are doing is practicing to be cats. They practice stalking and pouncing, and they exercise their bodies by rolling and jumping, and doing the things we've been talking about.

Children also need lots of time just to *get ready* to be grown-up. When they become teenagers, then they begin to practice being adults. It's your job to be a kid and there are things you need to do to get ready, just like kittens have to do the things we talked about, to get ready to be cats. Children need to be curious, imaginative, and playful. They need to learn lots of things, like getting along with different kinds of people, and how things work, and what the world is like. They need to roll, stretch, and exercise their bodies, and they need to study to help their thinking to grow. This takes lots of energy. Your energy has been mostly used in worrying about your little sister and taking care of her, and it's time now for that to stop, and time for you to start being a kid. Your mom and foster mother and I are going to help you to do that.

We know you've done a fine job taking care of your sister, but your mom's ready now to take over being Mom, and she wants you to use your energy to do kid things. Mom, why don't you talk to Lisa for a while about the good job she's done, and how it's time now for her to be a kid and learn to do kid things.

Parentified children do not usually have play or social skills, and many have convinced themselves that those things "are stupid anyway." They need to be given *specific instructions* on how to play, and cheered for their efforts as they learn. Group work is very effective, because the kids get swept up in the fun along with the others and are not singled out as deficient.

Organizations such as Education Through Music have excellent programs that teach children's songs and games to adults (see appendix A). Such instruction provides caregivers with ways in which they can relate to the child on the child's level, not on an adult level. The parentified child, in turn, is likely to be initially resistant to the new relationship, because she has been given lots of positive reinforcement for *not* behaving in childlike ways.

Before being asked to disengage from their caretaking roles, children need to be assured that those for whom they have assumed responsibility will continue to be cared for. When the assumed responsibility has been for a parent, the child needs constant reassurance that the parent will be fine without the child's caretaking and worrying. This can be demonstrated and concretized by having the child and therapist make a colorful poster that can be taken home and displayed by the child to keep the message alive. Having the parent participate in the exercise, or later sign the poster, makes it even better. One absent parent added three names to the child's poster when it was sent to him in prison.

"Who Can Help Take Care of Mom?" Poster

Janis, today we are going to take these beautiful marking pens and make a big list of every human being we can think of in your mother's life who can help her. Would you like to start, or should I? OK. It's my turn. I'll put down Mom's therapist. Who else? What about Mom herself? Who else? Sure, neighbors, the fire department, the crisis line.

Well, let's count all the people we've got here. That's sure a lot! Let's make the "Mom herself" part much bigger and decorate it. What do you think when you read this list? I'll tell you what I think. I think that it's almost time for you to give up your job of taking care of your mom. She needs to learn to use all the good helpers she has around her, and she also needs to learn to help herself. And you, my friend, need to learn to be a child.

Parentified children who have been removed from their parents are harder to wean from their feelings of responsibility than those children who have relatively continuous contact with a parent. The clinician should work with the parents whose interactions contributed to the dysfunctional relationship as much as possible, because doing so is more meaningful to the child and facilitates the process.

Caregivers, especially stepparents and foster and adoptive parents who equate a child's "good" behavior with their parental adequacy, will need guidance, support, and education to help them understand why the family is deliberately investing time and money to have their child change from a polite, nurturing housekeeper to a regular kid who gets rowdy, resists cleaning her room, and does not volunteer to clean up after the dog or take care of the toddler in the family.

Super Star

Children with distorted attachments can be very successful in their achievements. They identify with the role of a superstar, often in arenas which enable them to maintain control and avoid closeness with other people. Dependence on others represents loss of control to them. They may concentrate on areas such as computer programming or mathematics, or other activities where self-reliance is the norm. They have little tolerance for setbacks, mistakes, or less than an optimal performance, and they overwork, so that there is no time left for relationships. Their behavior is concentrated and focused, and can become driven and compulsive when stressed by their environment.

In addition to the therapeutic parenting described earlier, the clinician needs to coordinate the efforts of home, school, and others important to the child in focusing on things other than accomplishment when valuing the child. At the same time they must be careful not to minimize successes, for he would then probably exhibit even more driven behavior to achieve. The youngster needs to hear, "You are valued and cared about and liked, even when not excelling."

Puppets, psychodrama, and stories can be used to show that people, even adults and teenagers, can make mistakes and still be loved. Children make the relatively easy connection when their own experiences with pets are used as examples. For instance, the therapist reminds them their pets make messes and get into trouble, and that even though the child becomes exasperated or angry, he does not abandon the dog and still loves it.

Adults and children who are high achievers and who do not have attachment impairments often focus their energies narrowly and discipline themselves to defer current pleasures in order to achieve future goals. This same behavior is problematic for the attachment impaired child, because achievement substitutes for reciprocal, intimate relationships, and the child's self-image becomes linked to variable externals which require a concerted effort to maintain. It is important to remember the implication for these children of early loss, separation, and emotional distance.

Compliant Robot

Some children give up turning to adults to meet their needs when they have experienced a general unavailability of adults. They do not accept substitutes and do not turn to anyone. Separation from their primary caregiver elicits little or no response, and caregivers appear to be easily interchangeable. The childrens' facial expressions are immobile, inflexible, and seldom change. Because they are compliant, polite, and attractive, and because they follow the rules and do not make a fuss, professionals inexperienced with attachment impairment become confused when these children are neglected in institutional settings and experience placement and adoption failures. But, simply put, people do not like them.

Compliant Robots have no interest in interacting or having emotional contact with others. No matter how much is given to them, they give nothing back. Treatment calls for being attentive to any sign of the child's showing human interest, and then seizing the moment with physical, verbal, and social reinforcement.

Some children are able to connect emotionally with animals, which can be useful in initiating and maintaining connections that can grow to include people. The pet needs to be sturdy, affectionate, and diurnal, and needs to have completed basic training, and there must be a reasonable expectation that the child may claim it as his should attachment occur. The caregivers and therapist, through the pet, can gently and gradually make associations with which the child can identify.

> Eight-year-old Toni's history clearly demonstrated a distorted attachment pattern related to her multiple caregivers, numerous hospitalizations, and several failed placements since being abandoned by her parents. She had been identified as attachment impaired, and the clinician and new fost-adopt parents were aware of the prognosis. They were ready for a long, difficult attachment process with interventions done slowly and with utmost subtlety, feeling that this relationship was the child's last chance at finding a home.
>
> Toni was, as expected, compliant in her new home, and demon-

strated an unexpected, apparently genuine, affectionate interest in the family's eight-month-old golden retriever puppy.

The parents and therapist slowly and carefully made verbal connections between the situations of both puppy and child as being welcome newcomers in their home. The puppy was referred to as Toni's puppy. Toni's eventual identification with Rags enabled attachment interventions to be made and acknowledged, if not accepted.

Given Toni's low self-esteem, self-hatred, and inability to express anger directly, there was serious concern that she might abuse the puppy as she became emotionally connected to it. It was important for the caregivers to be made aware of this possibility, and to be given specific guidelines as to how they could intervene. Toni was told that people can sometimes feel like hurting a pet, but that animals are living things and need to be protected and taken care of, just as people were now taking care of her.

Toni was given primary responsibility for taking care of the puppy, beginning with its feeding. Fortunately, she saw this as a really fun part since it was the chore most likely to establish a successful relationship between her and the dog. Her responsibilities were expanded to include brushing, bathing, and exercising Rags. Cleaning up Rags's droppings in the yard was put off until the puppy attachment became more secure. The parents arranged for the veterinarian's office to support them by designating the child as Rags's mistress, and by actively acknowledging the child's great lovability from the puppy's perspective. Toni was then charged with, and assisted in, telephoning for a vet appointment and bringing Rags in for her appointment.

Toni's therapy appointments were made on Saturdays so that it would be possible for Rags to accompany her to a few sessions. She was encouraged to talk about the puppy's feelings of first being taken away from her original home and then finding another. The therapist's subsequent references to Rags in treatment became more powerful, because the puppy had actually been present. The child's feelings for her pet were used to help her understand the feelings, hopes, and expectations of her new parents. The process developed slowly from Toni's loving Rags to Toni's allowing her caregivers to love Rags (psychodynamically, they were in grandparent roles), and through the emotional joining, dependency, and shared love for the animal, Toni was able to experience the beginnings of a secure attachment.

These compliant, noninvolved children act disinterested and nonempathic toward others. Adults must continue interacting with the child *as if* the youngster were interested and *as if* they would someday have a positive relationship. The youngster's overly compliant style can be countered by offering alternatives, as well as by arranging for small increases in responsibility so that the child makes some of her own decisions. Clinicians and parents need to provide verbal and behavioral stimulation for these children and to be alert for the most subtle signs of emotional interest shown by the child. They should then grab the opportunity and in subtle ways, verbally, physically, and emotionally provide reinforcement.

Kid Cool

Kid Cool is self-centered, seeking possessions rather than relationships. His excessive urges for independence prevent his asking for help or receiving it. His contempt of sentiment stems from painful and futile attempts to form attachments with rejecting parent figures. This child can be surrounded by people and things, and behave in such a seemingly confident manner that the sparseness of his affectional ties are hidden.

Parenting Kid Cool means providing for his physiological needs without any expectation of, or attempt to engender, emotional response. The caring adults can remind the child that they are emotionally available and on standby; this position will probably remain unchanged until some initiative is taken by the child.

Kid Cool must be placed with adults who can tolerate his detached manner. Although caregivers generally attend to the advice of the clinician, most secretly believe that they can love the child into health. Caregivers will often become angry and frustrated, which further reinforces the child's belief that he is unlovable and that no one wants him anyway.

Clinicians, too, can become trapped into believing that the sheer force of their caring, clinical involvement will unlock the child and allow attachment to occur. And, as with the parents, their seeming ineffectiveness leads to frustration and often hostility, which the child can identify immediately, since he is so familiar with the process. Therapy for these children consists of strong support for the parents so that they will remain rock-solid providers and "hang in there" with the child, while feeling like the proverbial pregnant elephant whose gestation lasts for years, wondering at times if the effort is worth it, and hoping the result will not be stillborn.

Summary

The presence of an attachment disturbance should be clinically considered when treating traumatized children. A child's primary attachment, usually to a parent, is the emotional base from which he views and explores the world. Consequently, children are often frightened and overwhelmed by parental loss and separation. Reunification after separation can also be traumatizing. Whether the reunion is experienced positively or negatively, the process can create enormous conflicts and may also restimulate memories and emotions from past traumatic events.

Some children are attachment impaired because of early traumatic experience, that is, they have developed dysfunctional styles of interacting with the adults upon whom they are dependent. This impairment is evidenced through a wide range of behaviors, most of which are seemingly benign, in the sense that they do not physically harm others or appear to harm the child. A common thread between these behaviors, however, is that adults find it extremely difficult to relate to the youngsters and often have difficulty identifying the reason for their discomfort and dislike. With clinical probing, the reasons given usually reduce to some form of "The child gives nothing back emotionally." Large numbers of these children are found in out-of-home care and become placement failures, moved from home to home. This confirms their belief that no one wants them and that the world is indifferent and uncaring.

Clinicians need to understand the dynamics of attachment and the profound impact disturbances to the attachment relationships have on a child. Traumatized children can be further harmed by our attempts to help them when treatment requires interference with an existing attachment relationship or requires that they form a new attachment. The process of restructuring attachment patterns is long and difficult and is, for many children, their only hope of ever forming an intimate bond with another person.

13
Social Rehabilitation

Social rehabilitation has been achieved when unacceptable social behaviors have been replaced by those recognized as normal, usually through a combination of therapy and social-skills training. When traumatized children engage in behaviors that result in their being disliked by others, their belief that they are bad and unlovable is reinforced; modifying or eliminating these behaviors, therefore, becomes a treatment objective. There may be instances when dealing with the underlying issues is not realistic or is unnecessary, such as with a very young child, or one with limited ability or insight, or one who has not been taught appropriate behavior. In these and related situations, the clinical focus remains primarily on social-skills training.

For ease of discussion I have grouped the children who exhibit unacceptable behaviors that will require social rehabilitation into four categories.

1. *The Socially Inept Child* has not been taught, or has not learned, basic skills such as eating (they forage), playing (they have not learned to play), toileting (which happens anywhere), or how to interact socially with others.

2. *The Eroticized Child* has been taught unacceptable (for a child) sexual behaviors which can lead to continued exploitation.

3. *The Agitated Child* may have social skills, but his frantic style of interacting with others is so disruptive that it negates any positive interactions, and leaves the child feeling confused and hopeless.

4. *The Socially Inhibited Child* may have social skills, but believes she no longer has the right to have friends, or that no one would want to play with her. She feels stigmatized by sensory disabilities, medical problems, or events believed to be so shameful or so serious that having fun is now taboo.

Children in each of these categories could be helped by a comprehensive behavioral approach in which the child becomes a partner in a treatment process incorporating the basic steps of clarification, monitoring, identification, action planning, and follow through. A detailed example of this process is described in the example of John (chapter 9), who needed to gain control over his destructive behavior. That process can be modified to deal with other unacceptable behaviors.

Another important clinical intervention likely to be needed when treating those who fall into these four categories is assertiveness training. Not uncommonly, unacceptable behavior stems from the children's failure to ask directly for what they want. They manipulate instead, with behaviors ranging from passive to aggressive, in order to get what they need. Failure to ask directly for what they want may result from not feeling deserving, fear of rejection, not having permission to ask, or never learning how.

The clinician will have to spend time evaluating the underlying dynamics of the child's lack of assertiveness. He will also have to educate and elicit cooperation from the child's caregivers. Ideally, all family members will become involved in the child's assertiveness training.

Underlying issues often resolve themselves when the child learns by doing, that is, experiencing success when asking directly for what he wants. A step-by-step didactic approach to teaching assertive behavior is recommended. This should be followed by practice using role-play and rehearsal (using videotapes is especially helpful), and should be reinforced by clinical play themes, and at home and at school. Successes in assertiveness training should be celebrated.

The Socially Inept Child

Socially inept children are able to form positive relationships only to a limited extent. They have never learned basic social skills, and have developed patterns of behavior that are socially unacceptable. They operate on a survival level, foraging for food and defecating in corners, seldom making eye contact, without a concept of personal boundaries. These are usually youngsters who have been grossly neglected or raised with bizarre parenting practices. They have probably been removed from the parents who created the abnormal home environment, and their caregivers at the time of treatment are most likely relatives, foster parents, or childcare workers.

The success of social rehabilitation for this group is very much dependent on the caregiver, more so than for the other three groups. Providing specific skills training, consultation, and emotional support to the caregiver thus becomes a primary treatment function. Basically, the caregivers must be given care so that they, in turn, can nurture and guide the children, who then learn that they are valuable, and eventually care for themselves.

The clinician's most difficult task is helping the caregiver develop realistic goals within realistic time frames. Unless this is done, caregivers can become discouraged, and this discouragement is felt by the child; treatment is negatively affected and hopelessness sets in. Even though the clinician has carefully discussed the time and work required to help the child learn new social skills with the parenting adults, he may find that the caregivers, in their own minds, minimize the time and effort needed for change to come about. Not uncommonly, people who care for socially inept children become fiercely determined to love them back to normalcy: they expect their love and caring to quickly provide all that is necessary for healing. The child needs, and treatment requires, a high level of input from the caregivers that includes not only love, but also skills in therapeutic parenting. Although miracles do happen, the therapist is cautioned not to overlook the possibility of a parent's deep-seated belief that love alone will conquer all, and will do so quickly.

The first step toward rehabilitation of a socially inept child is to select a single behavior upon which to focus. It is unlikely that a child in this category will be exhibiting a physically dangerous behavior, but if so, that should be given priority. Barring the exhibition of such behavior, initial focus should be on something that is especially troublesome *to the caregiver*. (This may or may not be something that the clinician sees as being immediately important to the child.) The caregivers need some positive reinforcement, in the form of the child's behavior modification, so that they will continue to show interest in the process, and invest the high level of energy necessary for the child's healing.

For example, it may be most important to one set of parents that the child learn to make an emotional connection, so she will initiate contacts with the caregiver, make eye contact, and go to the caregiver to have her needs met. For other caregivers, the most important issue might be having the child learn to defecate in the toilet instead of in the corner.

Following are some basic principles for social-skills training. The clinician can find more detailed descriptions in works specific to this area, such as those by Dowrick (1986) and Krumboltz and Krumboltz (1972).

1. Separating the behavior into component elements allows the adults to clearly analyze and understand the tasks to be taught; they can see progress being made as each small step toward the final behavior is achieved. A child who has not learned toileting might first be taught to point to feces he has left in a corner. He is subsequently taught to pick it up and place it in the toilet. Finally, he is taught to use the toilet.

2. Rewarding any tendency toward learning the new behavior, and gently reinforcing beginning efforts, helps a child become successful. The child who stays in the room when a guest comes, rather than running out and hiding, is praised; the child who makes brief eye contact with a parent when talking, rather than turning away, is told how much that behavior is appreciated.

3. Ignoring unacceptable behaviors when such response is in order may be the most difficult part of the treatment program for some parenting adults. A child who does not talk during dinner but just gobbles down his food should be drawn into talking by others at the table. He is told how pleasant and interesting it is to talk with him; he is not chastised for being silent.

4. Modeling the behavior to be learned by actual demonstration, particularly by someone the child respects, facilitates learning. An older child in the family shows the learning child how he seeks out Mom and lets her know he is going out to play.

5. Rehearsing the behavior is another effective technique. The child role-plays, and in so doing accomplishes the behavior being learned. For example, the youngster goes through all the toileting motions and is praised for what she has done, or parent and child practice how she is to make eye contact when meeting someone.

6. Cuing signals are reminders established to help the child remember a behavior he is learning. His eating utensils could be placed on, rather than beside, his plate to remind him not to eat with his fingers, or a sign could be hung from the doorknob to cue the child to let his mother know if he is leaving the house.

7. Standards of performance should be established and be understood by the child, so that he knows exactly what behavior is acceptable and what is not. Telling a ten-year-old you are very pleased he is now using and flushing the toilet is important, but he also needs to be told that he should work on keeping the door closed while he is in the bathroom, and not unrolling lots of toilet paper and leaving it on the floor.

Caregivers need opportunities to ventilate their frustrations and safely talk about the times when they have "blown it," resorting to punishment, ridicule, or worse. That should take place not only with understanding friends, but also with the therapist. And, as with the caregivers' response to the children in their charge, the clinician does not blame; he acknowledges the behavior as unacceptable, teaches them specifically how to remedy a situation, rewards any tendency to improve, gives tons of encouragement and support, celebrates successes, and fights the urge to "do it himself" because it is easier.

The Eroticized Child

The clinician must continually remember that eroticized children may become sexually exploited by others, and that they experience profound rejection because of emotional or physical distancing from their caregivers.

These children are often and repeatedly abandoned by their caregivers, and moved from family care into successive foster homes, then into one or more group-home placements, and finally into institutional care facilities. Caregivers are panicked by erotic behavior in children, but rarely identify that as the real reason for having the child removed. This response compounds the child's difficulties, because the power of the erotic behavior is strongly reinforced when adults show that they are unable to deal with it. Each failed placement reinforces the child's feeling that she is to blame, and that she is unlovable and deserving of rejection. She does not get the treatment she needs, and is abused by the system charged with protecting her.

Furthermore, her behavior, combined with her neediness and placement history, may very well lead to her being sexually abused while in professional care.

The clinician must work with all adults who care for these children. In clinical consultation they can be advised that erotic behavior, as with any other objectionable behavior, should be addressed simply, directly, and without emotional charge. When confronted with this behavior the caregiver should surmise the child's intent as much as possible, and suggest alternate ways of expression. It may be appropriate for these interventions to be very gentle and soothing, or to be rather brusque. In any case, the adult should be firm, should state that the behavior is not acceptable, and should demonstrate or describe proper behavior, and express caring.

> A seven-year-old girl sitting on the childcare worker's lap grinds her buttocks against his groin. He suddenly spreads his legs and she falls to the floor. He picks her up, turns her to face him, makes eye contact, and says sternly, "That's not how we sit on laps in this house." He immediately puts her back on his lap, saying, "The way to do it is to keep your bottom still and watch TV." This should be followed shortly by, "I like holding you and feeling close. You are a very nice little girl."

> Ten-year-old Tom rubs his penis on his foster mother's leg. "Tom, I can see that you are a boy. If you want to rub your penis, do it privately in the bathroom. If you want to be close to me, then zip up your pants, bring a chair over here, and help me peel these potatoes."

> Eleven-year-old Linda, known to have been sexually abused by her father in the past, aggressively and sexually pursued her mother's lover. The mother and lover sought out the therapist, who told them, "Many adults who live with an eroticized child become overwhelmed with the child's behavior and withdraw from the child. They don't take direct action because they feel sorry for these girls and boys, knowing what they have been through. They feel the kids

can't help it, or that it would be harmful to deal with the behavior directly.

"Another worry adults have is that they will be accused by the little sexpot. Linda may be doing this to test whether or not you are going to abuse her. She may be testing out her new-found power. She may be jealous of Mom. She may want to please you. She may be trying to act grown-up. Or it may be some weird reason we haven't even thought of yet.

"It doesn't really matter. The behavior is unacceptable and has to stop. If we don't deal with it kindly, firmly, and directly, we are reinforcing it, which is not good. Think of it as something like nose-picking and it may be easier to deal with.

"Don't back off emotionally or physically. Maintain the affectionate and friendly interactions you normally have with her, or she will get the message that she is now either too hot to handle or she is damaged goods. Tell her that she isn't to jump on you, but that she can ask for a hug. If her hugs or kisses aren't appropriate, say so, and show her the right way to do it. And when Linda does give proper hugs and kisses, smile at her and tell her she's doing great. But don't wait for the perfect time alone to deal with the issue. A serious discussion usually doesn't work, in fact, it might even reinforce the behavior. Deal with the behavior only if and when it happens—in front of Mom or the little kids, in front of her friends, or at McDonalds'. If the issue were nose-picking, can you see how much unwanted importance and emotional charge you would be giving to the behavior if you had important, private, serious discussions about it?

"If you feel that some discussion is warranted, make it light, and pick a time when everyone is feeling good, not when the behavior has just happened. I tell kids that sex is supposed to feel good—that's why people are made the way they are. Its OK for children to have those feelings, but what they do about them needs to be limited. People have many feelings that they don't do anything about because it would not be OK. People think of killing their boss sometimes, and they think about just driving the car far away and never coming back to the squabbles at home. You could tell Linda, 'You might want to kidnap Michael J. Fox and have him all to yourself, but we just don't do those things, even though we might have the ideas and the strong urges.' I tell kids that it's kind of like driving a car: you can really want to drive one, and even know how to do it, but it's not OK until you are much older."

Young siblings often develop intense emotional and sexual bonds with each other. The relationship is like a marriage, with specific roles and dependencies. It can mean survival to the children by being a source of nurturance in an uncaring world. These disturbed attachments seem to develop between siblings who have suffered extreme abuse from their caregivers. No other adults are available to them, or those who are available are perceived as untrustworthy.

The sexualizing of their relationship occurs when the children have learned that sexual acting-out is the way to be affectionate. This learning may have occurred through the children's having been sexually exploited by adults, or from living in an environment in which they were exposed to explicit adult sexual behaviors.

Being removed from their families, despite a terrible home situation, can traumatize the children further and, in fact, be the triggering factor that sexualizes their already disturbed attachment to each other. There is no easy answer to the dilemma, and since it is such a charged emotional issue, the clinician must be particularly concerned that recommendations for the children are in *their* best interests and are not directed primarily toward relieving the adults who are charged with their care.

The risks to the children, and the amount of supervision available to insure their protection, must be realistically assessed when considering foster placement and/or separation of the siblings.

If a decision has been made to place these children in separate settings, enormous efforts must be made to insure that their loss is reduced. They should be allowed to spend significant amounts of time together and maintain contact by telephone. For example, they could spend a day at one sibling's foster home one weekend, and switch to the other home the following weekend. They should see the same therapist and engage in joint sessions for a while. They may be able to attend the same school or be involved in after-school activities together.

Treatment interventions are as set forth earlier. While respecting the survival value of the behavior, the clinician has to give a clear message that the behavior is unacceptable, and follow that by teaching acceptable behaviors.

> I know you feel safe with each other and that it makes you feel good to touch and suck each other's private parts, and that in your family people were sexual a lot. But that is against the rules in this family (group home, cottage). We want you to feel safe and good, and we want you to be close to each other. You two have had to take care of yourselves and each other for a while and that was very special. But now things are different. We are going to take care of you. We

are going to protect you, give you food, clothing, and exercise, and do fun things. Everything you will need is here for you. We will make sure you do your homework and your chores, and that you take good care of your bodies. Your job is to play, learn, help with chores around the house, make friends, and enjoy being sisters (brother and sister, brothers). It's fine if you want to hug, sit close when we're watching TV, give a big kiss on the cheek, or walk with your arms around each other sometimes. That's how sisters and brothers behave. But the sexual touching, sleeping together, taking baths together, and having secrets have to stop.

Now that things are different, you need to find other ways to feel comforted. It's kind of like when we were babies, we liked to have our bottle because that made us feel good. But we learned to feel good other ways. Lots of kids have a special little blanket or doll that they *must* have to feel good and safe. As we grow up we learn to stop doing some things and we learn to do new things. It would be kind of strange if I didn't learn that, and still had to carry around an old bottle or a piece of blanket or a doll. You two will always be brother and sister—nothing can change that—but you do have to give up the sexual touching with each other and find other ways to feel safe and good. It may be difficult for a while, but we're going to help you.

A youngster's vulnerability to sexual exploitation is best dealt with by teaching, over and over, that sexual interactions between a child and an older person are wrong and can be dangerous, and that the child will be carefully supervised for her own protection until she becomes mature enough to learn to protect herself.

In summary, the behavior of eroticized children is dealt with by taking the "charge" out of the behavior: by eliminating the seriousness, power, shame, fun, disgust, and blame. The children are matter-of-factly told that erotic behaviors are not OK, they are shown acceptable ways to interact, and they are told when they are doing a good job. Sexual feelings and urges are recognized, but placed in the context of feelings that people have, but upon which they do not act.

Therapists and caregivers must remember that children's normal sexual behaviors are also going to be present, and these should not be labeled pathological. It is helpful to remember that most of us did sexual things as kids that could be considered pretty weird when viewed from an adult perspective.

When an adult is caught off-guard by a child's eroticized behavior and is unable to think of anything else, a simple "Knock it off" is very much in order.

There are, however, at least two related situations that present significant clinical dilemmas and for which no, or only limited, solutions appear to be at hand.

1. The child whose rewards for erotic behavior cannot be matched elsewhere, for example, the ten-year-old boy prostitute who has received food, clothing, toys, attention, affection, "love," bodily pleasure, and power over an adult for his actions. The normal system cannot compete. This child is, and has been, deprived, and, as with other seriously deprived children, he measures caring, success, and survival in terms of material goods.

2. A child whose obsessive sexual behaviors are very pleasurable erotically and relieve tension, such as a 3-year-old who compulsively inserts anything and everything into his anus, or a child who compulsively victimizes others.

We can only hope that as our work with these children progresses we will become more skillful in intervening in these areas.

The Agitated Child

Agitated children are commonly described by adults as hyperactive, unable to sit still, disruptive, and as kids who do not pay attention or listen. Children describe them as bossy, pests, and no fun to play with because they just mess things up. The very presence of agitated children often fills a room with tension. Adults frequently respond to them with irritability and annoyance, or attempt to ignore them. These negative responses can trigger increased agitated behavior from the child, because of the additional tension. Although the children have strong needs for soothing nurturance, their wall of agitation blocks what little is available to them, and they frantically persist in demands for attention.

The clinician should consider that some or all of this behavior may have an organic base, such as an allergic response to foods, pollutants, or chemicals in the environment. However, the presence of a physiological reason for the child's behavior does not preclude the possibility of emotional problems, so that both physical and psychological evaluations may be in order. Even if the problem is identified as primarily physical, there may be a need for social rehabilitation to correct unacceptable learned behaviors that have become part of the child's repertoire and that require direct intervention.

Most agitated behaviors are seen in boys, and most boys believe that only babies, girls, and nerds engage in quiet, calm, soothing, and nurturing behavior. These "sissy" behaviors tend to make young males feel powerless, and powerlessness represents danger to them. They become locked into a deprivation cycle during which they need and long for nurturance and then feel vulnerable; the vulnerability leads to anxiousness and agitation, which in turn deflects available nurturing.

It is important that this cycle be interrupted. The child's attitude must be changed in a manner that allows him to equate calmness and nurturance with power. The therapist can hold up popular heroes as examples: Mr. Spock of the spaceship *Enterprise,* who frequently meditates, Luke Skywalker, who has learned to calm himself in order to use "The Force," and Yoda, the small, calm being with superior powers.

The therapist must convince the child that it is in the child's best interest to learn a different way of being in the world. Once done, the door is open for treatment.

Treatment is most effective when the therapist matches the child's high energy level during sessions, and channels it so that the energy can be brought under control. The therapist who has strong urges to quiet the child by strangulation during the first ten minutes would exercise good judgment by referring the case to someone else.

Clinicians should be certain that they respond to these children differently from the way others have responded to them. The experiences of agitated children have probably shown them that adults respond with a fairly predictable sequence of escalating negative behaviors, namely irritation, annoyance, hostility, yelling, physical restraint, loss of control, and, finally, abuse/rejection.

Self-Calming Techniques

The following exercises may be useful if the child is motivated to learn the "power" of self-calming and has developed a working relationship with the therapist. The child should be told that these exercises are tools he can use to give himself more options in dealing with his behavior.

Modified yoga. Children find animal postures, such as lion, cat, snake, bird, and fish appealing, and positive traits of the animals can be used to reinforce traits in the children. They can be told they are as wise as owls, as strong as lions, and so on. Begin at a controlled high-energy level and move toward calmness. The child and therapist stand in front of a full-length mirror; the child is directed to join the therapist in seeing themselves as lions, feeling the lion energy move up from the earth, pass into their feet, and spread through their bodies. They let the feeling build and build inside them, and then let out powerful roars. As the volume of the roars falls off, they move into a yoga posture and silently consider and create in themselves the quiet, languid strength of the lion. The child can feel the long, smooth muscles that are relaxed. He can think about how a lion balances his life with relaxation and play, while maintaining his power.

The lesson can be reinforced by having the child teach others, by taking a trip to the zoo, and by having the child research lions through books and videotape rentals. He and the therapist can modify the roar and posture exercise, so that the technique can be used in other settings when the boy needs to calm himself. (Modification can include a silent roar and a vertical stretch, or simply closing the eyes while slowly inhaling, and feeling the long muscles slowly stretch and relax.)

Deep breathing. Deep breathing is the easiest self-calming method to teach children. Give the technique prestige by telling the youngsters that many of those they admire—Olympic athletes, Michael Jackson, the Top Gun jet pilots—use this same technique when they need to calm themselves. Have the child breathe in deeply so that her abdomen blows up like a balloon, and then tell her to let the air flow out slowly, allowing her body to become more and more relaxed.

Visualization. The therapists works with the child to decide on an imaginary, peaceful place. Using relaxation and trance-induction techniques, the clinician has the child experience the inner peace connected to the image. The child can be taught a brief self-hypnosis technique that will enable her to recapture the experience when needed.

Sensorimotor play

Sensorimotor play can be used to penetrate a child's wall of agitation through joining, playfulness, intrusion, and providing physical nurturance. The therapist interacts physically with the child, at the child's level of energy, in a nonthreatening manner. Once joined, the therapist lessens the energy level in stages, until he is able to interact with the child in a way that is physically soothing. This technique is very similar to Jernberg's "Theraplay" (1979).

The process of matching the child's energy level and then gearing down to another level is similar to the process of mirroring noted in infant learning, wherein the parent joins the infant by matching his emotional state, facial expression, and body position. Once "connected," the parent makes a change which the infant follows. The parent shows pleasure, and continues joining and changing; it is a dance. Feelings of pleasure, connectedness, and nurturance facilitate the learning, and the infant feels acknowledged and appreciated.

> Eight-year-old Alex is jumping up and down, flapping his arms. The therapist matches his jumps and grabs his hand in the process saying, in rhythm with their movement, that after six more jumps they will arm-wrestle on the floor (slower pace). Near the end of the arm-wrestling, the therapist remarks on how the boy's wonderful shiny brown hair has gotten all messed up and, since the wrestling was her

idea, she'll just have to be the one to comb it (even slower pace). She then moves him to a chair where they sit directly across from each other to maintain eye contact, and she begins to slowly comb his hair.

The therapist makes soothing, trance-inducing comments during the combing. It's so *relaxing* to comb hair. I think your hair is a very special color. Look into my eyes. Oh yes, your eyes are just the right color for that terrific brown hair. It must be very *restful* for each hair to find its special place among all the others. They're just *resting* there, *calmly* and *peacefully* just being there, knowing that they'll be taken care of and admired. It's so special to be appreciated that maybe a thousand hairs are now feeling that they can just be *easy* and *calm,* knowing that they will be *soothed* and taken care of *gently* and *peacefully* by Alex, the Boy Wonder and champion arm-wrestler."

Another nonobvious way to provide basic soothing nurturance is to arrange for play that is messy—such as making painted footprints or hand-prints, or using gooey clay—and then helping the child clean up by slowly washing his hands and feet and carefully drying them, as you remark on the wonders of his toes and how well his ankles turn, and make other such comments. Then gently apply powder or lotion.

Snacks, especially foods such as oranges that the therapist slowly peels, sections, and feeds to the child, can provide powerful nurturing experiences.

Teaching a child how to soothe and calm himself not only enables others to like him better, but allows him to receive the nurturance and positive regard he needs for development.

The Socially Inhibited Child

A socially inhibited child may exist only in the mind of the parent or caregiver. The practitioner is cautioned to make this determination on his own, and not accept at face value the diagnosis of someone who could simply be describing the child in comparison to his own temperament or to that of the child's sibling. The initial assessment should include a history of the child's social abilities and interactions before, during, and after the traumatizing event. Background information will come from the parents, childcare providers, and teachers, and from the child himself.

Clinical impressions should also be based on observations of the child's play, and the child's response to direct questions.

One of the things we do here is help kids who feel uncomfortable making friends, or who can't seem to keep friends. We also work on helping children feel good about playing with others. Do you have any troubles or feel uncomfortable about playing with other kids since [the trauma] happened? How about friends? Do you have a best friend? Do you think it might be helpful for us to figure out why you are having a hard time being with other kids (or grown-ups)? Together we can figure out ways to make things more comfortable for you.

Socially inhibited children often have social skills, but fear ridicule and rejection by other children. They believe that they should no longer play and have friends, because of the seriousness of the traumatizing event. For some, their inhibition stems from having been separated from the world of friends and play. They feel extremely awkward about reentry and need guidance and support. Although a playing group may make an attempt to engage a socially inhibited child in play, withdrawn children, for the most part, tend to be ignored by other youngsters.

Once it has been established that there is a problem, and some progress has been made in gaining the child's cooperation, the reasons for inhibition need to be examined openly by the therapist and child. The openness of the process itself helps to lessen the inhibited behavior, whether or not insights are gained. The information obtained often reveals erroneous assumptions made by the child, which can be corrected and can reveal areas where skills training is needed.

Sensory- and physically disabled children usually experience social inhibitions related to their being the subjects of curiosity, having people not recognize their needs for assistance, or having people provide unneeded and unwanted help. It is important for these children to be taught assertiveness skills so that they can gracefully ask for help when needed and, equally important, let people know when it is not needed. These children will feel more secure when the clinician suggests exact sentences that they can say when others stare at them or ask embarrassing questions. The lessons can be backed up with modeling, role-play, rehearsal, and video practice.

Professional videotapes teaching withdrawn or shy children how to interact socially with others are available for use in clinical sessions—or a clinician can have a young therapy "graduate" make a short videotaped interview for the purpose of encouraging other inhibited children. The graduate can talk about how difficult socializing was for her initially, about some of the feelings she had at the time, and about how, with effort, things got better.

Group musical games are wonderful for getting children past social inhibitions. The rules of the game impose the structure, the sound sets the mood, the movement provides the energy, and the children experience the joy of shared play without much of the anxiety related to competitive games, and without having to verbalize with others.

Work with socially inhibited children as described in this section addresses the child's perceptions and feelings, without dwelling on them.

Socially inhibited children need to experience adequate social functioning with other children, and learn that children *do* want to play with them, that they can make friends, and that they must do some work to accomplish this. They should be told that they will have to learn to tolerate feeling awkward for a while, and that they must be able to accept the mistakes they will make. After the corrective experience is in place, the child and therapist can together recall the painful feelings related to the youngster's inhibitions, and in that way reinforce the value of working through difficulties. (This also provides an opportunity for self-appreciation for a job well done.)

Summary

Children's behaviors that are experienced by others as obnoxious, upsetting, or frightening, or that keeps people from making meaningful contact with them, need to be directly treated with social-rehabilitation techniques. Such behaviors are commonly found in traumatized children because they have been taught to behave in such ways by their caregivers, or because they developed dysfunctional styles of interacting that enabled them to cope with their traumatizing experiences.

Children can be resistant to giving up behaviors that represent past survival, their self-image, or their remaining emotional link with parents with whom they no longer have ongoing contact. Helping children change patterned social behavior is difficult and time-consuming work that requires dedication and skill on the part of both clinician and caregiver.

Unacceptable behaviors can be categorized by the way they are manifested—the socially inept child, the eroticized child, the agitated child and the inhibited child. Clinically addressing the conflicts and needs that have led to inappropriate social behaviors is generally insufficient. These children not only need to give up behaviors that alienate them from others and reinforce their negative self-images, but also need to be taught appropriate behaviors, need to learn that it is acceptable for them to behave differently, and need to be supported in their efforts to change.

14
Integration of Traumatizing Events

I ntegration of traumatizing events occurs when the experience is acknowledged as part of a person's life rather than being disowned, split off, or minimized.

There are four major steps that will facilitate youngsters' being able to integrate traumatizing experiences.

1. Clarify for children why it is necessary to slowly and carefully examine what happened to them.
2. Help the children re-create the traumatic elements in play and fantasy, where they can be victorious survivors rather than victims.
3. Enable the youngsters to acknowledge their own ideas, feelings, and behaviors related to the event.
4. Assist children in accepting the realities of their experiences without minimizing or exaggerating the significance of what happened, thus helping them to experience mastery.

Traumatized children do not integrate their experiences, because of the defense mechanisms they have had to invoke in order to deal with what transpired; but as long as these mechanisms remain in place, integration is impossible. These survival and coping mechanisms allow the children to avoid the unbearable, and keep from being immobilized. For example, growth and development require that young children believe that their primary caregiver will care for them and protect them. Children will often create that illusion for themselves when it does not exist in fact. When a traumatizing event occurs which threatens (in fact or in imagination) this sense of security, they use protective defenses to avoid acknowledging what happened, even to themselves.

Children need to protect themselves from the reality of the trauma, but this need does not remain fixed. Those who have been strengthened by nurturing environments, because of maturation, through professional help, or by change in circumstances, may increase their ability to deal with the trauma they experienced. Contrarily, a child may need to increase his denial of trauma with time if he senses a threat to himself or to his family, if new stresses make it impossible to deal with the harsh realities of the past, if the traumatic event has new implications with which the child is unable to cope, or if the child simply needs to deny reality in order to get on with his development.

For example, a child may deny having a life-threatening illness, then min-imize, and then acknowledge the painful reality of the event. The child may later again deny or suppress his awareness of his illness due to his need to pro-tect his parents, or because he cannot deal with the physical pain related to treatment and wishes to avoid the process.

At some point the cost of maintaining defenses begins to outweigh the benefits. A child who must continue to use defense mechanisms to survive his experience does so at great expense: it takes a significant amount of energy to deny reality, to block emotions, or to distort truth. Survival behaviors such as dissociative splitting, somatization, and avoidance of relationships impede and distort a child's development. Defending against childhood trauma can negatively affect a person's life through adulthood, because he needs to engage in continued attempts at mastery and/or attempts to support distorted ver-sions of reality. A man who was physically abused as a child may respond to authority and aggression as if he were still a child. Conversely, in attempting to "prove" to himself that his parent's abusive behavior was normal, he inter-acts in the same abusive way with his own children.

The clinician's role is to provide the necessary emotional security that enables the child to achieve as much awareness and understanding of reality as possible, within his developmental stage and functioning.

Clarifying Why Returning to the Pain Is Necessary

It is important that children and their caregivers understand why they need to go over the details of the traumatic events "in slow motion," and why they must work in therapy to tease out any forgotten parts. Confusion and resis-tance are created when a child is expected to proceed through a difficult pro-cess whose purpose has not been made clear to him. The youngster may feel he must have told his story incorrectly, since he is being asked to repeat it. He may think he was not believed, or that the therapist is satisfying his own morbid curiosity.

Working toward integration starts at the beginning of therapy and con-tinues throughout the treatment process. A child must be told early in treat-ment that the purpose of therapy is to help young people who have problems.

Many children experience unbearable tension waiting weeks, sometimes months, for the therapist to bring up the issue. The avoidance of direct discussion can be interpreted by the child as the therapist's inability to deal with the problem, thus strengthening the child's view that the traumatic event was too much and too hard to handle. The child's symptoms may escalate because of increased anxiety, and it is possible he will engage in reenactment behaviors, to force the issue and break the tension.

Many clinicians delay direct discussion of the traumatic events because they have incorrectly assumed any of several propositions, including

- the belief that the child will be more comfortable if they wait until a relationship has been formed to discuss the issue (this is sometimes done to meet the therapist's needs, not those of the child);
- the belief that most children can and will initiate discussion about such events when they are ready;
- the belief that approaching the issue disguised as play themes, or using other nondirective techniques, enables the child to integrate the experience; and
- the belief that more will be achieved if the therapist pretends she has no prior information and waits until the child brings up the event. (It may be a long wait.)

Discussing the traumatic issue as soon as possible in the treatment process relieves tension, provides assurances to the child, establishes the reason that the child is in therapy, affirms that they will directly discuss the issues and the child's feelings about them, and begins to set the foundation for their work. This is not to say that the child should immediately be pressured to begin work related to the trauma; if, however, a child is spilling over with a need to talk about his feelings, the clinician should, of course, be attentive and supportive.

Initial discussion of the traumatizing event is effectively accomplished when the discussion takes place while the child and therapist engage in quiet, parallel activity (such as side-by-side drawing or playing with clay). Interactive play, when the therapist and child are working on the same project together, is too demanding of attention and interferes with the process.

Parallel activity allows the therapist to make statements at a very slow, casual pace, so the child has time to absorb the information. The pauses are not experienced by the child as demands for response, or as tension producing, because the primary activity is the play. Such activity also allows the child to distract himself if necessary, that is, he can interrupt by calling attention to the clay or paint if he feels too uncomfortable.

The following example shows how a clinician can normalize the situation during a beginning treatment session. She tells the child that others come to her office to talk about various problems, including the issue(s) related to the child. The therapist lists various feeling responses common to children with similar experiences. She outlines how they will work together, specifically empowering the child in relation to the timing and pacing of treatment. At no time does she pressure the child to do anything other than listen, although it is likely that the child will make comments.

It is helpful to have a parent present in the playroom during this explanatory session, as this presence makes it clear to the child that there is parental approval for the process.

> Lisa, I know that your mom was very sick for a while, and then she died. I want to talk to you about how children come to see me because of lots of different problems in their families. Some kids have sad or afraid or confusing feelings about things that happen, and they find it helpful to have a safe place to talk about them.
>
> Children have all different kinds of troubles. In some families there is terrible fighting all the time, or for some, an accident happened. Maybe someone has been very sick or has died, like your mom. Some kids worry a lot because their parents drink too much, or have a problem with drugs. Sometimes a kid has been hurt by his parent. Kids come here too because of a problem behavior that we want to figure out, like maybe fighting all the time, or always being scared.
>
> When you and I feel like we know each other better, we can talk about what happened to your mom and what that means to you. Together we can figure out all the feelings you have about that. I know from talking to other kids who have had a parent die that their hearts and minds work to help them accept what happened. Their thoughts about the parent they miss so much are sometimes real strong. Sometimes the child sort of forgets it happened for a little while and then feels shocked when she remembers again what happened. Lots of kids feel that it was somehow their fault, although of course usually it's not, but they feel that way for a while. Some kids get really mad. Some boys and girls have strong feelings of God, or a guardian angel, or a higher power, which fills them with beautiful feelings that they just can't find words to describe.
>
> We'll do this work when you're ready. It will be kind of like driving a car together, or flying a plane as pilot and copilot. I'll choose the trip we'll be taking, with your help. Sometimes you can steer, but mostly you'll be in charge of the gas pedal and the brake. It's up to you to decide how fast or how slow we go, to do this work together. I may nudge you a little bit, but you always have the power to put on the brakes. You can say, "This feels too scary or sad to talk about

right now. Let's take time out or take a break for a while." And we will do that.

The same message is given to a very young child, but with fewer words and without the distraction of play. The following example accomplishes the same objectives but is simpler and more concrete so it can be understood by a child under age five, or by an older child who is so emotionally distraught that a simpler approach is needed. Here the clinician gives the child notice of the upcoming discussion, which allows the child to prepare for the transition from play to serious talk. The therapist makes certain she has the child's full attention before proceeding.

> Michael, in just a little while we will put away our wonderful drawings and go sit on those pillows and talk, because I have something very important to tell you.
>
> This is called the quiet corner, and it's the place for quiet talking and storytelling. I need to tell you something important for just a few minutes, and then I will read you a fun story. Right now I need you to listen very carefully. Are you ready?
>
> You and I are going to see each other lots of times. When you come here to see me we will play and we will work. The *play* will be driving these trucks, making worlds in the sandbox, telling stories, and other things. The work will be for us to talk about your mom's dying, and how that is for you.
>
> Kids have really big feelings about a parent being gone. Sometimes their feelings are so big that they feel upset. It's my job to help kids, and it will be your job to talk about your feelings and your ideas. Sometimes Dad is going to be with us, and sometimes just you and I will do the play and the work. How does that sound to you? Do you want to say anything about your mom and your feelings today—or should we just start our story?

The next dialogue typically takes place later in treatment, and is used to explain more specifically why an important part of the work is to reexamine events. The example could be used for most age groups, with the language made simpler for the younger child and more advanced for the teenager.

> Sometimes children wonder why they have to talk to someone about their troubles, even with a safe and fun person like me. I use a car accident to explain why (Use another example if the traumatizing event was a car accident.) If you were in a serious car accident, you probably would have a lot of feelings about it. You might feel mad, scared, excited, and lots more. You might even try to hide your feelings, or pretend that the accident didn't happen.

For a while you would have these feelings whenever you had to ride in a car. You might have them too if you just looked at a car. Maybe you would have the feelings if someone just said the word "car" or any word that reminded you of what happened. You could have feelings that made it seem as though the car accident just happened.

Having strong feelings about the accident that keep going on and on can keep a child so busy and worried that she can't do other things. But children need to use their energy to play, grow, and learn.

One of the things that can make it possible for the feelings to get less and less is sharing them with someone who can understand you and help you feel safe. You and this person can figure out what your thoughts, feelings, and worries were when it happened, and later on, too.

You would always remember that you were in a car accident, but you wouldn't have the feeling that it just happened. You would remember that you used to feel scared or excited or mad or whatever it was for you, but the feelings wouldn't be really strong, as if it just happened.

It is sort of the same thing for you and I to carefully talk about your mom dying. You will always remember what happened, but the feelings that you may have pushed away or locked up inside you, because they seem too much or unfair or not OK, will be possible to accept if we talk about them. They won't feel so big that you can't handle them. Some feelings and some ideas are just too big for kids to deal with by themselves—and you need to know that this is true for adults, too. Adults see therapists for the same reasons.

Does what I've said make sense to you? Do you want to ask me any questions about what I've been talking to you about? If I ever say anything that sounds confusing or kind of weird, it will help me if you let me know, and I will appreciate it if you tell me.

This has been an important, albeit subtle, interaction between therapist and child. Parents and caregivers, whether present during part of the sessions or not, may later quiz the child, in an attempt to help. The parent may believe that the therapist's approach to the traumatic material was insufficient or not understood by the child, and may attempt to redo the discussion. Such "help" can have negative consequences. It may scare or overwhelm the child, take the fun out of what transpired, or create conflict for the youngster.

Parents and caregivers who love and care for traumatized children find it intolerable when they do not know about or understand the treatment process. Parents must not only be respected and supported, but must be given information and specific guidance relating to the child's treatment. For instance, they should be told that the child is not to be quizzed overtly or covertly about their sessions, and that the caregiver is going to have to struggle, as do other parents, with learning to trust the process of healing. This clear direction is more apt to be successful if the parents are told why they should not question, and what actions they *can* take to facilitate the healing process. They need to be identified as part of the child's treatment team. The clinician may give the parents specific homework assignments, or suggest interventions to use with the child that directly deal with behaviors that the parents find most troublesome, such as bed-wetting or whining.

Restructuring the Traumatizing Event as a Victorious Survivor

Children usually cope with life's everyday difficulties through play and fantasy. Fears of losing a tooth, defending oneself against a mean sibling, avoiding playground bullies, and being treated unfairly by parents, among other things, are often played out with the child in the role of a hero who has supernatural strength and magical powers. In this mode the child can give himself exactly what he needs in order to reduce anxieties and to resolve conflicts. In the safe disguise of play, he can balance power, reward himself with fabulous riches, vanquish those who do not do his bidding, and devour his enemies. This experience of power and invincibility, and the process of confronting conflicts, allows the child to work and rework the issue until such negative feelings as fear, helplessness, and revenge are sufficiently under control to allow the child to deal with reality.

Traumatized children are not only unable to use this natural healing process because they are overwhelmed by their experiences, but they also seem fearful of fantasy and play, behaving as though they distrust their own imaginations. Many actively work at avoiding play, and act as though the dangers they experience exist not only in the environment, but also inside of them in the form of strong feelings such as terror, longing, hatred, and revenge.

Some children are blocked from expressing neutralizing play-anger because they believe the aggressor in their real-life trauma is so all-powerful that he will know what they have wished or thought or acted out in play, and will seek out the child and annihilate him. A youngster may believe that her own wishes and past play caused the trauma, and she must therefore avoid further play in order to survive.

Finally, some children have been raised in environments where play was not allowed, and that specific mechanism of self-healing seems unknown to them. Nontraumatized children gain power through imagery, rehearsal, and fantasy, to assist them in dealing with problems; so, too, must traumatized children be helped to play and fantasize.

The traumatized child cannot assimilate the external reality alone, nor can he singly face his internal demons. He needs to believe that the person helping him is able to control the internal and external dangers he experiences. The therapist provides the nurturance, guidance, limits, and support that allow the child to begin to use his own healing powers.

The therapist must actually join the child in play until the youngster has had sufficient actual experience to realize that her feelings will not destroy her, that she will not be punished for them, and that a past aggressor will not harm her because of her wishes and fantasies. A child might enthusiastically engage in playing the victorious survivor, with the clinician passively watching, during a session, and then wake up at two o'clock in the morning, terrified of retribution for her behavior. When the clinician actively engages in the behavior *with* the child, she is given—and receives—the message that the behavior must be OK.

A child can be instructed to reenact a trauma, only this time, she is told, she is the powerful person, the one who is master of the event. The clinician joins in, but the child is given the lead. The therapist can give a boost where needed.

> Today you are going to direct a puppet show about a girl who went to the hospital when she was very sick. A wonderful thing happened when she got to the hospital: she found she was just like Shira, Princess of Power, and she was able to tell everyone in the hospital what to do. You be the girl. What puppet do you want me to be?

> Last time you were here you got to make up the soap-opera story, so now it's my turn to come up with a story. I want the story to be about a boy who was in a plane crash, like you were, but this time you are going to have magic powers and you can do anything you want. You be the boy. Who should I be?

> I want you to do that dollhouse play again, only this time the little girl is going to be very powerful. She is going to tell that baby-sitter to get out of the house, that he can't trick her anymore, and that she is going to tell her mom. You can do anything you want in the play, but you must say those words, and you must be very powerful and stong. I will be the baby sitter and you be the powerful little girl. Knock knock!

> That's a wonderful world you made in the sand tray. You have a big monster over there, with all the people trying to protect themselves from him. Let's make a movie. Let's pretend you are Steven Spielberg and you are going to make a great movie for kids. First, the monster comes to town and scares all the people, and they run away to protect

themselves. Then the boy, with the companionship of his brave dog Skipper, gets everybody in town to help him, and they find a way to capture the monster. The boy is brave and smart, and knows how to ask people to help him. The town has a big party for the boy. At the celebration, where they just happen to be serving your favorite pizza, the people of the town have a meeting to decide what they will do with the monster. Since you're the famous director, you tell me who I should be.

The Clay Bombs exercise is loved by even the most inhibited child—and does nice things for the therapist, too. The child, in safe partnership with the therapist, releases aggressive feelings in a focused way by acting directly against an important drawing. The drawing may be of an abusive person, a person responsible for an accident, or a figure representing a disease. Displays of unfocused aggression are not effective and can create feelings of confusion and guilt in the child. I have found it helpful to have the parents present for this exercise, asking them to take a turn when the child and I have finished. Having the parents as witnesses validates the child's feelings; his witnessing their participation creates a powerful supportive memory.

A large piece of drawing paper, a felt marker, and a container of soft modeling clay are needed. For those who must be clean, wet paper towels will substitute for clay: they "thwack" nicely, and will stick to the paper.

Jenny, today we are going to make clay bombs. Most kids really like to do this. It helps us release mad feelings in a safe way and helps us exercise the big muscles in our arms, just like baseball pitchers do. And we can cheer each other on and make "Yahoo" noises like they do at baseball games. I'm going to draw an outline of the man you are most mad at. Yeah, that's right, him. I'm just going to outline his body first. What kind of expression should I put on his face? OK. Now, we're going to take this bucket of mushy clay and make up a bunch of bombs—about ten of them. We can use them over again. A little smaller than a baseball is good. OK, here are the rules. You have to stand across the room, and as you throw one of these clay bombs at Roger, you must say something to him. Then it's my turn. I'll go first. OK, Roger, here it comes . . . *I'm mad at you for what you did to Jenny!* OK, your turn . . . *I hate your hands!* . . . Great throw, Jenny, you got him right in the nose . . . *I hope you go to jail!* . . . *Jenny is never going to be tricked again by you or anyone else and I hope you have really scary dreams just like she did!"*

The therapist needs to lead a little until the child is able to make her most angry and original statements, with the clinician just a step behind. The therapist must be certain that he is facilitating the child's expressing her own feelings, and not his.

If the object of the bombs is a person to whom the child has positive feelings as well as anger, or with whom she has a psychological bond or loyalty conflicts, the clinician must spend some sessions exploring the positive side of the relationship before working to release the anger.

Dealing Directly with Traumatizing Events

Children are ready to directly acknowledge their own feelings, ideas, and behaviors related to traumatizing events, once they have learned to identify and express various feelings through indirect clinical work, and once they understand that feelings are not actions. They now recognize that people can have simultaneously opposing feelings. Those children whose impulse-ridden behaviors used to keep them (and their environment) in turmoil have, by this point in the treatment, developed the beginnings of control. Inhibited children should have begun to express some of their feelings.

It is very important to recognize that a child who has learned to substitute expressions of emotion for inhibition has not yet completed the healing process, although his accomplishment is a positive achievement. The child who has gained some control over impulse-ridden behavior is likewise not yet finished with treatment, although he, too, has taken an important, positive step. These changes are insufficient. Children need to *comprehend* what happened to them. They need to explore their ideas and feelings about the event, and talk about their behavioral responses to what happened. Once they grasp the reasons for their thoughts, feelings, and behaviors, they will be better able to understand and accept, emotionally and physically, the realities of what happened to them, and their own participation.

Structure, rules, and order can assist the child in exploring what really happened. Although this approach may appear insensitive because of its apparent lack of warmth, structure means safety to children whose life experiences have been chaotic and unpredictable. Children who are asked to slowly go over the specific details of what has been overwhelming, do so much more easily and willingly when they know they will stop working on the problem after a specified time. Intense, realistic work should be followed by a period of nondirective play therapy.

The following structured techniques are effective in clinical work with children. They add an element of fun and provide a little distance, which make the work less difficult.

Garbage Bag

The Garbage Bag exercise is a continuing exercise, used over the course of many sessions. The overpowering incidents that the child has experienced are literally contained (in a bag in the therapist's office), and because the events have become concretized, the child gains a much needed sense of control. The incidents, once written down, are not only contained by the therapist, but also cannot be successfully repressed. This exercise helps the child to clearly understand why he is reviewing the traumatizing event, and he gains a sense of accomplishment as each piece is mastered. The Garbage Bag is most effective when secrecy and shame are involved in what has happened in the child's life. Except for the quick overview described in the next paragraph, the technique should be invoked after the clinician believes a therapeutic alliance has been established, and after there has been some discussion with the child about the traumatizing event.

When first orienting a child to the playroom, I point to a shelf on which there are six or seven brown paper grocery bags that have been wildly decorated, and I say,

> Those are garbage bags made by other children. I can't tell you more about them yet. After you and I know each other better and we have done some work together, I can tell you. Perhaps you will decide to do the same thing as the other kids. They think it's very helpful.

We are usually into the second or third month of treatment before I feel it is time to begin the Garbage Bag exercise. A week prior to that time, I give it a buildup by saying

> You are doing so great. I think you are ready for the Garbage Bag. Next week when you come, I'll tell you all about it.

The next week I say

> Casey, when you finish that clay sculpture, we're going to do something very special. Do you remember the new thing you're ready to learn about today? That's right. You are ready to learn about the Garbage Bag.

The therapist, facing the child and seated so they are at the same eye level, opens a plain, unmarked paper grocery bag.

> What do you call the bag where all the old papers and food and smelly things go that your family doesn't want any more? Do you call it "garbage" or "trash" or something else?
>   Garbage bags are where you put old, nasty, yucky things. This is our garbage bag and I'm going to put in some old mashed potatoes that have been in the back of the refrigerator for three weeks and are gray now. [The therapist makes a face and mimes putting this in the

bag, which he holds open on one side as the child holds the other side, thus keeping it between them.] What are you going to put in? OK, it's my turn again. I'm going to put in a kleenex full of boogers. Ooh, yuck!

By this time the child has caught on, and relishes the game of permissible grossness. After a few minutes of filling the bag with vile, barely imaginable things, the therapist says

OK, now I want you to hold this bag by yourself, and using that terrific imagination of yours, tell me how much you think this bag of ours weighs? Move it up and down a little and just think about it. How do you think it would smell?

Now, I want you to imagine keeping this bag of garbage with you all the time. I want you to think about how it would be for you to take this to school with you, and to scouts, and to the movies. What would that be like? Now, imagine you are getting older. What kinds of things are you going to do when you're in high school? OK, imagine taking your bag of garbage to a football game. And imagine always having to take it along with you when you went anywhere in your car. Let's think about when you get out of high school. What might happen then? On dates? In college? OK, let's imagine that you are going for a job interview at the biggest computer corporation in the world, but you have your bag of garbage with you. What would that be like?

I have to tell you something important. Grown-ups come here too and talk about serious things that happened to them when they were kids. They have taught me something important. They say that what happened to them, like being abused, was kept a secret until they were grown up. They were not like you, Casey. No one found out about it, and they didn't have a safe place to talk about what happened. They say that keeping those thoughts and feelings inside them has been like carrying a bag of garbage around with them all their lives: that even though sometimes it felt good or they were made to feel like someone special and given presents, it was still like carrying around a bag of garbage. It's kind of like food. It can be good at first, but later it can turn yucky and rotten.

This is easily modified to deal with traumas other than abuse. For example,

Grown-ups who have had their sister or brother killed in a car accident sometimes keep some of their ideas and feelings about it locked up inside them all their lives. Some of their feelings and ideas made them feel yucky, and they thought they might get into trouble if anyone found out. Like feeling glad it wasn't them that got killed, or enjoying having a room to themselves, or thinking that their parents wished it was they who had died instead of the other child. They said having these feelings locked up inside them was like carrying around a bag of garbage with them all their lives.

See those garbage bags up there? The kids that come here decided that they did not want to be like those grown-ups I told you about. They wanted to get rid of those ideas and feelings. So here's the way we do it. This can be your bag. Next time you come we can decorate it with wrestler pictures, or feathers, sparkles, paints, drawings, whatever. What we want to do today is write down very quickly each thing that has happened to you that has been yucky in your life. Actually, you say it, and I'll write it down. I'll help you. We need to break up what happened into its pieces, so that each thing will be on a separate piece of paper. We need to do it fast today because I don't want you to get into a lot of feelings about what happened. Just the facts. Like they say on TV, "This is a brief report of the news to come at 11."

Then what happens is that each week when you come here we'll spend ten minutes working on one piece of garbage. I'll tell you when it's Garbage Bag time, and you'll go get your bag from the shelf. You'll reach in and pick out one piece of paper and we'll do some work on what the paper says. If you aren't ready to work on that thing yet, you can throw the paper back into the bag and pick out another one. When all the feelings about the piece of garbage you take out have been explored, and you don't feel excited or scared or whatever, just bored, then we will destroy that piece of paper. Some kids finish getting rid of the feelings in one or two sessions, while others need to work on a yucky thing for more sessions than that. How would you like to try that?

OK, let's go. What's the first thing your uncle did to you that you didn't like? OK, touched your penis. What did he touch it with? I'm going to write "touched penis with his hand." Here, you put it into your Garbage Bag. What's the next thing you remember? "Had me touch his penis." With what? OK, "with my hand." What's next? How about mouth? Any of that stuff? "Had me put his penis in my mouth." Casey, does your mom know about that one? One of the things that's important is that sometime during our work together, you and I need to let your Mom know all the things that happened to you. So, we're going to make a star on this one and any other garbage that your mom doesn't know about yet. After you and I feel like we're ready, we'll have her be here for one of our times together, and we can let her know the hard things that you were not ready to tell her about before. How does that sound? OK, let's move on. Did he put his mouth on some part of your body that wasn't OK? Let's see, "put his mouth on my penis." Does your mom know about that one? OK, then this one gets a star too.

Lots of kids who have been abused do sexual things with other grownups or with other kids. Do you remember anything like that? How about sexual weird things by yourself, or with animals or toys? Well, that may sound gross to you, but it happens. People do a lot of strange things. The important thing is that kids don't have to go around carrying yucky secrets like a big sack of garbage. And I know how to help kids control their own behavior. If you remember things like that later, you can let me know and we'll add it to the garbage bag. I've had boys call and leave messages on my answering machine, asking me to call them because they remembered something like that on the way home, or the next day.

I'll ask you sometimes if you've remembered anything new to add. This Garbage Bag doesn't just have to be old things or just sexual things. You can add new things, like trouble with your sister, your mom's being unfair, a terrible nightmare, or your dog's peeing on your foot. This is *your* Garbage Bag, and you and I are little by little going to take things out, look at them, push them around a bit, jump on them, whatever. When something's not such a big deal and it's getting boring, we'll just throw it away. Casey, you'll always remember those things that happened to you, but you can get so you don't feel like it's a big smelly mess that you always have to carry around with you. You can just leave it behind, and move on in your life.

List of Bad, Mean, Rotten Things That Can Happen to Kids

The List of Bad, Mean, Rotten Things reminds children that bad things happen to other kids, that what happened to them is just one of several terrible things that could have happened, and that things could be worse. The exercise is valuable because stigmatization is reduced with the reminder that others have had similar experiences; the trauma is "normalized" by being placed in the context of a range of experiences with which children must cope; and a sense of hope, control, and fun are conveyed in the process of concretely manipulating the list.

So as not to get bogged down with spelling and the child's need to write slowly and perfectly, the therapist should do the writing, while the child can do the cutting. The list should be limited to about six items when used with nonreaders, so that they can remember what is written. Stick-figure drawings next to the words can be helpful for nonreaders.

Today's game is to make a list of all the bad, mean, and rotten things that can happen to kids. Let's spread this roll of paper out on the floor and see how many things we can think of to put on our list. I'll do the writing, and we'll both do the thinking. Now, what bad, mean, rotten things can you think of? . . . OK, "being in a wheel chair," that's pretty bad. My turn. How about "parents always fighting"? . . . OK, that's a good one, "mentally retarded." Mine is going to be, ah, "being eaten by a lion." [It's always a good idea to add some outrageous items for fun, and you must make certain to include items that are clearly worse than what has happened to the child.]

That's great, no one has used that one before, "stolen by aliens and brought to another planet." I think I'll put in what happened to you, that's kind of awful, "parents put in jail." Most kids would feel bad about that. OK, yours is "having an ugly face." Let's see, help me out. I want to do another one about parents. What would be really awful. Thank you. That's certainly bad, "parent dies." Your turn.

Now, since I did the writing, you can do the cutting if you like. Cut across the paper, so that each terrible thing becomes a separate strip. That's great.

The game is for you to put the strips in order, so that we have a list with the very worst bad, mean, rotten thing on the top, then the next worst, then the not-so-bad, and end up with the one on the bottom of our list being the least bad thing.

Now, Tom, let's see. You have put "mentally retarded" as the worst, then "parent dies." That's interesting. Let's see, you have what happened in your family, "parents in jail," down here. That means that for you, Tom, "parents in jail" is not as bad as "mentally retarded," or "parent dying," or "eaten by a lion." But for you, it is worse than "being a faggot," "stolen by aliens," "having a liver transplant," "smelling like Keith," and all those other things. Would you like to change the list in any way? It's all right to do that. OK, you think "being a faggot" is worse than "parents in jail." I wonder why that's worse. Well, that's a good point, the teasing, but don't kids tease you some about your parents? What else is worse in your mind about being a faggot? Well, that's interesting, I guess it does last longer. I guess your parents will be home some day, and being gay is usually something people choose to be forever.

So, one of the things you think about when deciding how much awfulness each one has, is how long does the thing last: a short time, a long time, or forever? You're quite a good thinker. Any other changes you want to make? OK, let's tape these strips down on a big sheet of paper, put your name on it, and hang it on the wall until next week. When we take it down, we'll put our strips in your file. We can take the strips out again later and see what your thinking is then.

This exercise has added value when there are two or three children doing it together. They learn that it is acceptable to have different points of view, feelings, and experiences, and they are all to be respected. Working with more than one child is best when all contribute to a master list of terrible things. As the therapist then works with each child individually to rank order his list, the others can be engaged in another activity that does not require close supervision. Each child's finished list can be quickly copied, so that the strips can be reused by the other children.

Repeating the exercise at later times in treatment shows the clinician the child's changing perspective regarding his experiences. (The information obtained from these lists could provide a base from which several research projects might start, such as a look at children's perceptions of specific traumatizing events by age or sex.)

Experiencing Mastery

Children cannot work toward goals that are unimaginable or that appear hopeless. They must be shown concretely what they are working toward, and what it will be like when they have met their goals. They can learn from others that the process can be fun as well as hard work. They can experience what successful mastery can be like through play rehearsal and by interacting with other children who have successfully completed a course of treatment. Most of all, they can learn that there is hope and that goals are attainable.

Child Graduate Assistants

Children who have successfully completed their initial course of treatment can provide effective and much-appreciated healing experiences for others who are still actively engaged in the treatment process. They are living proof that another child really has accepted what happened to him, has completed therapy, and has moved on in his or her life. These "graduates" are models of success, can give comfort and support as children who have "been there," and can interest the treatment child in eventually becoming a graduate assistant himself.

The child graduate should be selected for prestige, that is, it should be someone that the child in treatment can look up to, such as someone of the same sex who is a few years older. The child graduate should have mastered traumatic events that are similar to those being worked on by the child in treatment.

The specific number of sessions and their content should be established prior to the beginning of attendance by the graduate.

Session One. The therapist will introduce the graduate child, Mary, as a person who was hospitalized for a long time and had treatment similar to Nancy's. They will get acquainted through various nondirective play activities, followed by snack time.

Session Two. Mary is to bring her scrapbook and talk with Nancy and the therapist about her experiences, fears, and successes. Nancy is encouraged to ask questions. Directed play, followed by snack time.

Session Three. Mary is to direct activities with input from Nancy. Commemorative seven-minute videotape is to be made for Nancy. Therapist provides closure and snack.

Rules. The children, parents, and therapist agree that Mary and Nancy may speak to each other over the telephone, but only for a limited time, usually not in excess of ten minutes. Everyone is also cautioned to remember that what happens in sessions is private, and not to be discussed outside the two families. (These rules would probably be inappropriate for adolescents. The teenagers and their parents should establish an agreement of confidentiality between them.)

Graduate assistants should be used only for short periods of time, and with clearly established objectives. This tight structure enables both children to meet their goal(s) and to feel successful. Initial enthusiasm by the child graduate or her caregiver may be quickly lost, and if meetings unexpectedly diminish or end, the child in treatment will probably feel rejected and blame herself. A few children have asked, and received, permission to have the graduate assistant attend a special event in their lives, such as a bar mitzvah, court appearance, dance recital, or adoption celebration.

The Elderly Child Remembers

The Elderly Child Remembers is a dramatic exercise that playfully allows the child to imagine a future for herself in which she has integrated her traumatic experience into the fabric of her interesting life. It is best accomplished with a small group, or with a child graduate assistant joining the child in treatment in an individual session.

It is helpful to have on hand some amount of dramatic play props for both boys and girls, such as hats, masks, scarves, jewelry, dishes, building materials, makeup, etc.

> Today we are going to imagine ourselves in a future time. You are going to be wonderful old ladies (or old guys) who are hanging out together having a good time. You have been successful in taking care of yourselves, in following your careers, and in raising your families. This is a time in your lives when you are very creative. There are many things you enjoy doing. You work part of the time and find your work interesting. Although you are old now, you have kept your bodies active and healthy. You have good friends that you enjoy spending time with, and today you are visiting with some of these good friends. You are in a restaurant [on a mountain top, fishing, on an airplane . . .] and are talking about your lives. You are going to talk about a long, long time ago when you were about eight [use current age of children] years old and feeling bad [worried, scared . . .] about the abuse [the operation, ever going home again . . .]. You are going to talk about how you felt way back then, how you got stronger, and then how you went on in your life to be successful. Talk about how it is for you now that you are an older person who is thinking back so long ago. And how does it feel when, as an older person, you think back to the (trauma) and remember that it was an important part, but just one part, of your very interesting life. First, let's get some props and costumes together. Should I be the waitress [friend, ranger, boat-cleaner]? Are we ready? Let's begin. Action!

Integration techniques lead to the child's being able to acknowledge his history, rather than disowning it or distorting it due to fear or shame. After achieving whatever understanding and acceptance is possible, the child may need to take his experiences and put them on the shelf for a while. But this time, the child is in control of the behavior and is not responding from a position of helplessness. Rather, he is in a position of choice and control.

A traumatized child who has effectively completed a course of treatment will have accepted the facts of the event, worked through what the experience meant to her, and engaged in grief work as well as work to consolidate gains. But she is also a child, and needs to have the burdens of the past lessened in order for her to have the energy to grow. From time to time she may therefore need to pretend that Mom and Dad will remarry, or that she was never abused, or that her sibling did not die violently. The clinician needs to teach the child that she will always know what really happened, but there will be times when she just doesn't want to think about it. She, like other children, will wish it had never happened, and may, in fact, enjoy pretending it never did.

Being a child includes enjoying pretend, magic, wishes, and fantasy. We can't change what really happened, but we do have control over how we think about it, how often we think about it, how we pretend about it, and whether or not we just want to put it away for a while.

Caregivers should be told that the child may occasionally need to act as if the event had not happened. If the behavior appears extreme and there is some worry about the child's reality-testing, empathic, sensitive questioning will usually clarify the situation. For example,

> I notice that when you and Kathy play together you usually say _____, and I wonder if you just wish that's the way things were, or if you put away for a while what really happened? Or maybe you think that's really how things were?

The child will generally acknowledge it as a wish.

An inquiry which confronts the child with precisely what she is attempting to avoid, usually elicits poignant, sad feelings. The questioning person should soothe the youngster, and reassure her that he, too, wishes it had not happened, and that it is fine to pretend, play, and wish—that that's what kids are supposed to do. The person should vigorously avoid further probing when it isn't necessary. This can be exploitive of the child's vulnerability, and give a confusing message. Making just a few statements can be enough, and empowering, for a child. A warm cuddle and assurances that the child can cope and is terrific are always in order.

Summary

Integration begins with the child's being strengthened by understanding the treatment process and actively participating in its planning. The emotional distancing and safety of art, play, and metaphor enables the child to cope symbolically with conflicts, provides a closer clinical bond with the therapist, and allows the child to experience pseudo-mastery. The experience lessens fears, and prepares the child for direct exploration of traumatizing issues. The sensitively paced exploration of thoughts, feelings, and behaviors is interwoven with activities that enhance the child's self-concept and provide pleasure. The child integrates his experience, sometimes "forgets" or pretends it did not occur, but knows it is all right to put off thinking about what has happened. Integration is difficult, sometimes moves too quickly or too slowly or even grinds to a halt until kick-started again, but it is essential!

15
Open-Door Termination

T he developmentally sequenced model described in chapter 2 considers termination to be the end of the first and most important part of treatment, not closure of therapy. "Open-door termination" indicates the completion of a phase of therapy, usually the longest and most important phase. As with the family physician, a professional relationship with the therapist is maintained, but is not necessarily active, over time. The clinician may be called upon by the family for consultation, or may provide regular, useful checkups, or may give the child a needed clinical boost during some developmental phase. When referring to termination or completion of treatment, the reference is to completion of the work necessary to resolve the current issues, but does not necessarily mean that the child has completed therapy.

Termination is not dealt with as the end of an intense, meaningful relationship. Instead, it is considered evidence of the successful completion of work well done.

References to termination should be made at various times during therapy, including when the child is told the reason for treatment, when the child helps in the planning, during mini-reviews of progress, when reference is made to child graduates, and in planning graduation. The youngsters are taught from the beginning that their work, with the help of the therapist, is to understand and accept what happened to them and to work on possible related problems, and that when that is completed, a phase of treatment is over. The children learn that their relationship with the clinician changes, but does not necessarily end.

Periodic mini-reviews of the progress of the therapy are very helpful to the child, to the therapist, and to the caregiver. These enhance a sense of accomplishment, provide opportunities for the child to recognize and appreciate his hard work, keep all parties motivated to continue working, enable us to make adjustments in the treatment plan, and serve as reminders that our goal is to terminate. A review can be a simple discussion of where we were at the beginning of therapy and where we are now, or might include looking at case records, videotapes, drawings, and any other physical evidence of the child's attendance at therapy sessions. The therapist can assist the child and caregiver in creating a progress report in the form of a psychodrama performance or puppet show for the family.

Termination occurs *when treatment objectives are met,* not when everyone feels comfortable or bored, fear is reduced, all known issues have been thoroughly addressed, or risks are completely eliminated. Everyone is aware that new issues, understandings, and confusions related to the trauma will emerge for the child as he or she matures. The child and caregiver are taught that such new issues will be the result of the child's emotional and cognitive *growth* rather than clinical failure. The child and caregiver learn how to identify possible difficulties and trouble spots that may occur in the future. This preparatory work helps them recognize new issues as problems to be dealt with, rather than as something frightening to defend against.

I generally plan with the child to have a final review of our work together during one or more sessions before the graduation ceremony. This is a more in-depth version of the mini-review. I find that our special relationship needs the solidification of doing this privately in individual sessions. We may open a part of the session to include other family members, but the bulk of the final review is between the child and the therapist.

A graduation ceremony representing completion of a phase of therapy is very useful, and is usually a fun way to commemorate what has been accomplished as well as memorializing the clinical relationship. The ceremony must be mutually and carefully planned, and can be simple or elaborate, based on the style of the therapist and the needs of the child. As with most important transitions, graduation has its excitement, poignancy, and worrisome aspects. The graduation ceremonies of my young clients have varied enormously, including such things as gift exchanges (simple, inexpensive items) between the child and therapist, food, instant photos, taking child and parent (or child only) to lunch at a neighborhood restaurant of the child's choosing, and inviting friends and relatives for a food/celebration/presentation by the child. The graduation exercise validates the child's work and represents a moving on in his or her life.

16
Crisis Intervention in
Large-Scale Disasters

I t is virtually impossible to plan an emergency mental health response that would be adequate and proper for all disasters. Each event is a unique event. But we *have* learned from those who study the needs of disaster survivors that victims seem to benefit greatly by immediate professional intervention (see Figley [1985], Eth and Pynoos [1985], and to the works of Terr [1979], Horowitz [1980], and Klingman [1981]).

Mental health practioners are generally inexperienced in providing professional assistance to a group of traumatized youngsters at the scene of a disaster. Clinicians who do become involved in such events must be perceived by their charges as being calm and in control, although they may be struggling with their own internal responses to what they have seen: dead, mutilated, and injured children. They must also be prepared to deal with being set on by frightened and enraged family members who make demands to which they cannot be responsive, or being aggressively pursued by media representatives.

A disaster scene experience may provide many therapists (particularly those in private practice) with their first experience in working cooperatively with professionals from other disciplines, whose objectives and limitations may not be the same as the goals and limitations of the clinician. Psychotherapists are, for the most part, accustomed to working autonomously and by appointment; unlike medical personnel and emergency workers, they do not easily follow orders or expect to stay on the scene for the time needed to get the job done. But even in the midst of confusion and chaos, common sense should prevail. For instance, a therapist would not interfere with a paramedic who is attempting to start an IV on a frantic child, but she should certainly make her availability known and offer to help calm the child if the paramedic would like that assistance. Such assistance should be by invitation only; paramedics, police, fire fighters, and other similar professionals most likely have had more experience dealing with terrified, out-of-control children than has the therapist.

I spent many hours discussing survivor care with Patricia Dixon, M.D., Chief of Pediatrics at Stockton's San Joaquin County Hospital, following the

the January 1989 Stockton schoolyard shootings. I also interviewed Ron Kiersten, Director of the county's Children's Mental Health Program, and several other child therapists from the Stockton community who were directly or tangentially involved in the incident. What I learned provided me with some new insights into what is needed for a prompt, well-integrated mental health response to a large-scale disaster involving children.

Emergency mental health support may be given momentary or may be offered for hours, such as when parents, relatives, or caregivers have to be identified, located, and then given time to reach the site; a salesman father and a meter reader mother may be difficult people to locate quickly, or some surviving children's parents may themselves be unknown victims—this might occur during a flood or tornado.

The unique aspects of each event can relate to many areas—physical, emotional, environmental, cultural, religious, and so on—each of which can be reasonably expected to create varied needs to which a clinician must be sensitive. An on-the-scene mental health worker must not only be innovative but also offer assistance quickly and effectively.

Generally speaking, psychotherapists at the disaster scene should (1) determine areas of responsibility and authority, (2) quickly obtain available information about the disaster and emergency response plan, and (3) assess and provide for the immediate mental health needs of the survivors. Other important considerations are the utilization of available resources and planning for post-disaster followup. The realities of the situation will dictate how much of which gets done, and in what order; all will probably be going on at the same time to some degree.

Authority: Who's in Charge?

A community may have an established emergency plan to be invoked in response to a large-scale disaster. Such plan will usually designate authorities and responsibilities. If not, this will have to be determined on-site. The person with senior authority will probably not be a mental health professional; however, a mental health professional may have been designated as responsible for overseeing the care of children outside of their medical needs. In disaster situations, important decisions need to be made quickly, and if those in authority are unavailable to perform this function, others need to step in.

Clinicians must guard against becoming participants in an Abbott and Costello "Who's on first?" routine, where disputes over who will make decisions renders the proffered assistance ineffective. Therapists should also guard against becoming immobilized on the scene, being reluctant to take control because they are waiting for the designation of, or appearance by, the ultimate clinical decision maker.

A common model in emergency medical responses provides for the highest ranking person on the scene to be in charge; the authority is handed over when a more senior person appears. If the medical authority model is not used, and there is more than one mental health professional present, a moment should be spent in identifying the leader, so that coordination and effectiveness can be established and maintained. The group leader will coordinate with other group leaders so that needed information can be readily obtained and disseminated.

Obtain Current Information

Child victims of disaster (like adults) experience enormous stress from the uncertainty of what has happened, and what will happen to them and to their families. Providing clear explanation of what is *and what is not* known has a calming effect, and can improve the survivor's ability to cope with the situation. It is important to quickly obtain whatever facts are available, including:

Present safety: Is the danger over? Is it contained? What precautions are to be followed regarding continued physical safety?

Reunification with parents: Have the parents been notified? What is the plan for reunification with the children? How? When? Where?

Damage: What is the extent of damage? How many were injured? Killed? Who are they? What was destroyed?

Immediate plan to care for children: Have appropriate medical assessments been made? Has a mental health professional been designated as leader to provide and/or to coordinate emergency services? Have decisions been made as to where children will be sheltered?

Assessment and Interventions

The needs of the children must be assessed as quickly as possible. Assessment must include both physical and emotional aspects. Although many of the decisions regarding physical considerations may have already been made and set in place, they may be modified for good cause.

Physical Considerations

If possible, it would be helpful to conduct medical examinations of the children in an environment with which they are familiar and where they are likely to remain in some proximity to their peers. This decision will likely be made by the attending medical practitioner, but a proper suggestion is in order.

Are the rooms where the youngsters are being sheltered safe and familiar and comfortable for the children? Are the children awaiting reunification with their families all together? Is the facility private to the extent that there will be no intrusion by media representatives and curiosity seekers? Is this some place where caregivers will be able to find their children?

Does the physical environment provide basic necessities? Are there adequate toilets? Is there good lighting? Water, soap, and towels? Heat or air conditioning?

Snacks can provide emotional nurturance to children who may be unable to accept direct nurturance from an unfamiliar adult. Eating snacks gives a feeling of normalcy, and can provide needed distractions as well as a sense of sharing with others. Some children, regardless of age, will benefit from the physical acts of being fed and otherwise cared for. Other children can and should be asked to help prepare and serve the snacks: This gives them a sense of power and control. Comfort foods such as cocoa, juices, and cookies are appropriate. The aroma of freshly popped corn may stir the most withdrawn child into interacting with others and, if it is appropriate and workable, older children can be the popcorn makers and servers. If detention is so long that meals are served, the foods should be those that are familiar and appealing to children. More frequent small meals are preferred over large meals served at lengthy intervals. The foods should be items that are easily eaten.

Blankets wrapped around children can provide emotional security. And blankets can be put together to form a protective nesting and resting place in a large room.

Children, particularly when in crisis, often find it impossible to say "no" to an adult, and will be compliant when asked if they want to do what the adult wishes. Adults generally tend to want children to be tidy and may be insistent that the youngsters remove clothing that is torn or stained with blood or dirt. They may not recognize the importance children attach to their own clothing. Children should only be asked to change what is really necessary—they need the comfort provided by wearing their own clothing. Young ones particularly may experience a loss of identity; they worry that their parents will not be able to find them if they are forced to give up their clothes and wear something unfamiliar. Older children may be emotionally regressed so that they, too, experience a loss of identity. Or they may feel a loss of control, perceive themselves as helpless, and feel intruded on when required to change or give up what they are wearing.

It is generally best to have and use recreational materials that will keep children somewhat connected to people present, or to the group as a whole. For example, children can sit together at a table while making clay objects, or coloring, or having stories read to them or playing cards. It may be helpful to have older children lead the younger ones in play, or read to them. Isolating activities, such as watching videotapes, may not be in order unless the group has been together for a long time and a break is needed.

Emotional Considerations

Although some of the activities identified above satisfy emotional as well as physical needs, the following discussion deals with what are elements clearly necessary to aid the emotional well-being of child survivors of a disaster at the scene.

Information. Children need accurate and specific information about their immediate safety, about what has happened, and about what will happen to them next. Adults tend to avoid giving any information to children until they are relatively certain they have all the necessary information believing, perhaps, that partial information will make children more anxious. This is not true in most cases. The pain of waiting for full and accurate information can be intolerable to children, and will increase their feelings of helplessness. Although all pertinent information may not be available when needed or desired, the survivors can be told, for example

- what is known
- what is not yet known
- what provisions have been made for obtaining further information
- how the information will get to where they are
- how the information will be given to them in the room
- how families are being contacted and that they will be told the children are safe and where they are.

In addition to the above, the responsible clinician might pass along instructions in the form of information such as,

> We are going to stay together in this room and we are not sure yet how long we will be here. We have three adults here who are helpers. They are going to help us find out more information, they will help some of the younger children with the bathroom and things like that, and they are going to arrange for food and get some other things we might need. Some of you children will be able to help too. I will introduce each of our helpers and then we will sit in a snug circle and see if you have some questions or some things you would like to say about what is going on.

Nurturing. Children, particularly when in crisis, need to be nurtured, and nourishment comes in as many forms as there are children. They can be highly resistant to some forms of nurturance and very responsive to others. It is important that the adults in charge be flexible and responsive to the children's individual needs.

As stated earlier, food gives most children a feeling of being cared for—it shows adults are aware of their presence and needs, and that adults will do something for them.

Cuddling and holding provides some youngsters (and their caregivers) with a needed sense of comfort, but the clinician should remember that this physical contact often elicits regressive behavior in children, and can result in their feeling more helpless. Since intimate physical contact may be unwanted or alarming to many children, it should be given only if a child indicates such attention is desired.

Physical contact in ways that promote feelings of power are generally more in order than cuddling and holding. Having the children sit in a circle with toes or elbows touching or holding hands can provide physical connection that enables a child to feel strongly connected to others, and thus powerful. The circle can be a power circle, a wish circle, a sharing of feelings circle, or some other group effort.

Children caring for children is a great intervention. The recipient is nurtured by what he receives in the way of food, play experience, attention, and so on, and the provider is nurtured by his experience of helping as well as by the expressed appreciation of the supervising adult.

Structure. Structure provides children with feelings of safety. When children feel uncertain and confused in crisis situations, structure gives them a sense of control and power since they know, step by step, what is going to happen next. Under normal circumstances, requiring regimented behavior would be oppressive to many children. But when all else is chaotic, it is comforting for them to know that a strong adult is in charge, is consistent in behavior, and has told them what they will do next. For example,

> I've made a chart for us to follow. At exactly ten o'clock the children at table one will put away their things and wash up for a snack (then explain how each group will proceed). During our snack, our helper, Mrs. Green, will go to the main office to see if there is any new information for us. After we clean up from our snack we will get into our talk circle. Mrs. Green will tell us any news and then we will talk for fifteen minutes. Then we will have a twenty-minute rest time. I will ask for five children to be helpers in putting out the blankets and pillows for everyone. The children at table two will choose the music we will play, softly, during rest time.

Limit Setting. Clearly identified and enforced limits help children to feel safe. Being out-of-control, or observing such behavior in other youngsters, is a frightening experience for children. And when the adult present is perceived as being unable to control the child's behavior, the situation becomes even more frightening and the behavior escalates. Adults need to set clear rules and enforce them consistently. They need to support the child's feelings and impulses while firmly identifying the unacceptable behaviors. A child can be comforted by knowing she is free to be enraged for a while, but will be externally controlled so no one will be hurt. The adult can say, for example,

> Mary, it's OK to be upset and mad and to want to leave here to go and find your mom. I know that is what you want to do, and I understand why. But you cannot leave this room. There are big, strong fire fighters out there working to take care of people. That is their job. Our job is to stay here taking care of ourselves so that people will know where we can be found.

Or a behavior can be limited, as by

> John, I can see that you are excited and that you seem to want to run around. Moving is OK, but you cannot slam into the wall and into other children. I'm going to join you over there in that corner and we'll do some football exercises for five minutes and see if that helps the jumpy, running-around feelings you have. We will mark off our exercise territory with those chairs. Should we ask a few of the others if they would like to join us?

Empowering. Children feel less helpless and more empowered when they know what is going on; when they are given choices; when they are *invited* to do things rather than being coerced or ordered; when they feel they are supported and not alone; when they can acknowledge their feelings and behaviors; and when they can take an active part in recovering their equilibrium after a traumatizing event.

The initial tasks in responding to crisis situations are to assure the children of their safety and create an environment that will enhance their ability to cope with what has happened. This process may include preparing children for what they will have to deal with in the immediate future, helping them to understand the reasons for some of these happenings, and some specific suggestions about how they can cope with these possible events. How much work can be accomplished in this area depends on the ages of the children, their abilities to participate, and the amount of time they will be in emergency care. The following examples of clinical interventions are more suited for use with children who are held in emergency care for more than a short time, or for those who have come together for follow-up sessions.

> Parents often have very strong feelings when something like this happens to their kids. I want us to do some very serious thinking about the kinds of feelings parents might have. You children yell them out and I'll write them down. I may add some too. OK. You've come up with a fine list. Let's start

with the first one, "really upset." Does everyone know what that means? Ok. I'd like everyone to stand up for just a few minutes. For exactly two minutes—I'll be the time keeper—I want each person here to act like a parent who is "really upset." Wait until I say go. I want you to use your expressive faces and your whole bodies, and say some words that will make you the best "really upset" parent that you can be? Ready? Go! You were wonderful. Now I'd like us to sit down and talk about what it's like to be a kid whose parent is being "really upset."

The listed parental response can be explored, along with the children's reactions to each. When dealing with "really upset," for instance, the therapist can explain how their parents will probably be very relieved when they learn their children are safe and unharmed, but will probably also be very angry, perhaps at the person who caused the disaster, or at the gas company whose tank truck blew up, or at the police for not preventing the disaster, and so on. The group discussion can then be focused on how children may misinterpret the feelings of adults, blaming themselves for having caused such feelings or being the source of the feelings. The therapist then engages the children in group problem-solving to figure out ways they can deal with their concerns, such as what to do when their parents come for them and express anger. How do they know the parents aren't mad at them? They can "check it out" by asking, "Are you mad at me?"

The children can be encouraged to tell adults directly when they need a hug, or to jump around, or when they need to *not* talk. It is beneficial and fun for children to rehearse asking for what they need. I might set up a role play where two children (safety in numbers) are tired of Grandma always hugging them and saying, "You poor, poor things" and going on and on about the accident. Two other children act out the role of parents. I tell them in advance that these parents really don't like to tell Granny anything, and they (parents) are really interested in the TV program they are watching, and both parents are almost deaf (this forces children to state their positions powerfully). Another role play might be about two kids who return to school and lots of friends want them to describe the grossest parts of the accident and they need to tell their friends they do not want to talk about those things.

Using similar group discussion and problem solving, the children can address other situations they will likely face, such as the persistent behavior of television reporters, or what to do when they want to talk about the event and everyone wants them to forget about it. They can talk about how it might be for them if they have scary dreams. Lists can be made of Things Kids Can Do To Help Themselves, which should include asking mom or dad for help. Some children may not be able to engage in these coping behaviors, so it would be helpful for the therapist to add

Sometimes children don't remember all the things on the list when they need to. That's OK. One thing on the list you can always remember is who you can ask for help. Asking for help when you need it is a strong and smart thing to do.

Techniques. Some of the techniques and exercises presented in chapter 17 may be very useful in emergency response situations. The reader is referred particularly to the Music, Movement, and Visualization exercises, and to the Self-Calming techniques described in chapter 13.

Resources

Information Exchange

Knowing where children are located and being able to reunify them with their families is vital to their well-being and should be a top priority after the child's physical safety has been established. It is essential that the clinician establishes a system of communication immediately if this has not already been done.

People

An available person, someone who is known to the children and who is trusted by them, can be a valuable resource. This person will probably be a teacher, parent, scout, or church leader. The clinician should remember that this adult is also likely to be in great need of emotional support, and thus what is expected of him or her should be realistic. The therapist should determine the person's ability to function cooperatively, with the therapist clearly in charge. The trusted person's role might be limited to their reassuring presence and providing the clinician with important information about the individual children or, if it appears appropriate, the trusted person may be able to execute specific assigned roles.

Volunteer adults with whom the children are not familiar may also provide assistance, but generally not for direct work with the youngsters. The therapist must be able to provide supervision for anyone working directly with the children. Since working in a group and developing a sense of cohesiveness between the children is beneficial, having a limited number of assistants actually working with the children is all that is needed. It would not be desirable to have a helping adult assigned to each child, each responding in their own unique way to what they presume "their" child needs. Those who do not work directly with the children can secure needed supplies, keep out intruders, obtain and report information, relay messages, and so on.

Children take their cues from adults about how safe or how much at risk they are, and how much they have been damaged by their experience. It is not helpful to have adults working with the children who are themselves so overwhelmed that they are unable to build on the child's coping abilities, or are unable to tolerate children acting-out or discussing the grim details of what they have seen and experienced. This acting-out or discussion is not actively encouraged immediately following the crisis, but occurs spontaneously, and needs to be calmly witnessed and contained.

Parents and other loved ones may not behave in ways we believe are optimal for their children, but they are family and provide love and security, whatever their behaviors. And the therapist should probably not attempt to intervene in the family's dynamics while administering emergency mental health aid.

Supplies

Generally, more is not better under these conditions. It is helpful to have an assistant who can deal with what is and what is not needed.

Post-Disaster Follow Up

What has been discussed to this point is emergency, on-site work with the surviving children. This is the time to prepare, as much as the situation will allow, for follow-up work. Some of the children will be able to handle the situation with equanimity and not need post-disaster assistance, while others will need professional help.

The mental well-being of those who are not direct victims of the disaster should be considered by the community mental health cadre. Siblings who were not present will likely need some attention, as will young friends from church, scouts, and so on. I have reports of children in Colorado having nightmares and being afraid to go to school after viewing television news specials about the Stockton disaster; obviously the therapist cannot get to these youngsters, but I include the information as an example of how far-reaching this type of tragedy can be.

A telephone hotline can be quickly and easily established after a tragedy. The telephone can be any existing crisis line or a number at a mental health office which would be available around-the-clock for a few weeks. The number could be disseminated by the media, which would also identify its use—providing consultation to parents and caregivers whose kids are upset and who need advice for dealing with them. Referrals would also be made as appropriate.

A group meeting for the youngsters in the community as soon as reasonably possible after the disaster may be of help to them. Knowledgeable adults providing factual information and answering questions is calming. This can be coupled with a mourning time, when the children can, as a group, express their sorrow about their losses. A concurrent group should be established for their parents, who can express their own concerns and feelings about what happened.

The young survivors will likely benefit from several follow-up group sessions with other survivors, perhaps twice a week for a while. As above, concurrent group sessions for parents and other adult family members is in order. Their support and guidance is an essential part of helping the children.

Summary

The framework presented here is directed toward helping the children feel physically safe and emotionally cared for during, or immediately after, a large-scale disaster. This is done by a strong adult in charge who will share information, seek to reunify them with their families, witness and contain their feelings and behaviors, and assist them in dealing with some or all of their present worries. Providing assistance to these children is difficult, and one can expect to find a range of behaviors from withdrawn children to those who are literally bouncing off the walls. Their needs for assurance and structure are the same; it is their fears that are expressed so differently. The work can be made more difficult by the presence of those who want to help but who are not properly knowledgeable or prepared. Therapists who work on-the-scene must not only commit themselves for the duration of the immediate crisis, but must make a commitment to heal themselves when the crisis is over.

17
Techniques and Exercises

T he techniques and exercises presented in this chapter are some of
many that I have successfully used with traumatized children. The
reader is cautioned to use these tools with care, since, as with any
clinical exercise, they can simply be interesting games unless linked, in some
way, to real life. The linkage requires sensitivity to the child's abilities, functioning, and readiness.

Many classic play-therapy techniques, although useful, are not included
because they are familiar to most readers or can be easily found elsewhere.
Exercises which have been described in other parts of the book are only
referenced here and not repeated in full. Comments, suggestions, and new
additions to the list from readers are not only welcome, but actively solicited.

Affirmations

Children can be helped to internalize positive messages by having them repeatedly write, say, or sing a specific sentence, such as

"I am a fun child who has a right to be happy."

"I am loving and kind."

"I have a rainbow of feelings."

"I have a heart full of love."

"I have a body and feelings and family and other things but I am more
than all of these."

The clinician and child should discuss the purpose of affirmation programming, the reasons it is useful, and work out a plan to evaluate its effectiveness. Booster messages can be put on T-shirts and banners, imprinted on
pencils, ordered on return-address labels, placed on family-made posters, etc.

Assertiveness

Assertiveness skills are important for youngsters who have been victimized, who function as caretakers for others, who feel insecure and undeserving of having their needs met, or who have learned inappropriate behaviors such as bullying or whining to get what they need. A classic behavioral approach that includes support from the child's home and school should be integrated with teaching specific skills. With younger children one might say, for instance, "Our job is to have you learn to get what you want by asking for it directly. What you're doing is not working." A more acceptable approach when dealing with teenagers would be, "We need to figure out how to train your parents to meet some of your needs. The way you've been operating with them doesn't work very well. The important thing is that we find a way that you can get them to cooperate, so you can get what you want. Let's examine all the creative ways you've tried so far."

Basket of Feelings

The Basket of Feelings exercise helps the child identify and sort out ambivalent and contradictory feelings. See chapter 11.

Behavior Control

Not uncommonly, children's traumagenic behaviors present serious risks to their own physical and emotional well-being, as well as to the well-being of others. Treatment needs to focus on gaining control of the behavior, which can be most readily accomplished by addressing the issue directly with the child, caregivers, and other significant adults who are part of the treatment/support team. Important elements of treatment include clarification, monitoring, identification of needs and conflicts, learning alternate behaviors, developing an action plan, and follow-up.

A child may need to be taught self-calming exercises (chapter 13) to help him reduce anxiety to a level at which behavioral change can occur. One such technique is described in chapter 9, in the discussion of John. Specific examples of treatment techniques for dealing with behaviors of socially inept, eroticized, agitated, and socially inhibited children can be found in chapter 13. Examples and techniques for treating attachment-impaired behaviors can be found in chapter 12.

Body Work

Body work includes exercises such as yoga, T'ai Chi, and aikido. Specific body therapies include bioenergetics, Rolfing, the Traeger Method, structured dance and sports, clinically directed movement, and physical touching, all of which remediate or enhance well-being.

Just as children need the props of play—such as toys, art materials, and sand trays—to provide the necessary emotional distance, so, too, do they need play-action situations to provide safe emotional distancing in body-work. By being a ferocious lion or a strong judge in a courtroom, a child experiences power that makes him less afraid of confronting his realities. The therapist and child who become clowns together (chapter 10) create a fun and safe atmosphere in which children of all ages can obtain significant physical release, and in which remedial attention can be given and accepted. Psycho-dramas can be created to engage virtually any movement helpful to the child. The therapist and child can be aliens, fish, dragons, trees, or vegetables; they can be made of steel, computer chips, rubber, sugar, or bubble gum.

Children have much to gain from the self-esteem, discipline, and mastery necessary in karate and T'ai Chi. Young children enjoy the animal postures of a modified version of yoga, as described in chapter 13. Most body therapies are based on the idea that changes in posture and in muscular tension will release emotional blocks and move preverbal and undifferentiated feelings into consciousness. Physical touching can provide emotional contact, valida-tion, support, and comfort for children when verbalizations are meaningless, because a child is too young, too frightened, or is distrustful of words.

Regular and structured physical activities can be a required adjunct to therapy. Gymnastics, ballet, and soccer are commonly prescribed. Low-impact aerobic exercises or jogging can become a regular joint activity for a youngster and her caregiver, and stimulates bonding as well as providing needed physical impact.

The clinician must carefully consider whether or not prescribing exercise could create or reinforce a negative dynamic, since many girls as young as eight are now expressing pathological concerns about their less-than-perfect shapes.

Direct physical manipulation of the child's body should be natural, and should be performed in a manner that does not create tension. The therapist should not avoid physical contact so much that the child gets the impression she might explode if touched, nor should the touch be tentative and ambig-uous, leaving the child confused about its meaning. The therapist may prefer teaching the child's caregiver how to manipulate the child's body and then working as a team, or the clinician may limit this work to group sessions, or to times when the child's parents are present.

Many movements can be accomplished without intense physical contact by having the child follow the therapist's directions.

Do you remember the Tin Man in the *Wizard of Oz?* Well, in my play for today you are the Tin Man, rusted very, very tightly. First, take some time to feel your body becoming very tight and feeling all rusted. And you cry, through your teeth, "Oil can, oil can." Then, using this pretend oil can, I will oil you one part at a time. As each part gets oiled, we need to have it get very loose and move freely. Round and round, up and down, really free. What do you think of that for today? You will be the director for the next play. Let's find some pieces of costume and then do it.

Chapter 10 describes work which will help children regain ownership of their bodies and improve negative self-images.

Breathing

Teaching children to focus on their breathing and to control their breathing patterns helps them disrupt negative patterns, relax, and experience mastery in the process. Many children develop significant tenseness in the throat, chest, and stomach areas. While sitting or lying on the floor with the therapist, the child is first asked to notice her breathing. She is then gently asked to find out what it is like to breathe in gently through her nose, slowly expand her tummy, then expand her chest as though there were a big balloon in there, and then slowly let the air flow out through her mouth. Each time the air flows out, she feels more relaxed. (This can be practiced while standing.)

Children can be encouraged to breathe this way as a daily exercise, and asked to try it when they next feel upset or afraid. The clinician checks in regularly with the child to see how she has put this into practice.

After the child can smoothly shift to diaphragmatic breathing, have her relax lying on the floor while you draw her attention to various body parts by saying

> What would happen if you could send your wonderful breath down to your toes? Imagine you are breathing right down into your toes. What is that like for you? What would happen if you could breathe into your legs? Imagine the air swirling all around in your ankles, knees, and thighs. Let's see what would happen if you breathed into your bottom, your private parts, and your tummy. Send the breath down slowly and gently, relaxing and being in control of your own body. What would happen if you breathed into your shoulders and sent your breath gliding down your backbone?

Child Graduate Assistants

Using children who have graduated from therapy to assist in the treatment of other children builds mastery and self-esteem in the assisting child, and provides a positive role model as well as a goal toward which the child in treatment can work. See chapter 14.

Child-Therapist Workchart

The child and therapist fill out a chart that reflects progress toward meeting clinical goals, on which both successes and areas that still need work are noted. See appendix E.

Clay Bombs

The Clay Bomb exercise helps children release powerful negative feelings directed toward the specific people whom they perceive as having hurt them. See chapter 14.

Clay Family

The Clay Family is a projective technique that can be helpful in working with the child's relationships with members of his family. The child is asked to make a representation of each member of his family in clay, without making anyone a human. Giving an example or two is generally in order, such as, "Someone could be a lamp, or a cat." I have found it best to sit silently beside the child during the sculpting. When the work is completed, the child can be asked to elaborate the ways in which each family member can be likened to the sculpted object.

An adolescent girl represented her stepfather (who had sexually abused her) as a zit, a gross thing with no value; her father was an oak stump who could have been something strong and useful, but who cut himself down with drugs; her three-year-old brother was a dragonfly who was beautiful and flitted around; she represented herself as a wooden box that was just beginning to open; her mother was a basically harmless garter snake that was unpleasant to have around, and that was constantly trying to slither into the box to find out what was in there. The girl used these symbolic representations to talk about herself and members of her family for many months following the exercise.

Clowning

Clowns have permission to do almost anything. Putting clown makeup on a child fosters safe touching, eye contact, and a shared creative experience. Therapists are cautioned against using whiteface with children under age six, because they often experience this as a fearful loss of identity. Just colors are fun for the little ones, with a red circle on the nose usually mandatory. Clowning encourages emotional freedom, is fun, and provides a safe way for the child to be silly, mean, tricky, or sad. This activity combines psychodrama and movement in powerful ways that are enjoyed by most children and is suitable for all ages. See chapter 10.

Color Your Life

In Color Your Life, a child is asked to make a list of feelings along one side of a piece of paper. Each feeling is written in a different color, so that the list actually becomes a legend associating a color with a feeling. A large circle or mandala is then drawn on the page, and the clinician asks the child to let the circle represent him, and to show how he feels *now* by using just colors rather than representational drawings. He can later be asked to show how he remembers feeling on the day of the trauma. Another mandala can show his guesses about how each member of his family is feeling. Family members can be invited to join in this activity, and comparisons can then be made between a picture of one person's guesses about another's experience, and that person's own portrayal of the experience.

Another version utilizes a 4- to 6-foot strip of butcher paper. The therapist instructs the child to use this long strip to represent his life, expressing his feelings and experiences with colors. The child is directed to begin at the left side, representing when he was born, and continuing to the right side, identified as present time. It is best not to discuss the work until the child has finished.

Children often clearly identify a number of meaningful events through childhood with colors, and later say, for example, "This is when I went to the hospital, this is the divorce, this is when I lost my tooth, this is when my sister was born, this is my new bike."

Community Therapy

Involving the child's community for one or more sessions can be a powerful experience. A community therapy session becomes a strong, positive memory of people caring. An example of the technique used with a suicidal adolescent appears in chapter 9.

Community intervention is essential in refugee camps and with other displaced people, so that children can experience cultural continuity and group cohesiveness when they have lost everything else. Songs, games, storytelling, and religious rituals are all healing experiences.

Child populations that experience violence or disaster as a group can be greatly helped by community therapy. A school bus accident or the suicide of someone the group collectively knows can be coped with best by structuring a group experience that includes opportunities to hear the facts, to express feelings, to ventilate, and to participate in group rituals such as saying goodbye.

Computer Story Writing

I'm grateful to Hugh Clegg, child therapist from Washington, for sharing this technique of using a computer for writing stories.

A word processor provides needed emotional distancing while adding novelty and fun. The child and clinician jointly write a story: the child writes one sentence and the therapist the next. They alternate in this manner until the story is completed. The child consciously or unconsciously brings her conflicts and concerns into the treatment arena through the story. The clinician can decide whether to end with a proud reading of their creative effort, or whether further work and interpretation directly related to the story should ensue.

Dance

See "Movement."

Doctor

Children are able to work through both nurturing and sadistic impulses using a doctor's kit. The kit allows child and therapist to rehearse an upcoming medical procedure, or play out what has actually been experienced, in order to gain mastery. Children who feel emotionally disabled, as well as those with physical incapacities, have used the physically disabled play theme to work through their worries about helplessness, dependencies, and distorted self-images.

Victoria Coad and Pat Levinson, child therapists from the San Francisco Bay Area, helped me realize the value of having actual medical equipment in the playroom doctor's kit for those children whose fears are related to medical procedures they have experienced. Available materials can include several sizes of plastic syringes (without needles), lots of strange tubes and connectors, an oxygen face mask, a stethoscope, various gauze sponges, and rolls of rubber and gauze bandages. (The number of rolls of bandaging material should be minimal, or an inordinate amount of time will be spent rerolling them at the end of a session!) It is also helpful to have available a washable doll that can be painted to represent blood, burns, or incisions. The doll-sized wheel-chair and crutches manufactured by Mattel are very useful.

The medical items themselves stimulate intense play. Destructive children may play out tender, nurturing themes as well as torture; sexually assaulted children may act out revenge fantasies by replaying the anal/vaginal/oral rape by means of "medical" intrusion. Such play can be incredibly gross to witness, but provides a forum in which children can play out their conflicts.

The youngster can feel empowered when he acts out a modified version of what happened to him. This time he can be the doctor in charge, telling the medical staff what to do. He can say all the things he wanted to say to them when he was a patient, or he can retell what happened to him by taking a doll through the process. He describes as much detail as he can, telling how the doll feels and what the doll worries about, and the therapist responds by saying that any doll (kid) would feel the same way in a similar situation.

Dollhouses

Young children do best with small dollhouses, such as the Fisher Price models. Using two houses enables them to demonstrate and play through conflicts related to their fragmented lives, such as their home environment before the traumatic event and home life now, or home and another place, such as the hospital, daycare, or school.

Even very young children can demonstrate their pain related to custodial conflicts, by having a "mom's house" and a "dad's house," or foster care versus parent's home. I often videotape this play, and then invite the parents to attend a showing.

Drawing

A large basket filled with various marking pens is virtually irresistible to younger children and adolescents. I find it useful to have a large roll of butcher paper and a box of computer paper available. Drawing side-by-side with a child, or sharing the creation of a picture story, is fun and helpful in expressing feelings. See "Color Your Life," "Inside/Outside."

Dream Work

Children generally enjoy talking about their dreams, and the therapist can obtain much useful information by having them draw what they have dreamed, or act out a dream with puppets.

Children who are afraid of characters that appear in their dreams can be given a little "magic" to help them. I suggest to a youngster that when frightening figures appear in a dream, the dreamer should just slightly twitch his nose or blow gently toward the unwanted characters and watch them become smaller and smaller, until they are so small the youngster can pick them up in her hands and tickle them and make them laugh. It is better to make a suggestion in which monsters are mastered rather than eliminated, for elimination is often not possible, either in real life or in dreams.

Older children can gain insights when they join the clinician who asks if they would like to figure out some possible ideas about the dream. With permission, the therapist proceeds to write down key words while the child tells of his dream. They then go through the list, using the Gestalt technique of naming each object or feeling from the dream, and the youngster is asked to talk about what it would be like to be that object. The therapist takes notes during this process, and when they are finished he reads them back to the child, asking if any of what he has said has some meaning in his own life.

For example, the elements listed from a child's dream were a cruise boat, a tidal wave, a shark, a lifeboat, and a feeling of being really scared. The child talked as if he were each of those things.

As a cruise boat, "I'm full of people and everyone's having a good time. I like going different places." As the tidal wave, "I'm powerful and cause a lot of damage, and everyone is afraid of me." As the shark, "I eat up boats and people, and I'm lonely, but I don't notice it because I'm hungry all the time." As the lifeboat, "I am very small, and no one usually notices me or thinks I'm important until something happens. I worry that I won't be able to hold so many people, and that I won't be able to do the job I'm supposed to do." As to being really scared, "People don't like me to be around."

The child is asked to listen carefully while the comments are read back slowly, without mention of the objects, and to think about how any of the comments he made might have meaning to him in his life right now.

The Elderly Child Remembers

The Elderly Child Remembers exercise helps children to experience future mastery and to put a traumatic experience into the perspective of one event in a lifetime. See chapter 14.

Family Work

Many exercises described in this chapter can be adapted for family work, such as "Psychodrama," "Opera," "Drawings," and the "Clay Family." This work can be a diagnostic experience as well as providing insight for members who can look at both process and product.

One old standby is to ask each person in the family to state what he likes best about each of the other family members. The responses are written on large sheets of paper so that everyone can see them, and elaboration and comments are solicited, in a light, discovery mode, from those present. This exercise can become intense when one person cannot think of anything positive he likes about another. It is important that this be brought out, although it may be difficult to deal with. After everyone has had a turn, each person is asked to identify one thing they would change about each of the other family members. This can provide rich material for therapy, and gives the messages that people are appreciated although not always perfect, and that everyone has an opinion others should listen to. See the example of family work with Rob, chapter 7.

Feelings

Traumatized children often have significant difficulty coping with all their feelings. Like war veterans, they seem to shift between feeling everything with great intensity, and feeling nothing at all. Clinical work includes helping them to differentiate feelings so that they are not experienced as an amorphous, frightening mass; teaching them that feelings are not actions; helping them to tolerate the physical sensations related to their feelings; helping them to understand that present feelings can trigger their reexperiencing past events for a while; helping them to remember that the danger is past; and teaching the children that they can experience feelings without going out of control.

Utilizing the safe emotional distancing provided by play, children can explore the feelings of fictional characters, and then examine with the therapist what children in general might feel in similar situations. The child will then be better prepared to discuss her own feelings. Being able to identify and discuss feelings is a step toward mastery.

Related exercises include the "Basket of Feelings," "Color Your Life," "Guess What Sexually Abused Kids Worry About?," "Feelings: Inside and Outside," and "Feelings: Where Are They in My Body?"

Feelings: Inside and Outside

Feelings: Inside and Outside helps the child portray hidden or unexpressed feelings nonverbally. See chapter 10.

Feelings: Where Are They in My Body?

Feelings: Where Are They in My Body? is an exercise to help a child develop an awareness of sensations related to emotions and a facility for discussing his feelings. See chapter 10.

Field Trips

Any reasonable outing that enhances treatment by providing education or desensitization, or which contributes to a stronger connection between the child and therapist, should be considered. I believe it is wise to include the child's parents, friends, or siblings in such an outing. Caution must be exercised against the clinician's inadvertently slipping into a "good-time" parenting role that causes deep resentment in the caregiver. With many children the clinical objective is to strengthen the parent-child bond, and field trips may dilute this objective unless the parent comes along, with the therapist as the parent's ally. Trips may be planned to the art museum, mall, hospital, jail, court, rehabilitation ward, etc. I once took a child and his mother to a store which sold snakes and other reptiles, so that the child could ask The Expert if snakes ever, ever live in toilets. This reality check enabled the child to get back on track after his regressed toileting.

Fingerpainting

The art form of fingerpainting has the wonderful advantage of allowing a child to create, destroy, and recreate. It provides an opportunity for messiness, and generally conveys the message that here, at least, mistakes cannot be made. Fingerpainting should not be used, however, with children who are barely containing frightening, primitive feelings, because this medium elicits regressive behaviors and emotions.

When a therapeutic alliance has been established and the child is prepared to have feelings emerge, fingerpainting can facilitate fantasy expression, with little skill needed. The child can fingerpaint alone, can have the therapist join him with his creation, or they can paint side-by-side.

Garbage Bag

The Garbage Bag exercise is designed to contain the elements of the traumatizing event and enable the child to work on them at his own pace. It also empowers the child, and helps to reinforce the reason for therapy. A detailed description of this exercise can be found in chapter 14.

Genogram

A genogram is a diagrammatic representation of a family tree, drawn with squares representing males, circles for females, and solid lines joining these symbols to represent relationships. Drawing the family in this way makes the child feel important, and is a simple, concrete way for the child and therapist to observe together the unique family constellation. I ask the child to help by giving me information while I draw the genogram so I can understand who's who in the family. The process is done slowly—it may sometimes take three sessions to complete a genogram since they are frequently complex, containing marriages, divorces, remarriages, step-relationships, and so on.

I put the first names and ages in the circles and squares, and ask the child to say one or two characterizing words about each person, and I write the responses—typically "grouchy," "funny," "alcoholic," and so on—directly onto the genogram. I also include the child's teacher, best friend, and pets, using dotted lines to connect them appropriately.

Putting the genogram on the playroom wall during several sessions helps me to remember the child's complex family relationship.

Guess What Other Sexually Abused Kids Worry About?

Guess What . . . provides a safe, structured way to educate the child and answer questions they may have been afraid to ask. See chapter 10.

Guests in Treatment

Inviting a guest to a treatment session who is a positive authority figure for the child, can be helpful not only during the session but, by reference, at later times as well. Adults and teenagers who have experienced traumatic events similar to that of the client child can be positive role models, giving the child a sense of identification by discussing their feelings and hopes. The child in treatment recognizes that another person having similar problems has been able to cope successfully.

Although usually harder to arrange, it is helpful to invite other professionals to sessions when they can provide the youngster with information about what happened to them, or what they can expect. For example, a medical person with anatomical models can teach about body functions or birth planning. The family's religious adviser can give a religious perspective (see the discussion in chapter 7) and the child's attorney can discuss relevant legal matters. If impossible to do so in person, these professionals may be amenable to a conference call between themselves, the child, and the therapist. The therapist should be prepared to "interpret" what is being said for children who do not understand.

I have found it empowering in a small therapy group to invite a police officer, court mediator, or district attorney to a session so the youngsters can offer advice to them on how to better interact with the children that they deal with professionally, and to give the children an opportunity to ask the guest questions. See Child Graduate Assistants.

Helping Others

Traumatized children can help others who have had similar experiences to do all the things we know about from our self-help programs, such as building self-esteem, achieving mastery, reinforcing growth, and so forth. Eugene Porter, psychotherapist from the San Francisco Bay Area, has taught me the value of having children make videotapes or write articles to be shown to other youngsters. Child "graduate assistants" provide an opportunity for children to help others through identification, and by providing some of the advantages of group work when a group is not available.

House-Tree-Person

Therapists have used the House-Tree-Person projective drawing technique with children for almost fifty years. The technique's appeal is that it is fun, simple, and results have been standardized. The child is asked to draw as good a House (and later, a Tree and a Person) as he can. Although the therapist directs what to draw, the child has latitude in determining details. The objects to be drawn are familiar to the child, are commonly found in free drawings by children, and provide stimulus for exploring feelings and conflicts with the therapist. The therapists can use qualitative interpretations of these drawings (see Hammer, 1958) or can ask the child questions about various details in the drawings; have the child speak as if he were the house, tree, or person, and describe what life is like; or ask the youngster to tell a story about the house, tree, or person he has drawn.

It's Just Not Fair

It's Just Not Fair is an exercise that provides a means by which the therapist is able to validate the child's experience and help him engage in regressive expressions of feelings. See chapter 10.

List of Bad, Mean, Rotten Things
That Can Happen to Kids

The List of Bad, Mean, Rotten Things is an exercise that helps remove stigmatization, and gives the child the sense that he is not alone. Senses of hope, control, and fun are conveyed. See chapter 14 for a description and example.

Make a Machine

The therapist starts by making repetitive body movements, with corresponding sounds, such as raising and lowering one arm and bowing forward every time the arm is lowered, sounding "whsssssh" when the arm goes up, and "aaahhhhhh" with every bow. The child joins the machine, perhaps by placing her hands on her hips after each bow and putting a leg forward after each arm raising, both movements accompanied by different sounds. There is no limit as to how many people can become part of the machine. This exercise promotes joining and body control.

Making a Friend of the Scar (Bald Head, Wheelchair, etc.)

Making a Friend of the Scar is designed to assist the child in accepting and integrating painful results of the trauma. See chapter 10.

Metaphor

See Storytelling.

Mime

The child and therapist can create fine pieces of drama through movement alone. Children enjoy the equalization of power that occurs when miming adults are prevented from using their superior word skills.

Modeling

Examples of successful treatment can provide motivation for confronting and mastering traumatizing events. The clinician can introduce models through invited guests (Guests in Treatment, Child Graduate Assistants), videotaped interviews of other children describing their trauma and therapy (Video), and the work or success of fictional characters from books, movies, or other sources.

The therapist continually models behavior for the child. I commonly find situations for modeling trust, limit setting, nurturing, and how to cope with anger. Boundary modeling occurred, for example, when a young boy snapped my bra strap. I immediately and forcefully said

> That is not acceptable behavior. I don't allow anyone to touch me in ways I don't want them to. Joey, you sit right here beside me and keep your hands to yourself. If you were wanting to be playful or needing my attention, there is an OK way to do that, and I'll show you how later.

The child misbehaved as he did for important reasons, but a clear boundary had to be immediately established in a way that did not shame the youngster.

Another modeling example occurred when three adolescent girls were acting in a way that was sexually inappropriate with their male therapist in group therapy. His immediate, nicely exaggerated response was

> "Whoa! Give me a break! You girls are too much. And my wonderful wife wonders why I come home all tired out! Turn it down, girls. You have bodies that would be the envy of any mature woman, but my God, it's like having puppies that you know are going to be champions, but they just haven't figured out how to coordinate everything and they're just all over you. It's OK to enjoy what you've got, but it's not OK to come on to me, especially when you gang up. Now, to turn the heat down a bit, we are going to sing a kid's song. Let's go.

In this instance the clinician believed that the young teens were dealing with developmental issues that they were unable to wrestle with at home, or with other males. He therefore wanted to validate their sexuality while setting a limit to their being seductive with him. To have had a serious or lengthy discussion with them might have led to denial, and feelings of shame.

Movement

Movement allows the child to express and explore feelings and conflicts in an indirect and safe way. The fun of movement in a therapy setting can take away the fear of being there, and the mirroring between child and therapist lessens the child's sense of lonely isolation. Children can play out joy, curiosity, pleasure, playfulness, fear, disgust, panic, or despair through directed movement, and feel a sense of release and personal power as they do so. Verbal expressions of these emotions may not be possible because of their age, their functioning, or family injunctions.

Clinicians and their child clients should together think up ways to broaden the range of movement and nonverbal emotional expression. They can examine fast and slow pacing, and explore their surrounding space, by jumping and walking on tiptoe (to occupy the upper parts of their space), spinning and turning with arms outstretched (to fully use the intermediate space), and rolling and wriggling on the floor (to use the low space). Style can be rigid, jerky, fluid and smooth, or floppy.

Background music is an enhancement to this exercise, and environmental sound albums are fun for children. The child and therapist may wish to use movement to express what is being experienced when listening to music.

Useful scenarios that can help get things started include being underwater where an octopus has many arms for hugging, and there are sharks and starfish and caves for exploring, and hidden treasure to be found; or being wind-up toys, like soldiers and ballerinas; or walking through a forest where there are lions, tigers, and bears (Oh my!); or exploring gravity-free outer space, where you float around; or seeing alien slime balls grow; or becoming a hero.

The theater arts include creative games and exercises for loosening and expanding actors' movements and emotions. Some are just plain fun, suitable for individual and group work. See "Make a Machine," "Mime," "Throw a Face."

In addition to increasing the positive aspects of the child's self-image, decreasing muscle tension, and improving coordination of fine and gross motor skills, dance and movement accept the child "as is" and lessen her sense of lonely isolation. See "Body Work," "Music"; See also "Movement and Music" in chapter 10.

Music

Religious and military leaders are aware of music's ability to lift the spirit, lend strength, and give hope until the listeners can create their own. The rhythm and beat can alter a mood from depression to wellness, and create rousing feelings of strength, aliveness and energy, as well as relaxation. The words in a song can slip in under a child's defenses and subliminally strengthen him until the real thing comes along. Music and song can teach children that others have had similar experiences, and have come to understand them, and they can come away with the sense of a shared emotional experience.

Children love to sing. Despite some self-consciousness, making music and singing is fun, and is a safe way for children to feel connected with others. This form of healing is particularly well suited to work with traumatized children, since it does not require body contact, self-disclosure, or competition.

Child therapists can readily build a small library of audio tapes to use in treatment with children. Classical music should not be ignored: Schumann's *Third Symphony* is heroic and playful; *Don Giovanni* ranges from despair to loving to the demonic; *Peter and the Wolf* certainly tells a story; and Strauss waltzes are restfully stirring. The clinician's library should also contain some New Age music, and environmental sounds of the sea, wind, or meadow, for use as background to movement exercises. Or the music can be songs written especially for children, such as Sesame Street songs and Peter Alsop's songs (appendix G). It is important that the clinician find the music enjoyable so his feeling is communicated to the child.

The Richards institute program, Education through Music, is designed primarily for teachers of children's music, but instructs students in the use of children's singing games that empower children, build self-esteem, give pleasure, and facilitate the creation of internal discipline. (For the address of the Richards Institute, see appendix A.) See "Movement," "Opera." See also "Singing with Movement" and "Movement with Music" in chapter 10.

Normalizing Events

Experiences that are especially stigmatizing need to be placed in a context with which the child can live. Helping the child understand that he is not alone, and that the trauma he suffered has happened to others who have survived, is essential. Giving the child a cognitive grasp of exactly what happened is empowering, and normalizes the event. Understanding that lots of weird and different things happen to people who survive the experience is a part of the normalizing process. Straightforward, unashamed, direct discussion is the key to helping children accept what happened as unusual, but still within the realm of human experience; this allows them to integrate the event into their lives. See "List of Bad, Mean, Rotten Things That Happen to Kids" in chapter 14, and "Normalizing the Genital Area" in chapter 10.

Opera

Opera requires several people. I have found that it works best with families and groups of older children. Participants are told that they will play out a story in song. The therapist is the director and sets the theme, and at times may have to direct the action. Each person is assigned a role and is expected to join the others in singing. They create variations that play off what another is singing: they can increase or decrease the volume, change the tempo, and otherwise contribute to the opera.

The following opera was created by a family to help a child release herself from guilt feelings related to a sibling's death from cancer. In clinical sessions prior to the staging of the opera the child spoke of feeling guilty and partly responsible for her brother's death.

The wise owl (child in treatment) was assigned the role of convincing the little bunny (an older sibling) that it was not her fault her brother bunny died. The bear (father) and the deer (mother) were to help her with this chore. They used a tambourine and a triangle to round out the sound. The opera began with the whole group singing, "We miss Tom, we all miss Tom. He's gone and it's hard and we all miss Tom." Each then did a solo about what they especially missed. The bunny, following whispered stage directions from the therapist, began to sing about the times when they had fights and she knew he now hated her, and so did everyone else. The family chorused, "Not true, not true, it's simply not true." The basso bear kept repeating the refrain, "Brothers fight, sisters fight, it happens everywhere." The wise owl and the deer chorused, "So what, so what, sooooooooo what. It's not your fault." The bunny's single line solo, "I'm glad I've got my own room now" was followed by more "So What" choruses. The bear began, "You feel bad, but you didn't do it.", which the owl and deer joined. The grand finale was a chorus of "We love you bunny, when you're funny, when you're sad, when you're good, when you're bad. We love you. We all miss Tom, we miss him, we miss Tom." The opera ended and was followed by a quiet family discussion of tender feelings, while refreshments were served.

The opera was not carried off as smoothly as it appears in writing: brief stops were called so that family members could consult with each other. The family asked to repeat their opera at another session, wanting the pleasure of having it performed with more polish and, at the request of the child in treatment, the performance was videotaped for a keepsake.

Pets as Treatment Team Members

Pets can be very useful in teaching nurturance, empathy, and responsibility, and how to accept affection. A pet is an uncritical listener, and a "voice" through which the child can speak by explaining how the pet feels. Pets can make useful affectional connections for children in out-of-home care who need "someone" they can trust who does not represent a loyalty conflict between the new caregivers and the child's real parents.

One colleague uses her golden retriever as a cotherapist, with a great deal of positive effect. Her young clients tell the dog things in the therapist's presence that they just would not tell her. I have had children bring their pets to one or two of their sessions when there was an indication that it would be clinically beneficial. For example, I had a twelve-year-old boy bring his dog after he told me he had had his fill of "shrinks," and I needed to do something different to help me make a connection. Another client was a fragile, needy child who was terribly blocked from showing how she felt; I had her bring her bird along to meet my bird. In both instances, the children were able to speak freely of how life had changed for their pets since the trauma.

Prescribing a pet as part of the treatment plan is contraindicated when it is likely that the child will abuse it, and when an adult is unavailable to monitor interactions. A young adolescent girl experiencing intense conflict expressed her rage toward her mother by throwing her guinea pig, a recent gift from her mother, against the wall and killing it. She was relishing her demonstration of power and hate while at the same time, identifying with the helplessness of the animal.

Setting a child up with more than he (or the pet) can handle, can lower self-esteem and, if he abuses the animal, can convince him that neither he nor the adults in his environment can control his behavior. See the discussion about Toni's pet in chapter 12.

Posters

Children enjoy making posters to take home. These help keep the clinical connection vital, can be used for positive affirmations, and can reinforce goals which the child wishes to achieve. The posters may be lists the child makes as part of a work exercise, such as a "List of What I Like About Myself" and a "List of What I Have Trouble With." Refer to "Who Can Help Take Care of Mom Poster" in chapter 12 for a clinical exercise in which a poster is used to assist in disengaging a child from his parentified role in the family.

Psychodrama

Hats, masks, scarves, feather boas, leather jackets, frilly dresses, and other props can entice a child into joining the therapist in creating dramas. The theatrical presentations can be the child's spontaneous creation in response to an instruction like

Today, you're the director. Tell me what role you would like me to play. Do we need to use any of our dolls for roles? How do we begin?

Or the therapist may be more directive by starting with something like

Today let's do a play about a little forest creature who is lost and cannot find his parents. Tell me what role you would like to play.

Or,

Let's do a play about a child who was abused. What role do you want to play? How should we begin?

The therapist may use psychodrama as an adjunct to another mode of clinical interaction.

Do you suppose you and I could take some of the creative ideas from your sand tray and create a ten-minute play?

Or,

Let's see if we can take each of the family members you've painted and create a play where each one is a different character. They could be fantasy figures from a magic land, or creatures from the sea, or just different kinds of people. You and I could each play the parts. Let's figure out each one and come up with some costumes. How do we begin?

The therapist enters the world of the child, where communication is conducted in the child's own language. Children as animals, heroes, and fairy princesses are able to play out their conflicts, speak the unspeakable, display emotions and behaviors that have been blocked, practice new ways of being, and demonstrate their hurts and wishes.

Young teenagers have chosen to sit quietly and discuss their concerns when we were both dressed in character roles. Whole families have dressed up and spontaneously created dramas in which all of them contributed to the direction of the action.

Puppets

Puppets can stimulate a child into interacting with the therapist. They provide the emotional distance needed to allow therapist and child to send and receive messages safely. Fear, guilt, and timidity can be lessened by the child's projection of feelings through the puppets and his identification with them. A reluctant child can be approached in a silly, nonthreatening way by a puppet that, for instance, nibbles the child's shoelace or talks to his watch.

String-type puppets tend to be too complicated for children and for the therapist, but hand- and stick-puppets are readily available and easy to use. Any doll in the playroom can be hand-held and used as a puppet. The slow, creative process of a child's making her own puppet out of papier-mâché, plasticine, socks, or any variety of materials deepens the child's identification with her puppet and makes the process more powerful.

Children so easily relate to puppet play that a "theater" is not really required for fun and effective work. If desired, a makeshift stage can be created by spreading a cloth between two chairs. I had a wooden box with a curtained front and a wooden top, part of which could be flipped open. The child could crawl into the box and hold hand-puppets up through the top opening. Most children did not feel the need to remain concealed, and often stood beside their performing characters. At other times this theater doubled as a hiding-box, where the child could take a needed time-out, or could sit unobserved while talking to the therapist or to a parent attending a session.

Relaxation

Children benefit from relaxation training by a reduction in the tension they experience, and by learning that they can have some control of their body tension. This in turn gives them a sense of mastery. See Breathing. See also "Self-Calming Exercises" in chapter 13.

Releasing Feelings

The body and emotions can be allowed a full range of physical and emotional expression in the safety of the clinical setting, through fantasy play or through direct expression. The therapist and child can, for example, be lions who terrify someone who once frightened or hurt the child, or they can be wizards who change aggressors into insects. They can throw clay at a target representing someone ("Clay Bombs" in chapter 14) or the child might be a very strong heroine who cries rivers of tears and then explodes like a volcano, to let the world know how she feels about her drug-abusing parents. See "It's Just Not Fair!" and "Guess What Other Kids Who Have Been Sexually Abused Worry About?" in chapter 10.

It is important that the therapist be sensitive to the child's need not to "kill off" a person who has been nurturing to him. Time can be spent helping the child acknowledge and honor the positive parts of the relationship, and then carefully directing the release of the child's negative feelings toward a specific behavior or part of the person, rather than against the whole individual. In this way the child does not lose the part of the relationship that has been nourishing.

Restructuring Trauma

Children often cope with their problems in play by reenacting a difficult situation with the child as the controller, enforcer, super hero, or revenge-seeker.

Traumatized children need the safety and protection of the clinician for assistance and guidance in performing this natural process of mastery and integration. Any play therapy techniques that appeal to a particular child can be used. For example, the therapist can ask the child to create a puppet show, computer story, or psychodrama about a boy (use same sex as child) who has experienced a traumatic event (the same as that endured by the client child). In the reenactment, the child has all the power he needs to take care of himself: for example, he could turn into a powerful genie when he was bitten by the dog, or could order around the hospital staff who treated him when he was injured. See chapter 14 for further discussion.

Self-Calming

See Relaxation and Breathing. See also "Self-Calming Exercises" in chapter 13.

Sensorimotor Play

Sensorimotor play, action play, is particularly important because the experiences of children are frequently not linguistically encoded in their memories, and are consequently unavailable through discussion. Or a child may not be ready yet to verbalize his experience. Utilizing sensorimotor therapy, clinicians are able to join with the child, building self-esteem, giving important messages, and providing either stimulation or soothing experiences. See further discussion and examples in chapter 13.

Singing

See Music. See also "Singing with Movement" in chapter 10.

Spirituality

Children who have experienced profound and frightening changes in their lives, such as the loss of a home or a parent, life-threatening diseases, body disfigurement, or abuse by a loved parent, need to understand that they are *more* than their families, their possessions or their bodies. They need to feel that there is a core to their being that cannot be lost or taken away, and that they have an inner wisdom upon which they can rely. This knowledge of a spiritual self can be developed and nourished using examples from the natural world. Children are encouraged to consider and experience patterns of existence and the interconnectedness of life.

Awareness of life patterns, transformation, unity, and inner wisdom can be developed even in very young children. The child's attention can be directed to pertinent areas by comparing his situation to natural events. For example, if the child is struggling with loss or change in his life, he might be asked, "If a tree loses its leaves, is it still a tree? When a caterpillar changes into a butterfly, what happens? Is something lost or gained—or is life just different for that creature?" Discussions about all the things a body does to protect and nourish itself can develop some sense of inner wisdom. The clinician can point out wonderingly how our bodies automatically take care of themselves by rapidly closing an eye when something flies toward it, or sweating, shivering, or sneezing when needed. Marveling with the child about the phenomena of seeds sprouting, eggs hatching, and the earth moving can contribute to his understanding of himself as part of the universe.

Children can be asked to talk about times in their lives when they have felt deep joy or peacefulness, a feeling of oneness, or sense of a presence. They can be taught and encouraged to recapture those experiences through music, art, meditation, or, if it is part of the youngster's background, through prayer. Acknowledging children's natural spirituality validates and strengthens their experiences. Helping them savor peaceful, powerful experiences assists them in coping with their difficulties. They can learn to embrace what they fear in themselves and observe the flow of their various feelings.

Even children who have not been exposed to religious teachings often believe that they are being punished by God. This can be explored by saying, for example, "Some children who have been (use relevant experience) have important ideas about God and what happened. I wonder if you had some thoughts about God and your being taken away from your mom." This can create an opening for discussion of the child's feelings and conceptualizations. Should the child deny such concern, the clinician can leave the door open for later work with a statement like, "Sometimes kids have ideas or thoughts or dreams about this after we talk about it a little in our sessions. So, I might ask you about this again later, or if you think of anything later and want to talk about it, let me know."

Direct work with the spiritual nature and beliefs of a traumatized child is commonly needed, as that area is often damaged or may be the only place where needed strength can be gained.

Storytelling

Metaphor embedded in story is a powerful teaching tool and a good way to transmit empowering messages. Stories capture the child's imagination and are easily remembered; since they do not obviously and directly relate to the child's issues, the youngster does not actively defend against the presented ideas. Some common themes I use include:

> The brave knight who sensibly wore his armor in battle and felt so comfortable and safe that he began to wear it all the time. He became so accustomed to it that he eventually forgot he could take it off. He had all sorts of silly misadventures clanking around in his safe, but not always necessary, protection.

A champion runner named Flojo trained very hard. She practiced every day, ate the right foods, and wore beautiful lightweight running clothes. She had a friend who very much wanted to be a champion runner too, and Flojo wanted to help her become a winner. Her friend had a fine healthy body and brave heart, but she was a worrier. The story continues with our champion slowly and sensitively teaching her friend that she could run without her umbrella, sunglasses, muffler, flashlight, rainboots, lunch, and sunburn lotion. Flojo also points out that there may be some discomfort and that some precautions can be useful, but that knowing what to do or how to find help is just as valuable as having accessories, and does not get in the way of having fun.

And then there is the story of the little rainbow who was taught to display only one of his many beautiful colors, because if anyone saw all the colors that were part of him, he would be resented and might even get into serious trouble. Through a series of adventures the rainbow learns to honor and display all of his colors, and becomes a much appreciated and interesting rainbow.

Children can be encouraged to tell stories that are completely their own creation, or they can be given some direction such as, "Tell a story about a wonderful animal who lost something very important to him and had lots of feelings about it."

See chapters 7 and 9 for examples of clinical story use. Gardner's storytelling techniques (1986) and an entire book devoted to the use of metaphor with children (Mills and Crowley, 1986) are fine references.

Telephone

Young children and teenagers find toy telephones useful props for communicating with the therapist or with someone else they are not ready or able to speak with directly. The phones can be used to rehearse what needs to be said, to verbalize what they wish they had been able to say, or to tell what they really feel but choose not to say.

I use my telephone answering machine as a clinical tool with children. I have found it effective to tell children that they can leave *brief* messages to report a success or a just-remembered aspect of their trauma that they wish to discuss further, or to report some difficulty that they would like to work on in their next session. This empowers the child and strengthens their connection with me between sessions.

I routinely make telephone contact with any adolescent who is scheduled to meet me for the first time. I tell them I like to introduce myself by telephone first, because most teens are a little uptight about meeting a therapist, and that if they know a little bit about me and what we are going to do beforehand, things will go a little easier. I describe myself and the office and playroom, and tell the teenager what we will and will not do during our first meeting. For example,

> I don't ask kids to talk about the details of what happened to them because I know a lot of it anyway, and it usually works best to get to know each other better before talking about that stuff. I don't have a couch to lie down on and I don't read minds. We'll talk some in general about how things are going for you. We'll talk about therapy and how it works; and I'll tell you how the teenagers that come to see me have found it helpful. You probably have some questions you want to ask me. This is what I look like . . . Do you have any questions you'd like to ask me now?

Supportive telephone contact between a child graduate assistant and a child in therapy is discussed in chapter 14.

Throw a Face

Children and leaders sit in a circle. The leader begins by facing the person next to him, making a silly or horrible face and then, with a quick forward thrust of his face, "throwing" it to the next person. This person "catches" the face by immediately copying it while jerking her face back as it is "caught." The catcher slowly modifies the facial expression while turning to the person on the other side of her and "throws" the new face to a new catcher. This utterly ridiculous exercise is an icebreaker, leads to lessening of protective armors, lets children know that it's OK to have fun, and enables the child to feel that she can relate to the clinician.

Ventilation

See "Releasing Feelings" in this chapter.

Video

Video equipment provides many opportunities for effective, creative interventions, and is great fun. It can be used to record puppet shows, psychodrama, storytelling, sand-tray creations, paintings, and sculptures. The child can rehearse new behaviors on videotape, or a graduate (or near graduate) can make a brief videotape for the express purpose of having it shown to other youngsters who are entering treatment for the same or similar problems. The tape contains lots of positive messages, and its use encourages the new child to make a similar tape when he graduates.

An older child can make a documentary about his own experiences. Commercial tapes can be used to educate the child about hospital procedures. Children may want to make a tape to send to a parent or sibling with whom they are unable to have physical contact. Clinical progress can be recorded for future review or for sharing with those at home. A child's successes can be commemorated. Heilveil (1983) and Gardner (1986) describe their creative uses of video in therapy with children.

Water Play

A low, child-sized sink is, in my view, the ultimate in playroom equipment. A sink full of water, bubbles, squirt guns, and toys for projective play (boats, divers, people, sharks, treasure chests, etc.) is wonderful for younger children and for those who need to engage in regressive play. Water is soothing, healing, and easier to clean up between sessions than sand.

What People's Bodies Do When They're Scared

What People's Bodies Do is designed to educate the child, normalize and defuse anxiety related to her responses to fear, and integrate her experience. See chapter 10.

"Who Can Help Take Care of Mom?" Poster

Making the poster is a technique to assist the parentified child in letting go of that dysfunctional role. See chapter 12.

Worry Wall

The child writes her "biggest worry right now" on the back of the therapist's business card and tacks it on the playroom wall, at a height representing the intensity or size of the worry. See further description in chapter 12.

Yoga

See discussion in chapter 13.

18
Theoretical, Developmental, and Experiential Foundations: A Personal History

My clinicial curiosity, which prior to being degreed and licensed was plain old nosiness, always leaves me wanting to know something about the personal and professional development of the authors whose works I read. This brief chapter outlining my professional work and growth is offered for those of you with a similar curiosity. I give up this information knowing that I am sabotaging my now not-so-secret wish to be mysterious.

If you do not share this interest about authors, stop after the following: thank you for reading *Treating Traumatized Children,* and I hope the information presented will be of use to you.

For the really curious, please note that the teachers, colleagues, and mentors named in this chapter are, with two exceptions, all represented by at least one entry in the reference section. The exceptions are Judy Fjell and Peter Alsop, who have some of their fine songs identified in appendix G.

Most of my formal academic education in child development and child treatment was obtained while completing a master's program in international social work, and during two years of advanced clinical training in family therapy during the mid-1970s.

Those portions of my master's program which related specifically to my future work with children included a study of social policy and health and education planning as these areas relate to children's well-being. The mental health approaches I studied at the time included the works of Freud, Erickson, Klein, Fraiberg, Axline, Moustakas, and others. The principles of community organization, cultural self-determination, and the global perspective that I adopted through my work in the International Social Work Program at the University of Hawaii have influenced my clinical work.

A year of study and research in 1976 as an East-West Center Scholar in Honolulu led to an internship with the United Nations in Bangkok. This professional experience included providing consultation in the development of a mental health program in Fiji, and participation in the implementation of a social services program in Nepal. During later travel in Southeast Asia I was invited to look at children's programs in refugee camps.

During the two years' training at the California Graduate School of Family Therapy, I was strongly influenced by the works of Satir, Ackerman, Haley, Minuchin, Bowen, Boszormenyi-Nagy, and others. I learned how extensively a traumatic event that happens to one family member is felt by the entire family and more importantly, I learned about the generational influences, fierce loyalties, and unholy alliances that family members use to influence one another.

During the 1970s and early 1980s, family therapists generally ignored the individual treatment needs of children. This was apparently a reaction to the usual model of child treatment in which the child had a confidential relationship with his therapist, who rarely communicated with the child's parents. In another model commonly followed at that time, the child guidance model, the parents would be seeing a therapist other than the one seeing their child, and the two clinicians would confer.

It became clear to me that one cannot treat a child in isolation—that the complex dynamics of the family system impinges so greatly on the life of the child that failure to involve those important people will yield poor results. And, as a social worker, I learned to incorporate the effects of social systems, the community, and public policy in my diagnostic procedures and treatment plans.

I am an inveterate conference-attender, and consider seminars, workshops, professional meetings, and other get-togethers to be an important part of my education. These meetings make learning fun, and the presenter is available to clarify, to respond, and to bump up against when there are differing clinical views. I treasure the professional relationships that sometimes begin their development during such meetings.

During the early 1970s a three-year teaching assignment in the Truk District of Micronesia, I conducted a research project dealing with local high school student suicides and alcohol abuse. This resulted in a program sponsored by the Community College of Micronesia, in which I directed the process of helping elementary schoolteachers develop an indigenous approach to mental health for children, and designed a school counseling program.

My later work as part of a specialized treatment team in child protective services in California from 1976 to 1980 gave me a rich, albeit exhausting, experience in providing therapy for abused children and their families. My graduate courses had not provided the theoretical understanding or treatment approaches needed to work with the issues and conditions that I frequently encountered. Since we usually worked in cotherapy teams, I received invaluable on-the-job training from well-seasoned colleagues. I sought out the writings of Kempe, Helfer, Steele, Greene, Mrazek, and others who were the recognized experts in child abuse.

Many of the treatment methods espoused by child-abuse experts were in direct opposition to much of what I had learned in graduate school. I found, for instance, that to be effective, a clinician often has to allow dependencies to occur, that a commitment beyond the clinical hour is essential, that a therapist needs not only to be able to give parents practical suggestions related to child rearing, but also has to be able to re-parent the adults when needed, while being exquisitely careful not to be patronizing in the process.

I received this training at a time when professionals within the public welfare systems were just becoming aware of the extensiveness of sexual abuse incidents within the respective communities and around the country. Developing treatment methods and techniques, in the absence of clearly established theoretical bases for this problem area, caused considerable anxiety among those of us who became very involved in treating these victims. The absence of people who knew the right thing to do was some solace to us as we worried about doing "the right thing"; we were painfully aware that no one else had the answers either.

I worked with two colleagues to establish a county-wide, comprehensive treatment program for victims of sexual abuse and their families in the late 1970s. We learned about the dynamics of intrafamilial abuse as they emerged during our work. The staff often met in consultation to seek help about confusing interactions, to argue over methods, to present new ideas, and to develop treatment plans. Our work with these families sharpened our skills in being respectfully confrontational and directly supportive at the same time.

The knowledge and experiences gained from this were invaluable, and led to the publishing of *Treating Traumatized Children and Their Families*, which I wrote with a colleague Maria Nasjleti in 1983. This book has been adopted as a text by many universities in the United States and in Canada.

The "pioneers" in dealing with sexual abuse were contemporaries who helped me to learn and to grow, through their writings, consultations, and, with some, appreciated clinical arguments. These include researchers such as Finkelhor, Abel, Groth, Goodman, and Saywitz, and theoreticians and practitioners such as Summit, Sgroi, Berliner, Gil, Corwin, MacFarlane, Goldstein, Porter, and others.

I learned firsthand the debilitating effects of burnout on body, mind, and spirit working in a government agency with noble goals but limited resources. I also worked in the private sector, where I spent two years in the early 1980s supervising a diagnostic program for children in residential care. The professional staff at Children's Garden in Marin County, California, were the best I have met in the residential care business, with regard to both their theoretical approach and their practice. In addition to their day-to-day caretaking and treatment, they have engaged in intensive research to delineate levels of attachment ability in children, and treatment for attachment impaired children, as well as studying the dynamics of failed adoptions.

My role in supervising the diagnostic process for these children included working as team coordinator with the psychiatrist, psychologist, neurologist, pediatrician, teachers, and house staff, for damaged children who had been removed from their homes. It was here that I learned to truly appreciate the value of having various disciplines working together within a holistic approach. Veteran foster parents and childcare workers enriched my experiences about how it is for children in out-of-home care. I learned to value their insights and their dedication to the children in their charge. I learned that a severely traumatized child needs more assistance than can be provided by seeing a therapist for an hourly clinical session once or twice a week.

While working with children in out-of-home care, my professional awareness grew with regard to the treatment needs of children sustaining multiple losses that included not only their homes, families, and communities, but also their pets, toys, and clothing—everything they had ever had. This loss was too frequently followed by the loss of foster home after foster home, with children literally having fewer belongings to take with them each time their plastic garbage bags were packed for moves to other foster homes. They needed to have something that could not be taken from them. They were often too emotionally bereft to have a sense of themselves apart from the influences of their immediate environment. Such children in residential care are like child victims of war who spend significant parts of their early lives in refugee camps. What we can give them is an understanding of a higher power (perhaps God, perhaps not), and recognition of the spirit within them that is constant, able to transcend the child's fragmented, unstable situation, and provide a deep sense of self, unrelated to what was done to them and what they did.

A shift to private practice in the early 1980s opened two new areas of learning for me. I specialized in providing consultation and training, as well as evaluating children for various judicial systems. This work requires that I stay current with the research and practical areas of my profession, and pushed me to become knowledgeable in related areas. I struggled along with my colleagues to develop professional standards and guidelines for determining whether or not abuse had occurred in a family. I learned, slowly and with some difficulty, to respect both the roles and limitations of various professionals in the medical, law enforcement, and judicial systems, and am grateful for what they taught me. Most of us, I learned, care a great deal about children and do not want them to be hurt, and it is important for us to respect our different roles and work together to help the children. (I even learned to grudgingly accept the value of having my knowledge, methods, and opinions regularly challenged as part of the adversarial legal process.)

I have become more and more involved in providing treatment for babies, the two- and three-year-old-victims of abuse. I looked to the studies of the infant by Stern and his colleagues, to Main's work with babies and their interactions with their parents, and reread Fraiberg's work on young children and their parents. I developed some forms of sensorimotor play and remedial parenting techniques for the young child and for the older child whose treatment needs included physical nurturing, stimulation, or learning the fundamentals of play.

Learning what is clinically effective from child clients is not difficult. Their straightforward responses—active expressions of pleasure and interest, ignoring me, saying no, vigorous attempts to leave the room—provide immediate, clear feedback that rarely needs to be studied or evaluated to determine meaning.

I work with children dynamically, and maintain a large playroom that might be any child's idea of heaven. I generally do not believe in passive observation alone, but instead encourage the youngsters to do something, with me taking an active part in whatever they choose. I may have to direct them to an area, such as using puppets or dressing up or painting, but then I usually join the activity and connect with the child in that manner. I thought that my style of working with young children was unique until I became acquainted with Jernberg's Theraplay and saw concurrent evolution in progress. She had successfully used similar techniques of planned intrusion that were fun, intense, action-filled, soothing, met some basic needs of the child, and gave the child strong, positive messages about himself.

By this point in my professional development I had become profoundly aware that many of the children I treated were damaged at every level of their being, and that treatment had to reach all of these sensory and psychic areas. Van der Kolk's work on the biological, psychological, and sociological impact of trauma stimulated my thinking, and led to my directly working with the body. I turned again to Moreno's work and developed psychodrama techniques for young children. I sought out the body-people, to learn what could be adapted for those children who felt they had lost the right to their bodies. I returned to Lowen's work and conferred with Trager and Reichein therapists, as well as with dance and movement therapists.

Nonclinical professionals taught me about the healing work they have done with children. For example, musician-composer Judy Fjell has developed powerful techniques for working with children who live in shelters with their battered mothers. I spent a week at the Richards' institute where, along with delightful music teachers, I learned children's songs and games. In seeking consultation with music therapists I found that most specialized in working with children who had organically based disabilities. I tentatively, and then with gusto, experimented with the use of classical music, rock and roll, Sesame Street songs, and the sensitive, appealing work of Alsop, and used these audio tapes as background to directly teach, and to lead us in movement to help children express the unspeakable.

My consultations with art-play therapist Levinson taught me about working with hospitalized, burned children and she helped me to appreciate anew the works of Levy, Rubin, and others.

I began to incorporate parents into the treatment team and to tell children up front that they must take an active part in their treatment: that play therapy is not all play. I tell them why they see me, what we are doing, and where we are going. I was smug in the success and uniqueness of my approach and then found Richard Gardner's work, which affirmed my own while reminding me that what I was doing was not entirely unique. His writings are filled with wonderful, creative techniques for helping children address their problems.

I studied and tracked down colleagues for consultation and got fat at numerous lunches and marathon discussions with other professionals who were also struggling with clinical horrors, such as child victims of ritualistic abuse who had been drugged and reported participation in murders and abuses against other children. This led me to yet other areas of study. I went to the research and writings of those who have specialized in traumatized children such as Terr, Spiegel, Eth, and Pynoos, and to people who were learning and teaching us about dissociative disorders—Kluft, Braun, Sachs, Putnam, and others.

As the reader has undoubtedly recognized by now, I utilize and encourage a direct, holistic approach to treating children, and firmly believe that such an approach not only benefits the children greatly, but is the best way to treat ourselves as we go about our professional activities. Drawing something with a youngster during a session cannot hurt the child, and it can make her more comfortable and trusting of me, and more likely to be spontaneous and open. And the drawing itself can be important, revealing problems or conditions that might not have been exposed otherwise, or not until a much later time. A clinician need not be an expert in a modality in order to incorporate its use in the treatment process; we can get comfortable with art therapy and psychodrama and sand tray play and many of the other methods we avoid for any of a number of reasons. Learning some music therapy allows us to use music when working with children—and they love it! When we learn something about art therapy we have grown professionally and personally and are able to give our clients something more.

I do not propose that we take extensive coursework in all of these areas, but I strongly suggest gaining some familiarity with many of them. One of the most important things we need to learn is how little we know and, consequently, when to consult with the experts, but we may also learn to recognize potential problems in the youngsters we treat, and that is our purpose.

Perhaps the richest part of my life, the memories of which keep me humble and appreciative, is the parenting of my own children, now grown. I cannot think of any other experience that provides the emotional stretch of parenting. It includes unbelievable joy, exquisitely poignant moments, fear, and leads to homicidal thoughts, if not urges. Every emotion is there. As I was a late-bloomer academically, I came to hear, "Gee, Mom, too bad you didn't know all that neat stuff when we were little!" I entered the professional world as a seasoned parent and believe it was this, together with a respect for what others had to teach me, that made it all work.

I currently live on the Kona coast of Hawaii, where I offer seminars for professionals in related disciplines who wish to learn, share, and reach a more comfortable level in working with children and their families. I give occasional lectures and workshops in other places, but home for me is on the Big Island.

My formal studies, varied professional work, and on-going conferences and readings (in an attempt to keep up), are all part of my compost pile. There have been many highs and lots of tears. As with compost, I turn it over now and then and it gets better.

Bibliography

Abel, G.; Mittelman, M.; Becker, J.; Cunningham-Rathner, J.; and Lucas, L. 1983. The characteristics of men who molest young children. Presentation to the World Congress of Behavior Therapy, December, Washington, D.C.

Ackerman, N.W. 1966. *Treating the troubled family*. New York: Basic Books.

Ainsworth, M. 1964. Patterns of attachment behavior shown by the infant in interacaction with his mother. *Merrill Palmer Quarterly* 10: 51–58.

————. 1973. The development of infant-mother attachment. In *Review of Child Development Research Vol. 3.* ed. Caldwell, B., and Ricciuti, H. Chicago: University of Chicago Press.

Ainsworth, M., and Wittig, B.A. 1969. Attachment and exploratory behavior of one-year-olds in a strange situation. In *Determinants of infant behavior*, ed. Foss, B.M. London: Methuen.

American Psychiatric Association. 1986. *Diagnostic and statistical manual of mental disorders,* 3d ed., rev. Washington, D.C.: American Psychiatric Press.

Anthony, E.J. 1974. The syndrome of the psychologically invulnerable child. In *The child in his family: Children at psychiatric risk,* ed. Anthony, J.E., and Koupernik, C. New York: John Wiley & Sons.

Anthony, E.J., and Cohler, B.J., eds. 1987. *The invulnerable child.* New York: Guilford Press.

Armstrong, T. 1985. *The radiant child.* Wheaton, Ill.: Theosophical Publishing House.

Axline, R.M. 1955. Play therapy procedures and results. *Am J Orthopsychiatry* 25: 618–26.

Axline, V. 1956. Play interviews as described by child participants. *J Cons Psychology* 74: 53–63.

Azarnoff, P., and Flegal, S. 1975. *A pediatric play program.* Springfield, Ill.: Charles C. Thomas Co.

Bank, S.P., and Kahn, M.D. 1982. *The sibling bond.* New York: Basic Books.

Benedek, E. 1948. The silent scream: Countertransference reactions to victims. *Am J Soc Psychiatry* 4: 49–52.

Benson, H. 1975. *The relaxation response.* New York: Avon Books.

Bergen, M. 1958. Effect of severe trauma on a 4-year-old child. *Psychoanal Study Child* 13: 407–29.

Berliner, L., and Stevens, D. 1982. Clinical issues in child sexual abuse. In *Social work and child sexual abuse*. ed. Conte, J.R. and Shore, D. New York: Haworth.

Bettelheim, B. 1977. *The uses of enchantment*. New York: Vantage Books.

Blatner, H.A. 1973. *Acting in: Practical applications of psychodrama methods*. New York: Springer Publishing Co.

Block, D.; Siber, E.; and Perry, S. 1956. Some factors in the emotional reaction of children to disaster. *Am J Psychiatry* 113: 416–22.

Boszormenyi-Nagy, L., and Spark, G. 1973. *Invisible loyalties: Reciprocity in intergenerational family therapy*. New York: Harper & Row.

Bowen, M. 1977. Theory in the practice of psychotherapy. In *Family therapy: Theory and practice*, ed. Guerin, P. New York: Gardner Press.

Bowlby, J. 1958. The nature of the child's tie to his mother. *Int J Psychoanalysis* 39: 350–73.

———. 1963. Pathological mourning and childhood mourning. *J Am Psychoanal Assoc* 11: 500–541.

———. 1969. *Attachment and loss. Vol. 1, Attachment*. New York: Basic Books.

———. 1973. *Attachment and loss*. Vol. 2, *Separation anxiety and anger*. New York: Basic Books.

———. 1977. Making and breaking of affectional bonds: etiology and psychopathology in light of attachment theory. *British J Psychiatry* 130: 201–10.

———. 1979. On knowing what you are not supposed to know and feeling what you are not supposed to feel. *Can J Psychiatry* 24: 403–8.

———. 1980. *Attachment and Loss*. Vol. 3, *Loss, sadness, and depression*. New York: Basic Books.

Braun, B.G. 1984a. Multiplicity: Form, function & phenomena. Chicago: Associated Mental Health Services.

———. 1984b. *Towards a theory of multiple personality and other dissociative phenomena.*   : Psychiatric Clinics of North America 7: 1, 171–93.

———. 1988. The BASK model of dissociation. *Dissociation* (2): 16–23.

———. 1986. *Treatment of multiple personality disorder*. Washington, D.C.: American Psychiatric Press.

Braun, B.G., and Sachs, R.G. 1985. The development of multiple personality disorder: Predisposing, precipitating and perpetuating factors. In *Childhood antecedents to multiple personality*, ed. Kluft, R.P. Washington, D.C.: American Psychiatric Press.

Burgess, A.W. 1975. Family reaction to homicide. *Am J Orthopsychiatry* 45: 391–98.

Burgess, A.W., Hartman, C.R.; Wolbert, W.A. and Grant, C.A. 1987. Child molestation: Assessing impact in multiple victims, Part 1. *Archives Psychiatric Nursing* 1(1): 33–39.

Burton, L. 1968. *Vulnerable Children*. London: Routledge & Kegan Paul.

Carson, M., and Goodfield, R. 1988. The Children's Garden attachment model. In *Challenging the Limits of Care*, eds. Small, R.W. and Alwon, F.J. Needham, Mass.: Albert Trieschmen Center.

Coles, R. 1967. *Children of crisis: A study of courage and fear*. Boston: Atlantic Monthly Press.

Corwin, D., Berliner, L., Goodman, G., White, S. 1987. Child sexual abuse and custody disputes. *J Interpersonal Violence* 2: 91–105.

Danieli, Y. 1985. The treatment and prevention of long-term effects and intergenerational transmission of victimization: A lesson from Holocaust survivors and their children. In *Trauma and its wake: The study and treatment of post-traumatic stress disorder,* ed. Figley, C.R. New York: Brunner/Mazel.

De Mille, R. 1955. *Put your mother on the ceiling.* New York: Penguin Books.

DiLeo, J.H. 1983. *Interpreting children's drawings.* New York: Brunner/Mazel.

Dowrick, P.W. 1986. *Social survival for children; A trainer's resource book.* New York: Brunner/Mazel.

Dunn-Maxim, K.; Dunne, E.J.; and Hauser, M. 1983. *When children are suicide survivors ** Suicide and its aftermath: Understanding and counseling the survivors.* New York: W.W. Norton.

Earle, E. 1979. The psychological effects of mutilating surgery on children and adolescents. *Psychoanal Study Child* 34: 527–46.

Epstein, H. 1981. The private passages of the hostages. *Life Magazine,* March.

Erikson, E. 1963. *Childhood and society.* New York: W.W. Norton.

———. 1977. *Toys and reasons: States in the ritualization of experience,* New York: W.W. Norton.

Eth, S., and Pynoos, eds. 1985a. *Post traumatic stress disorder in children,* Washington, D.C.: American Psychiatric Press.

Evert, K., and Bijkerk, I. 1987. *When you're ready.* Walnut Creek, Calif.: Launch Press.

Fagan, J., and McMahon, P.P. 1984. Incipient multiple personality in children. *J Nerv and Mental Disease* 172: 26–26.

Feder, E., and Feder, B. 1981. *The expressive arts therapies.* Englewood Cliffs, N.J.: Prentice-Hall.

Ferenczi, S. 1949. Confusion of tongues between adults and children. *Int J Psychoanal* 30: 225–30.

Feshbach, S. 1955. The drive-reducing function of fantasy behavior. *J Abnor and Soc Psychology* 50: 3–11.

Figley, C.R. ed. 1985. *Trauma and its wake.* New York: Bruner/Mazel.

Finkelhor, D. 1985. *Child sexual abuse: New theory and research.* New York: Free Press.

———. 1986. *A sourcebook on child sexual abuse.* Newbury Park, Calif.: Sage Publications.

Finkelhor, D., and Browne, A. 1986. Initial and long term effects: A conceptual framework. In *A sourcebook on child sexual abuse,* ed. Finkelhor, D. Newbury Park, Calif.: Sage Publications.

Fraiberg, S.H. 1951. Applications of psychoanalytic principles in casework with children. *Quart J Child Behavior* 3 (Apr): 15–54.

———. 1959. *The magic years: Understanding and handling the problems of early childhood.* New York: Chas. Scribner's Sons.

———. 1978. Libidinal object constancy and mental representation. *Psychoanalytic Study Child* 24: 9–47.

Frederick, C. 1985. Children traumatized by catastrophic situations. In *Post traumatic* stress disorder in children, ed. Eth, S., and Pynoos, R. Washington, D.C.: American Psychiatric Press.

Friedrich, W.N., Beilke, R.L.; and Urquiza, A.J. 1988. Behavior problems in young sexually abused boys. *J Interpersonal Violence* 3: 21–28.

Freud, A., and Burlingham. D.T. 1943. *War and children*. London: Medical War Books.

Friedman, P., and Linn, L. 1957. Some psychiatric notes on the *Andrea Doria* disaster. *Am J Psychiatry* 14: 426–32.

Galdston, R. 1965. Observations of children who have been physically abused and their parents. *Am J Psychiatry,* 122: 440–43.

Gardner, G.R. 1971. Agression and violence—the enemies of precision learning in children. *Am J Psychiatry* 128: 445–50.

Gardner, R.A. 1986. *The psychotherapeutic techniques of Richard A. Gardner.* Cresskill, N.J.: Creative Therapeutics.

Gaston, E.T., ed. 1968. *Music in therapy.* New York: Macmillan.

Gelinas, D.J., 1983. The persisting negative effects of incest. *Psychiatry* 46: 312–32.

Gil, E. 1983. Outgrowing the pain. Walnut Creek, Calif.: Launch Press.

Ginott, H.G. 1961. *Group psychotherapy with children.* New York: McGraw-Hill.

Goodman, G.S., and Hepps, D. 1985. *Children's eyewitness testimony: The effects of trauma on memory.*Unpublished manuscript, Univ of Denver.

Goldstein, S.L. 1987. *The sexual exploitation of children,* New York: Elsevier.

Gottman, J.; Gonso, J.; and Schuler, P. 1976. Teaching social skills to isolated children. *J Abnor Child Psychology,* June 179–97.

Green, A. 1978. Psychiatric treatment of abused children. *J Am Acad Child Psychiatry* 17: 356–71.

———. 1983. Dimensions of psychological trauma in abused children. *J Am Acad Child Psychiatry* 22: 231–37.

Groth, A.N., and Burgess, A.W. 1977. Motivational intent in the sexual assault of children. *Criminal Justice and Behavior: An International J Correctional Psychology* 4: 253–64.

Haley, J. 1978. *Problem solving therapy: New strategies for effective family therapy.* New York: Harper & Row.

Hambridge, G. 1955. Structured play therapy. *Am J Orthopsychiatry* 24: 601–17.

Hammer, E.F. 1958. The house-tree person projective drawing technique: Content interpretation. In *The clinical application of projective drawings.* ed. Hammer, E.F. Springfield, Ill.: Charles Thomas.

Heilveil, I. 1983. *Video in mental health practice.* New York: Springer Publishing Co.

Helfer, R.E., and Kempe, C.H., eds. 1968. *The battered child.* Chicago: Univ of Chicago Press.

Hendricks, G., and Wills, R. 1975. *The centering book: Awareness activities for children.* Englewood Cliffs, N.J.: Prentice-Hall.

Horowitz, M.J., and Kaltreider, N. 1980. Brief treatment of post traumatic stress disorders. *New Directions for Mental Health Services* 6: 67–79.

Husain, S.A., and Vandiver, T. 1984. *Suicide in children and adolescents.* New York: Spectrum Publications.

Hyman, I.A.; Zelikoff, W.; and Clarke, J. 1988. Psychological and physical abuse in the schools: A paradigm for understanding post-traumatic stress disorder in children and youth. *J of Traumatic Stress* 2: 243–67.

James, B., and Nasjleti, M. 1983. *Treating sexually abused children and their families.* Palo Alto, Calif.: Consulting Psychologists Press.

Janov, A. 1973. *The feeling child.* New York: Simon & Schuster.

Jernberg, A. 1979. *Theraplay.* San Francisco: Jossey-Bass.

Jernberg, A.; Allert, A.; Koller, T.; and Booth, P. 1982. *MIM manual: Adult-school age child.* Chicago: Theraplay Institute.

Jones, D.P.H. 1986. Individual psychotherapy for the sexually abused child. *Int J Child Abuse & Negl* 10: 377–85.

Jones, D.P.H., and Macquiston, M. 1985. The predicament of the child sex abuse victim. In *Interviewing the sexually abused child,* ed. Jones, D.P.H., and Macquiston, M. Denver: Kempe Center Publications.

Juhan, D. 1985. *The Trager approach: Psychophysical integration and mentastics.* Mill Valley, CA: Trager Institute.

Kagan, J. 1984. *The nature of the child.* New York: Basic Books.

Kalff, D.M. 1980. *Sandplay.* Santa Monica, Calif.: Sigo Press.

Kaufman, G. 1980. *Shame: The power of caring.* Cambridge, Mass.: Shenkman Books.

Kempe, C.H., and Helfer, R.E. 1972. *Helping the battered child and his family.* Philadelphia: J.B. Lippincott.

Khan, M. 1963. The concept of cumulative trauma. *Psychoanalytic Study Child* 18: 54–88.

Kivnick, H.Q., and Erikson, J.M. 1983. The arts as healing. *Am J Orthopsychiatry* 53: 602–17.

Klingman, A., and Eli, Z.B. 1981. A school community in disaster: Primary and secondary prevention in situational crisis. *Professional Psychology* 12: 523–33.

Kluft, R.P. 1984. Multiple personality in children. *Psychiatric Clinics of North America* 7: 121–34.

———. ed. 1985. *Early antecedents of multiple personality disorder.* New York: American Psychiatric Press.

Kluft, R.P.; Braun, B.G.; and Sachs, R.G. 1985. Multiple personality, intrafamilial abuse, and family psychiatry. *Int J Family Psychiatry* 5: 283–301.

Koocher, G.P., and O'Malley, J.E. 1981. *The Damocles Syndrome.* New York: McGraw-Hill.

Kramer, E. 1974. *Art as therapy with children.* New York: Schocken Books.

Krell, R. 1985. Holocaust survivors and their children: Comments on psychiatric consequences and psychiatric terminology. *Ann Progress in Child Psychiatry & Child Devel* 631–41.

Kris, E. 1956. The recovery of childhood memories. *Psychoanal Study Child* 11: 54–88.

Krueger, D.W. 1983. Childhood parent loss: Developmental impact and adult psychopathology. *Am J Psychotherapy* 37: 582–92.

Krumboltz, J.D., and Krumboltz, H.B. 1972. *Changing children's behavior.* Englewood Cliffs, N.J.: Prentice-Hall.

Krystal, H., and Niederland, W. 1968. Clinical observations of the survivor syndrome. In *Massive psychic trauma,* ed. Krystal, H. New York: International Universities Press.

Kübler-Ross, E. 1969. *On death and dying.* New York: Macmillan.

———. 1975. *Death: The final stage of growth.* New York: Macmillan.

———. 1983. *On children and death.* New York: Macmillan.

Langmeier, J., and Matejcek, Z. 1973. *Psychological deprivation in childhood.* New York: Halsted Press.

Lazarus, R.S. 1966. *Psychological stress and the coping process.* New York: McGraw-Hill.

Lederman, J. 1969. *Anger and the rocking chair: Gestalt awareness with children.* New York: Viking Press.

Levinson, P. 1986. Identification of child abuse in the art and play products of the pediatric burn patients. *Art Therapy,* 3: 61–66.

Levinson, P., and Ousterhout, D.K. 1979. Art and play therapy with pediatric burn patients. *J Burn Care and Rehab* 1: 42–46.

Levy, S., and Levy, R.A. 1958. Symbolism in animal drawings. In *The clinical application of protective drawings,* ed. Hammer, E.F., Springfield, Ill.: Chas. Thomas.

Lifton, R. 1967. *Death in life: Survivors of Hiroshima.* New York: Random House.

Lister, E.D. 1982. Forced silence: A neglected dimension of trauma. *Am J Psychiatry* 139: 867–72.

Lowen, A. 1975. *Bioenergetics.* New York: Penguin Books.

Lynch-Fraser, D. 1982. *Danceplay.* New York: New American Library.

Macfarlane, K., and Waterman, J. 1986. *Sexual abuse of young children.* New York: Guilford Press.

Mahler, M.S. 1971. A study of the separation-individuation process and its possible application to borderline phenomena in the psychoanalytic situation. *Psychoanal Study Child* 26: 403–26.

Mahler, M.S.; Pines, F.; and Bergman, A. 1975. *The psychological birth of the human infant.* New York: Basic Books.

Main, M. 1975. Exploration, play, cognitive functioning, and the mother-child relationship. Presentation to the Society for Research in Children, April, Denver, Colo.

Meiselman, K. 1978. *Incest.* San Francisco: Jossey-Bass.

McWhirter, L., and Trew, K. 1982. Children in Northern Ireland: A lost generation? In *The child and his family: Tomorrow's parents,* ed. Anthony, E.J., and Chiland, C. New York: John Wiley & Sons.

Mervis, B.A. 1985. The use of peer-pairing in child psychotherapy. *Social Work.* March: 123–8.

Michel, D. 1976. *Music therapy.* Springfield, Ill.: Chas. C. Thomas.

Miller, A. 1984a. *For your own good: Hidden cruelty in child-rearing and the roots of violence.* New York: Farrar, Straus and Giroux.

———. 1984b. *Thou shalt not be aware: Society's betrayal of the child.* New York: Farrar, Straus and Giroux.

Mills, J.C., and Crowley, R.J. 1986. *Therapeutic metaphors for children and the child within.* New York: Brunner / Mazel.

Minuchin, S. 1974. *Families and family therapy.* Cambridge: Harvard University Press.

Modlin, H.C. 1983. Traumatic neurosis and other injuries. *Psychiatric Clinics North America* 6(4): 661–82.

Moreno, J.L. 1946. *Psychodrama Vol 1.* New York: Beacon House.

Moustakas, C.E. 1959. *Psychotherapy with children.* New York: Harper & Row.

Mrazek, P.B., and Kempe, C. eds. 1980. *Sexually abused children and their families.* New York: Pergamon Press.

Newman, C.J. 1976. Children of disaster: Clinical observations at Buffalo Creek. *Am J Psychiatry* 133: 306–12.

Oaklander, V. 1978. *Windows to our children.* Moab, Utah: Real People Press.

Orbach, I. 1988. *Children who don't want to live.* San Francisco: Jossey-Bass.

Pearce, J.C. 1980. *Magical Child.* New York: Bantam Books.

Pfeffer, C.; Plutchik, R.; and Mizruchi, M.S. 1983. Suicidal and assaultive behavior in children: Classification, measurement, and interrelations. *Am J Psychiatry* 140: 154–57.

Pfouts, J., Schopler, J.; and Henley, H.C. 1982. Forgotten victims of family violence. *Social Work* 27: 367–68.

Philpot, A.R. 1977. *Puppets and Therapy.* New York: Plays, Inc.

Plank, E. 1977. *Working with children in hospital.* Chicago: Yearbook University Press.

Pollock, G.H. 1986. Childhood sibling loss. A family tragedy. *Pediatr Ann* 15(12): 851–55.

Porter, E. 1986. *Treating the young male victim of sexual assault.* Syracuse, N.Y.: Safer Society Press.

Price, K. 1988. Empowering preadolescent and adolescent lukemia patients. *Social Work,* 33: 275–76.

Putnam, F.W.; Guroff, J.J.; Silberman, E.K.; Barbar, L.; and Post, R. 1986. The clinical phenomenology of multiple personality disorder: 100 recent cases. *J Clin Psychiatry* 47: 285–93.

Pynoos, R., and Eth, S. 1984. The child as witness to homicide. *J Soc Issues* 40: 269–90.

Rapp, D.J. 1979. Food allergy treatment for hyperkinesis. *J Learning Disabilities,* 12: 42–50.

———. 1985. Allergies: Are some children pains in the class? *J School Administrators Association of New York State,* 16: 29–32.

———. and Bamberg, D. 1986. *The impossible child.* Buffalo, N.Y.: Practical Allergy Research Foundation.

Reich, W. 1949. *Character Analysis.* New York: Orgone Institute.

Robertson, J. 1975. *Young children in hospital.* London: Tavistock Publications.

Rothstein, A., ed. 1986. *The reconstruction of trauma: Its significance in clinical work.* Madison, Conn.: International Universities Press, Inc.

Rubin, J.A. 1978. *Child Art Therapy.* New York: Van Nostrand Reinhold.

Rutter, M. 1980. Parent-child separation: Psychological effects on children. In *New directions in child psychotherapy,* ed. Harrison, S., and McDermott, J. New York: International Universities Press.

Sachs, R.G. and Braun, B.G. 1986. The use of sand trays in the treatment of multiple personality disorder. In Dissociative disorders 1986: Proceedings of the third international conference on multiple personality/dissociative states. Chicago: Rush University.

Saywitz, K. 1988. The child witness: Experimental and clinical considerations. In *Childhood assessment: Through the eyes of the child,* ed. La Grecca, A.M. New York: Allyn & Bacon.

Schaefer, C., ed. 1981. *Therapeutic use of child's play.* New York: Jason Aronson.

Schaefer, C.; and O'Connor, K.J., eds. 1983. *Handbook of play therapy.* New York: John Wiley & Sons.

Schetky, P.H. 1973. Preschoolers' responses to murder of their mothers by their fathers: A study of four cases. *Bul Am Acad Psychiatric Law* 6:45–57.

Sgroi, S.M. 1982. *Handbook of clinical intervention in child sexual abuse.* Lexington, Mass.: Lexington Books.

Shore, M. 1967. *Red is the color of hurting.* Bethesda, Md.: National Institute for Mental Health.

Sheehy, G. 1986. *Spirit of survival.* New York: Wm. Morrow and Co.

Solomon, J. 1942. Reactions of children to blackouts. *Am J Neuropsychiatry* 12: 361–62.

Spiegel, D. 1984. Multiple personality as a post-traumatic stress disorder. *Psychiatric Clinics North America* 7: 101–10.

Spiegel, D. 1986. Dissociation, double binds, and post traumatic stress in multiple personality disorder. In *Treatment of multiple personality disorder,* ed. Braun, B. Washington, D.C.: Psychiatric Press, Inc.

Steele, B.F., and Alexander, H. 1981. Long term effects of sexual abuse in childhood. In *Sexually abused children and their families,* ed. Mrazek, P.B., and Kempe, C.H. New York: Pergamon Press.

Steen, C. and Monnett, B. 1989. *Treating adolescent sex offenders in the community.* Springfield, Ill.: Chas. C. Thomas.

Stern, D.N. 1985. *The interpersonal world of the infant.* New York: Basic Books.

Sternberg, F., and Sternberg, B. 1980. *If I die and when I do.* Englewood Cliffs, N.J.: Prentice-Hall.

Summit, R. 1983. The child sexual abuse accommodation syndrome. *Child Abuse Negl* 7: 177–93.

Taylor, P., and Jampolsky, G., eds. 1978. *There is a rainbow behind every dark cloud.* Millbrae, Calif.: Celestial Arts.

Terr, L. 1970. A family study of child abuse. *Am J Psychiatry* 127: 665–71.

———. 1979. Children of Chowchilla: A study of psychic trauma. *Psychoanal Study Child* 34: 547–623.

———. 1981. Forbidden games: Post-traumatic child's play. *J Am Acad Child Psychiatry* 20: 741–60.

———. 1983a. Chowchilla revisited: The effects of psychic trauma four years after a school-bus kidnapping. *Am J Psychiatry* 140: 1543–50.

———. 1983b. Life attitudes, dreams, and psychic trauma in a group of "normal" children. *J Am Acad Child Psychiatry* 22: 221–30.

———. 1983c. Time sense following psychic trauma: A clinical study of ten adults and twenty children. *Am J Orthopsychiatry* 53:244–61.

———. 1984a. Children at risk: Psychic trauma. In *Psychiatry update,* Vol. 3, ed. Grinspoon, L. Washington, D.C.: American Psychiatric Association.

———. 1984b. Time and Trauma. *Psychoanal Study Child* 39: 633–65.

———. 1988. What happens to early memories of trauma? A study of twenty children under age five at the time of documented traumatic event. *J Am Acad Child Adolesc Psychiatry* 1: 96–104.

van der Kolk, B.A. ed. 1984. *Post traumatic stress disorder: A psychological and biological sequelae.* Washington, D.C.: American Psychiatric Press.

———. 1987. *Psychological trauma.* Washington, D.C.: American Psychiatric Press.

van der Kolk, B.A., and Greenberg, M.S. 1987. The psychobiology of trauma response: Hyperarousal, constriction, and addiction to traumatic reexposure. In Post traumatic stress disorder: A psychological and biological sequalae. Washington, D.C.: American Psychiatric Press.

Wallerstein, J.S., and Kelly, J.B. 1980. *Surviving the breakup: How children and parents cope with divorce.* New York: Basic Books.

Williams, T., ed. 1987. *Post-traumatic stress disorders: A handbook for clinicians.* Cincinnati, Ohio: Disabled American Veterans.

Winnicott, D. 1960. *The maturational process and the facilitating environment.* New York: International Universities Press.

Yates, A. 1981. Narcissistic traits in certain abused children. *Am J Orthopsychiatry* 51: 55–62.

———. 1982. Children eroticized by incest. *Am J of Psychiatry* 139: 482–85.

———. 1987. Psychological damage associated with extreme eroticism in young children. *Psychiatric Annals* 17:4, 257–61.

Ziv, A.; Kruglanski, A.; and Shulman, S. 1974. Children's psychological reactions to wartime stress. *J Pers Soc Psychol* 30: 24–30.

Appendix A
Resources

International Society for
the Study of Multiple Personality
and Dissociation
2506 Gross Point Road
Evanston, IL 60201
(312) 475–7532

Education Through Music
Richards Institute
P.O. Box 6249
Bozeman, MT 59771

Society for Traumatic Stress Studies
P.O. Box 2106
Dayton, OH 45401–2106
(717) 396–8877

Appendix B
Behavioral Checklist to
Help Aid Identification of
MPD in Children and Adolescents

DEAN BEHAVIORAL CHECKLIST
FOR CHILD AND ADOLESENT MPD

BEHAVIOR OBSERVED IN PLAYGROUND SETTING WITH PEERS

Check if Observed

Isolates and talks to self .... _____

Talks to self .... _____

Stares .... _____

Does not recognize playmate .... _____

Slaps or hits self or pulls own hair .... _____

Makes strange sounds .... _____

Appears awkward at times.. _____

Terrified when other children are disciplined .... _____

Albilities to perform change.. _____

Becomes aggressive suddenly .... _____

Withdraws suddenly .... _____

Afraid to go near equipment .... _____

Afraid to go into certain places even with escort........................... _____

Makes enemies then makes friends (polar behavior) .... _____

Startles easily as if daydreaming .... _____

Uses objects to hit others .... _____

Good kid bad kid extremes .... _____

BEHAVIORS IN CLASSROOM

Denies own work .... _____

Denies own drawings... _____

Uses left hand — switches to right hand, denies switch

  or hold pencil differently from time to time............................. _____

Stares .... _____

Does not recognize teacher... _____

Denies relationship with peers .... _____

Gets confused often .... _____

Seems to be in another world .... _____

Appears hypnotized when viewing video's, movies, won't respond to own name ...... _____

Refuses to sit in assigned seat, claims it is not his

  (may use alter's name as assigned person....."That is Jane's.") .... _____

Refuses to fall asleep during nap time..................................... _____

BEHAVIORS IN CLASSROOM (Continued)

Regresses easily and rapidly . . . . _____

Does not want to be touched . . . . _____

Confusion about birthdate ("No I was born in June not in January.") . . . . _____

Visual changes, sits close "I can't see!" then sits far away

"I can see better back here!" . . . . _____

Talks to self . . . . _____

Include any behavior's in playground checklist . . . . _____

DRAWINGS

Two selves — "This is me and this is me." . . . . _____

States "We are going to the river." When asked who the other person is may respond

"I don't know." "A person in my dream." "A person I play with I don't know her

name." "A person in my head." . . . . _____

Pictures with knives, blood, killings . . . . _____

Denies own drawings — "I didn't do that." . . . . _____

Faces inside of each other . . . . _____

Distinct separation of two parts of body . . . . _____

Morbidity . . . . _____

Objects, animals, martians aggressive towards people . . . . _____

Identification with astraunaut, martian etc. (statements "I am this martian,

you don't understand I am really a martian." . . . . _____

Acknowledgement of drawing only part of a picture . . . . _____

Drawings that seem to have been drawn by several individuals . . . . _____

Drastic changes in choice of paints or materials from one drawing to the next . . . . _____

Refuses to sign picture (may not be willing to acknowledge that several

alters participated in the production.) . . . . _____

Use of both hands while drawing . . . . _____

Any symbol depicting trauma:

dark skies . . . . _____

large mouths . . . . _____

teeth . . . . _____

excessive heart shapes-(hidden threats) . . . . _____

"twin towers" -(wish for union of self with parent or union of parents, etc.) . . . . _____

snakes, monsters, sharks, trees-(sexual) . . . . _____

omissions . . . . _____

eyes-(paranoid or afraid) . . . . _____

Males — vaginal shapes, looks trapped . . . . _____

females — phallic objects penetrating forms . . . . _____

clowns — shame . . . . _____

BATHROOM

Sounds and different voices, even though one child is in the bathroom . . . . _____

Fear of going to the bathroom alone . . . . _____

CARETAKERS/PARENTS

Does not recognize mother or father or caretaker . . . . _____

Does not recognize grandparent or relative who picks up child . . . . _____

GENERAL BEHAVIOR

Does not recognize own jacket or toy "That belongs to Jane (alter)." . . . . _____

May seem like an odd child . . . . _____

May seem like a perfect child at times . . . . _____

May tell other children "I have special powers!" . . . . _____

Spends a lot of time defending self . . . . _____

May deny self in picture of class . . . . _____

Changes subject often . . . . _____

Looks at you as if she/he never saw you before . . . . _____

May claim to hear noises that aren't there. (This may be a primitive form

of communication by an alter or may be voice alter.) . . . . _____

Pretends to have an imaginery friend at school . . . . _____

Fluctuates in ability to perform . . . . _____

Gets lost easily . . . . _____

EATING BEHAVIOR

Eats apple one day, states "I don't like apples." . . . . _____

Refuses milk or other drinks that you have observed the child enjoying at other times.

Has tantrum when parent put lunch together that he/she states she does not like . . . _____

Starts to eat food, seems to enjoy it, then spits it out claims he/she never did like it . . . _____

Odd eating behavior, eyes roll or move a lot while eating, appears to be having

difficulty staying focused on mealtime . . . . _____

DEAN ADOLESCENT INVENTORY SCALE/D

DATE _____   *Circle One*

1. I have been afraid to tell anybody about some of my experiences. ...... TRUE FALSE

2. Sometimes I hear arguing in my head and it confuses me............. TRUE FALSE

3. When I was very young, I pretended to have a playmate that nobody
    knew about. .... TRUE FALSE

4. Sometimes when I am writing I feel like someone else is guiding my
    hand.. TRUE FALSE

5. Often times when I look into the mirror my haircolor seems to change.... TRUE FALSE

6. When I am eating food, there are times that ''I'' cannot taste the food. .. TRUE FALSE

7. When I am playing sports with friends, sometimes I can do real well in
    one game and then the next time I play it I feel like the game is new to
    me. .... TRUE FALSE

8. Sometimes when I sleep at night I feel like I am awake and I am having
    conversations with people. .... TRUE FALSE

9. I am upset when people claim they know me and I have never met them
    before. .... TRUE FALSE

10. My handwriting changes often.................................... TRUE FALSE

11. I have looked into the mirror and have seen someone other than myself. .. TRUE FALSE

12. Something terrible happened to me but I don't know what it was. .... TRUE FALSE

13. I don't remember a lot of things that other people tell me happened to
    me. .... TRUE FALSE

14. Sometimes I will be with friends and I can't remember how I got there. .. TRUE FALSE

15. I feel like I have totally lost a portion of my memory.................. TRUE FALSE

16. When I get dressed I have a difficult time deciding what to wear because
    it seems like parts of me want to wear something different than what I
    want to wear. .... TRUE FALSE

17. I have heard that people who hear voices in their heads are crazy and
    sometimes I think I may be crazy because I have heard voices too. ...... TRUE FALSE

18. I feel like nobody has ever been able to help me. .... TRUE FALSE

19. I have bad headaches and nobody has been able to find out why. .... TRUE FALSE

20. I feel that there are things that happened to me that I could never tell
    anyone, but I don't know what they are. .... TRUE FALSE

21. My legs and arms and sometimes my hands move and I don't move them. . . . . TRUE   FALSE

22. I have watched myself doing things and talking to people but could not talk. . . . . TRUE   FALSE

23. Time is discontinuous for me. . . . . TRUE   FALSE

24. I do lots of things at once and don't really understand how I can do this. . TRUE   FALSE

25. I have been accused of stealing but I know that I have never stolen anything. . . . . TRUE   FALSE

26. Things have appeared in my room that I am accused of stealing but I know that I did not steal them. . . . . TRUE   FALSE
27. My parents tell me I lie all the time. . . . . TRUE   FALSE

28. I like to lie. . . . . TRUE   FALSE

29. I have stolen things to get my parents mad. . . . . TRUE   FALSE

30. I like to cause trouble for people. . . . . TRUE   FALSE

31. Sometimes I can watch myself getting into trouble and I can't stop it. . . . . TRUE   FALSE

32. My vision changes all the time but nobody believes me. . . . . TRUE   FALSE

33. I have eaten entire meals and don't remember eating. . . . . TRUE   FALSE

34. I have favorite things in my room at home, but some of the things I feel belong to someone else. . . . . TRUE   FALSE

35. My parents have accused me of talking to myself. TRUE   FALSE

36. I have been abused by many people. . . . . TRUE   FALSE

37. Sometimes when I go to school I am not aware of what the teacher is talking about as if I had lost part of the lecture. . . . . TRUE   FALSE

38. In school I have a bad memory for subjects that I thought I knew well. . . . TRUE   FALSE

39. There is a violent part of me that I have not told my doctor about. . . . . . . TRUE   FALSE

40. Sometimes I feel like I may have done something terrible but I don't know what it could be. . . . . TRUE   FALSE

41. I panic when I get around certain people and I don't know why. . . . . TRUE   FALSE

42. I have had several times when I was not sure who I was or even what my name was. . . . . TRUE   FALSE

43. Sometimes I call myself by another name. . . . . TRUE   FALSE

44. I always pretend that I remember things even though I just can't remember them. . . . . TRUE   FALSE

45. Sometimes I am talking to a friend and I don't know what happens but I just disappear and come out later somewhere else.................... TRUE FALSE

46. People tell me I stare a lot... TRUE FALSE

47. My teachers in school are always trying to get my attention. .... TRUE FALSE

48. Many times I feel that when people are talking to me they are talking to someone else. .... TRUE FALSE

49. Once I saw a person killed in real life. .... TRUE FALSE

50. I hide things from myself all the time. .... TRUE FALSE

51. My friends don't really care about me because they don't really know who I am. .... TRUE FALSE

52. I have witnessed someone dying in real life......................... TRUE FALSE

53. I don't like to talk about anything that causes me to get upset because sometimes it makes me disappear into myself....................... TRUE FALSE

54. When I disappear into myself I can hear people calling me but I have no control to speak out, and this scares me a lot....................... TRUE FALSE

55. I have been raped and can't talk about it........................... TRUE FALSE

56. My biggest fear is that someone will hurt me. .... TRUE FALSE

57. Sometimes I am working on an activity and then I just can't think at all about what I was doing because my mind is blank.................... TRUE FALSE

58. I have become full of rage and have not been able to understand why. ... TRUE FALSE

59. I have been told that I roll my eyes. .... TRUE FALSE

60. Sometimes I want to do one thing and my body seems to want to do another thing... TRUE FALSE

61. If I can ever find out what is wrong with me I will work hard to get better. TRUE FALSE

62. Some people think I am a problem to society but they can't help me either. .... TRUE FALSE

63. Sometimes I find myself eating food that I don't like. .... TRUE FALSE

64. I can't always smell odors even when I don't have a cold. .... TRUE FALSE

65. Sometimes I answer questions on exams and don't know where the answer comes from. .... TRUE FALSE

66. I have been involved in cult activities and it scares me to admit it. .... TRUE FALSE

67. I have been threatened to keep a big secret. .... TRUE FALSE

68. I have lost days at a time and have no explanation for it. .... TRUE FALSE

69. Most people that have tried to help me don't ask me the right questions about myself. . . . .   TRUE   FALSE

70. I have been constantly present during the taking of this test. . . . .   TRUE   FALSE

71. There is a part of me that is childlike and I am embarrassed when people tell me I acted that way again. . . . .   TRUE   FALSE

72. I have been told by someone in me to do things that I am not willing to do. . . . .   TRUE   FALSE

73. I rarely see things that aren't there. . . . .   TRUE   FALSE

74. Voices in my head sometimes are so clear I am frightened by them. . . . .   TRUE   FALSE

75. I feel good about taking this test because I feel like you may be able to help me. . . . .   TRUE   FALSE

76. Sometimes I feel like there are many different parts to me. . . . .   TRUE   FALSE

77. I get upset when I am extremely angry with someone I love and I can't explain what happened because I don't know. . . . .   TRUE   FALSE

78. I have tried to use drugs to cover up my experiences. . . . .   TRUE   FALSE

79. There is one part of me who wants to use drugs and I try to keep that part under control. . . . .   TRUE   FALSE

80. I have heard voices in my head that have convinced me to kill myself. . . .   TRUE   FALSE

81. Sometimes I burst out laughing and can't stop. . . . .   TRUE   FALSE

82. I find myself crying and don't understand why my eyes are wet because "I" wasn't crying. . . . .   TRUE   FALSE

83. Many times I have no feeling in part of my body and I can't explain why.   TRUE   FALSE

84. I have found letters that I don't remember writing but they were signed by me. . . . .   TRUE   FALSE

85. The question that upset me the most was question No. _____ . . . .   TRUE   FALSE

86. I don't remember taking this test before. . . . .   TRUE   FALSE

87. My biggest fear today is that nobody will find out what is wrong with me then I will think I really am crazy. . . . .   TRUE   FALSE

88. I believe that when I was a small child something happened to me that may have caused me to do these strange things. . . . .   TRUE   FALSE

89. I have to be reminded many times about things that I should have done that I thought I did. . . . .   TRUE   FALSE

90. There are some people that I need to stay away from because I have thought about killing them. . . . .   TRUE   FALSE

91. I have been beaten severely. . . . .   TRUE FALSE

93. Part of my body works at times and I can't get the other part to move. . .   TRUE FALSE

94. I cover up a lot for myself because I don't know the truth anymore. . . . . .   TRUE FALSE

95. I don't think anybody has my experiences and knowing that frightens me.   TRUE FALSE

96. I know that I do not lie to my parents, but they tell me I lie all the time. . .   TRUE FALSE

97. Sometimes I feel like I am asleep all day and another part of me took
     over and participated in the day for me. . . . .   TRUE FALSE

98. I will be very happy if you find out what is wrong with me. . . . .   TRUE FALSE

99. I don't want any of my firends to know about my problem. . . . .   TRUE FALSE

100. I have never really felt a feeling, I just pretend I do. . . . .   TRUE FALSE

101. I feel I have lost control over myself and I need help. . . . .   TRUE FALSE

Richard P. Kluft, MD, and Frank W. Putnam, Jr., MD, are the originators of the Childhood MPD Predictors List, which was originally published in *Psychiatric Clinics of North America* (1984). The Dean Behavioral Checklist for Child and Adolescent MPD is based on their work, and was developed to enhance understand of some of the behavioral aspects of this disorder. There is no scoring; the items are only to provide a systematic approach to behavioral observations with children who may be showing symptoms of MPD.

The Adolescent Inventory is being utilized only as an assessment adjunct while additional information is gathered from several populations of adolescents, including those suspected of MPD, post traumatic stress disorder, and dissociative disorders.

Developed by Gwen L. Dean, Ph.D. (MR19987, licensed MFCC). Adult, Family & Child Counseling Center, 18436 Hawthorne Boulevard, No. 108, Torrance, CA 90504. Reprinted with permission.

Appendix C

HOW TO RECOGNIZE WHY A CHILD'S BEHAVIOR ACTIVITY AND LEARNING ABILITY CHANGES

Look for a Child Who

has typical allergies or allergic relatives.

acts like "Dr. Jekyll—Mr. Hyde."

earns "A's" one day, "F's" the next.

cannot write, draw or do math, at times.

has poor school grades in relation to I.Q.

craves certain foods or odors.

is too tired, hyper, irritable, depressed or vulgar.

never seems to feel well.

Look for

red earlobes or cheeks.

dark eye circles.

puffy bags under the eyes.

eye wrinkles.

glass, glazed eyes.

nose rubbing or nose wrinkle.

Is the Cause Inside School or Home? Ask if the Child Is

better outside than inside?

better if camping, vacationing, or in a hospital?

worse in certain school or home rooms?

worse from any indoor chemical odor?

Is the Cause Outside School or Home? Ask if the Child Is

better when indoors?

worse when outside?

worse during pollen season?

worse from any outside pollution?

worse when it is damp?

worse from outside chemicals?

Is the Cause a Food? Ask if the Child Is

too fond of a particular food or beverage?

better if not eating?

worse after certain foods, snacks, parties?

the same inside, outside, at home, on vacation?

reacting to a food which caused problems in infancy?

When you figure out the cause, you can do something about it.

From *The Impossible Child* by Doris J. Rapp, M.D., FAAA, FAAP with Dorothy Bamberg, R.N., Ed.D. Published by the Practical Allergy Research Foundation, P.O. Box 60, Buffalo, N.Y. 14223-0060, 1986. Reprinted with permission.

Appendix D

THE CHILDREN'S GARDEN ATTACHMENT MODEL

Assessment

In assessing attachment potential, the three major areas are:

1. Reciprocity—Does this child give emotionally? Can this child let anybody matter to him? Can he respond to affection?

2. Separation response—Is there a response to possible or actual loss or separation?

3. Ability to explore—Is the child curious about his environment? Is he free enough to take the risk inherent in learning and mastering new tasks?

In examining these, we have found a number of specific questions to be essential to the development of attachment assessment. Each of the questions is a behavioral manifestation of one of the three major areas. The following list of thirteen questions develops an attachment profile of a child:

1. Does the child show protest behavior at separation from the primary caregiver? Does he show any response at being separated from a person who has provided him with nurturance and security?

2. Does the child have difficulty tolerating emotional intimacy, instead seeking objects as an expression of caretaking? Is it more important to this child that he have an object given to him than an emotional response from the person taking care of him?

3. Does the child engage in molding with the primary caretakers? (Molding refers to what an infant will do when he relaxes while being held by an adult.)

4. Does the child show affection spontaneously? Will the child initiate a hug, a kiss, or a touch?

5. Does the child seek affection in an indiscriminate manner? Does the child show selective preference toward adults?

6. Does the child respond with satisfaction to adult intervention? Does he look for others to help him when he needs help? Does he show pleasure in the attention given him?

7. Is the child clingy? Does the child allow the adult to have any body space? Does he seem to get enough gratification from the adult to permit him to separate even briefly?

8. Is the child able to engage, unsupervised, in age-appropriate play? Can he get along with peers? Does he wish to have peer interaction or does an adult have to be present to intervene and to set limits?

9. Is the child free to explore the environment? Is he curious about the world around him? Is he free to learn in school? Does he take pleasure in new challenges and new tasks?

10. Can the child assimilate and utilize new information? Does he learn from experience? Does he retain information?

11. Does the child show empathy? Is he responsive to the emotions of others?

12. Can the child enjoy successful or pleasurable experiences without engaging in negative behavior afterwards? Can he allow himself to have a good time? Does he seek to destroy pleasurable interchange?

13. Does the child imitate other children's behaviors which he sees reinforced by adult approval? Can he spontaneously initiate behaviors based upon a sense of himself? Can he utilize his behavior as a means toward achieving positive recognition?

The answers to these questions, when related to both the attachment definitions and the three major areas as we have defined them, provide information regarding the child's availability for affectional interchange.

Carson, M. and Goodfield, R. 1988. The Children's Garden Attachment Model in *Challenging the Limits of Care*. eds. Small, R.W. and Alwon, F.J., Needham, Mass.: Trieschman Center. Reprinted with permission.

Appendix E

About three-quarters of the way through treatment, the therapist helps the child fill out this work-chart, discussing each question. This exercise helps focus the treatment by identifying gains made and work yet to be accomplished before termination. Children feel proud of their accomplishments and are reminded that separation from active treatment is imminent. Statements can be added or modified to address the treatment objectives of a specific child. The parents are also given a work chart, with the same questions in more adult language.

	Met	Needs Work
1. I know that what happened was not my fault.		
2. I can talk both about the good feelings and bad feelings I have for important people in my life.		
3. I can cuddle and feel good with the people in my family.		
4. I know I'm the kid, and Mom and Dad are the parents.		
5. I like and feel safe with these grown-ups who don't live in my house: _____ _____ _____		

	Met	Needs Work
6. I can use words to ask for what I need.		
7. I can use words to tell how I feel.		
8. I have a wonderful body and I know how to take care of it.		
9. I can make friends and keep them.		
10. I can enjoy school and do my work.		
11. I like myself.		
12. I know what really happened to me and I don't have to hide it or show it off.		

PARENT/CAREGIVER WORK-CHART

The issues referenced in this chart are the same as those found in the Child/Therapist Work-Chart illustrated previously, except that this chart is presented in adult language. The parents or primary caregivers are asked to complete this at home and discuss it with the therapist during a special consultation meeting, at about the time the child and clinician are working on their chart. The parents at this structured meeting are asked to discuss areas of concern and areas where they are pleased with the child's growth. As with the child's chart, this one can be added to or modified to match the treatment objectives of a specific child.

The therapist may find it useful to follow this parent meeting by having the parent join the child's next session, to discuss similarities and differences in their charts, work together to plan a course of action, and begin to discuss graduation.

	Met	Needs Work
1. Child does not own any responsibility for the traumatizing event.		
2. Child is able to acknowledge and express both positive and negative feelings toward those who are close to him or her.		

	Met	Needs Work
3. Child has secure and affectionate relationship with parents and close attachment to siblings and other family members.		
4. Clear and appropriate role boundaries exist between child and parent.		
5. Child has positive relationship with adults other than those in immediate family.		
6. Child is able to ask directly for needs to be met.		
7. Child is able to express feelings directly.		
8. Child has a positive body-image.		
9. Child has been able to reestablish or develop social skills and improve peer relationships.		
10. Child has been able to function well in school setting.		
11. Child has improved mastery and self-esteem related to traumatizing event.		
12. Child is able to acknowledge traumatizing event without minimizing or exaggerating its importance.		

Appendix F

PARENT/CHILD SUPERVISION GUIDELINE

The purpose of professionally supervised contact between parent and child is to ensure that

1. The child is free to have an enjoyable experience with the parent;
2. The child is physically safe;
3. The child is not exposed to behaviors that would be unduly stressful and emotionally upsetting.

Certain parental behaviors are necessary to assure that these objectives can be met. These behaviors are based on valid psychological principles which are directed primarily toward the welfare of the child, yet also address the feelings and concerns of the parents.

1. The parent is not to be alone with the child or engage in whispered conversations.
2. The parent can invite, but not demand or coerce, physical contact with the child.
3. Presents and other visitors may be very stressful by virtue of their unexpectedness and/or inappropriateness. Prior approval of the supervisor must be obtained.
4. Because past events may have caused stress/trauma and the child is uncertain about the future, references to past events and future plans should be avoided in discussions with the child. The visit should focus on the present so that the child experiences a calm and pleasurable visit.

If the behaviors of the parent do not conform to this guideline, or in any other way jeopardize the physical or emotional well-being of the child, the visit will be terminated.

Developed by Beverly James and Claudia Gibson. Copyright 1987.

Appendix G

Safe, Strong and Free!

Safe, strong and free! That's how we all should be!
Safe, strong and free in our lives!
Safe, strong and free! That's how we all should be!

Rich or poor, young or old, on a city street or a country road,
Man or woman, boy or girl,
We should all feel safe in this old world!
(refrain)

At home or school, work or play
In the middle of the night, in the middle of the day
With strangers, friends or family
We should all feel safe as safe can be! (refrain)

No more secrets that shouldn't be
When we are safe and strong and free
So let's work until we understand
How to stop all those hurting hearts and hands! (refrain)

Words and music by Judy Fjell. © 1984 (BMI). Available from Honey Pie Music, P.O. Box 1065, Davis, Ca. 95617-1065. Reprinted with permission.

No One Knows for Sure

There's a camel in the desert
Who could really use a drink
Her hump is all dried up
And her name's Irene I think,
If she doesn't get some water
Or some juice or soda soon
I don't think she'll last much longer
I don't think she'll last till noon . . .
And the sun is burning brightly
And the desert sand's so hot
And Irene's so awfully thirsty
She might die right on the spot . . .

But no one knows for sure,
Something might come along
That could save the day and help her out
And fix whatever's wrong . . .
'Cause no one knows for sure,
We've still got time to hope . . .
And Irene might see a giant milkshake
Over the next slope . . . well . . . she might!
'Cause no one knows for sure . . .
No one knows for sure!

There's a monkey named Mc Caffree
Who's lived a long, long time
And he's got a broken tail
That makes it pretty hard to climb
So he's careful in the jungle
When he climbs where monkey's go
But he missed a vine and fell into
The river down below!
And the crocodiles surround him

And Mc Caffrey, he can't swim
And he's driftin' toward the waterfall
Guess that's the last we'll see of him . . .
(chorus) And Mc Caffree might see Wonder Woman . . .
And she might have her rope . . .
Well, she usually carries it with her and . . .

There's a kid I know named Ev'lyn
One of my fav'rite friends
They put her in the hospital
For testing once again
And the doctors and the grown-ups
Well, they were sad when they were through
They told her she was very sick
No one knew what to do
To make her feel better
So that she could run and play
And Ev'lyn knew that she might die
But she'd look at me and say . . . .
(chorus) And maybe Dr. Seuss and me'll invent
A Sooper-Dooper Kind-a Soap!
. . . and I'd wash behind my ears, even . . .
'Cause no one knows for sure,
No one knows for sure . . . no one knows for sure!

My Body

My nose was made to sniff and to sneeze
To smell what I want, and to pick when I please!

(chorus) My body's nobody's body but mine
You run your own body, let me run mine!

My lungs were made to hold air when I breathe
I am in charge of just how much . . . I need!!!

(chorus) My legs were made to dance me around
To walk and to run, and to jump up and down!
And my mouth was made to blow up a balloon,
I can eat, kiss and spit, I can whistle a tune!

(chorus) No one knows better than me
it tells me "Let's eat!" it tells me "Go Pee!"

(chorus) Don't hit me or kick me, don't push or shove
Don't hug me too hard when you show me your love!

(chorus) Sometimes it's hard to say "No!" and be strong
When the "No!" feelings come, then I know something's wrong!
'Cause my body's mine from my head to my toe
Please leave it alone when you hear me say "No!"

(chorus) Secrets are fun when they're filled with surprise
But not when they hurt us with tricks, threats and lies.
My body's mine, to be used as I choose,
Not to be threatened, or forced or abused!

(chorus) Our body's one body, one voice is heard
We sing for freedom, when we sing these words!

Index

Page numbers in italics indicate figures; page numbers followed by t indicate tabular material.

About the Author

Beverly James is a clinical social worker who has specialized in evaluating and treating traumatized children for the past twelve years. She has authored a number of articles and coauthored *Treating Sexually Abused Children and Their Families*. Currently director of the James Institute in Kona, Hawaii, her training skills have brought her national and international recognition.